This collection fills an important gap in our understanding of the role of uncertainty in the science–society nexus. It illustrates the growing awareness that, in this context, uncertainty is essentially a political concern to be addressed by better governance rather than a scientific problem to be solved by improved techniques. Scientific uncertainty will continue to be a challenge for contemporary societies as long as the legitimacy of policy decision-making and action is based on trust in science.

> Professor Silvio Funtowicz, Centre for the Study of the Sciences and the Humanities, University of Bergen; formerly EU Joint Research Centre, Ispra

What should we do with uncertainty? Not abolish it with facts, this wide-ranging essay collection argues. Introduced by two of our most incisive analysts of alternative social futures, the book delves into today's most significant governance challenges and shows how uncertainty leads us to reimagine the politics of modernity. In these turbulent times, this is a book to read, savor and read again.

> Professor Sheila Jasanoff, Pforzheimer Professor of Science and Technology Studies at the Harvard Kennedy School

The old world order is fading into history: what a new one will look like is currently uncertain. In fields as diverse as climate change, finance, urban futures, pandemics, mass migration and many more, the future looks less predictable and demands alternative approaches. This well-timed book lays out what they might be.

> Professor Dipak Gyawali, Academician, Academy of Science and Technology, Kathmandu; formerly Nepali Minister of Water Resources

The Politics of Uncertainty questions the framing of uncertainty that has largely been transformed into calculable risks. Across a wide spectrum ranging from finance and banking to practices of modelling disease and climate change, the authors highlight the failings of institutions of illusionary control. Their urgent appeal deserves to be widely heard: by embracing uncertainty a culture of care can emerge, paving the way towards sustainability.

> Emeritus Professor Dr Helga Nowotny, Chair of the ERA Council Forum, Austria; former President of the European Research Council

Our world is deeply uncertain. Yet the concept is barely understood. This extraordinary volume brings together a cross-disciplinary, international group of thinkers on the leading edge of thinking about incertitude. The book's essays challenge us to recognize the unique risks and, more radically, the emancipatory opportunities associated with what cannot be known or domesticated.

> Professor Ilene Grabel, Distinguished Professor of International Finance, Josef Korbel School of International Studies, University of Denver; author of multiple prize-winning book, *When Things Don't Fall Apart* (MIT Press)

That even the best of global scientific knowledge and attendant policy cultures are always beset with contingency and ignorance has been a long and unfinished learning struggle. That this recognition is vital for practical effect in the development of sustainable and just human democratic futures has seen even stronger resistance, or denial. This collection integrates leading insights on the diverse, evolving challenges presented by these persistent conditions – a truly unique resource.

Emeritus Professor Brian Wynne, Centre for the Study of Environment Change, University of Lancaster; former special advisor to the House of Lords and Royal Society on science in society

While risk and uncertainty are often described in technocratic ways that create fear or the feeling of being overwhelmed by complexity, this book offers us a new way to reimagine how society can engage with uncertainty in an open way that prioritises alternative visions, questions the sources of data and the direction of science, debates the distribution of benefits and opens the possibility of participation and experimentation along the way. It could not come at a better time.

Professor Mariana Mazzucato, Founding Director, Institute for Innovation and Public Purpose, University College London; winner of 2014 New Statesman SPERI Prize, 2015 Hans-Matthöfer-Preis and 2018 Leontief Prize

THE POLITICS OF UNCERTAINTY

Why is uncertainty so important to politics today? To explore the underlying reasons, issues and challenges, this book's chapters address finance and banking, insurance, technology regulation and critical infrastructures, as well as climate change, infectious disease responses, natural disasters, migration, crime and security and spirituality and religion.

The book argues that uncertainties must be understood as complex constructions of knowledge, materiality, experience, embodiment and practice. Examining in particular how uncertainties are experienced in contexts of marginalisation and precarity, this book shows how sustainability and development are not just technical issues, but depend deeply on political values and choices. What burgeoning uncertainties require lies less in escalating efforts at control, but more in a new – more collective, mutualistic and convivial – politics of responsibility and care. If hopes of much-needed progressive transformation are to be realised, then currently blinkered understandings of uncertainty need to be met with renewed democratic struggle.

Written in an accessible style and illustrated by multiple case studies from across the world, this book will appeal to a wide cross-disciplinary audience in fields ranging from economics to law to science studies to sociology to anthropology and geography, as well as professionals working in risk management, disaster risk reduction, emergencies and wider public policy fields.

Ian Scoones is a professor at the Institute of Development Studies at the University of Sussex and is co-director of the ESRC STEPS Centre.

Andy Stirling is a professor at the Science Policy Research Unit at the University of Sussex and is co-director of the ESRC STEPS Centre.

PATHWAYS TO SUSTAINABILITY SERIES

This book series addresses core challenges around linking science and technology and environmental sustainability with poverty reduction and social justice. It is based on the work of the Social, Technological and Environmental Pathways to Sustainability (STEPS) Centre, a major investment of the UK Economic and Social Research Council (ESRC). The STEPS Centre brings together researchers at the Institute of Development Studies (IDS) and Science Policy Research Unit (SPRU) at the University of Sussex with a set of partner institutions in Africa, Asia and Latin America.

Series Editors:
Ian Scoones and Andy Stirling
STEPS Centre at the University of Sussex

Editorial Advisory Board:
Steve Bass, Wiebe E. Bijker, Victor Galaz, Wenzel Geissler, Katherine Homewood, Sheila Jasanoff, Melissa Leach, Colin McInnes, Suman Sahai, Andrew Scott

Titles in this series include:

Agronomy for Development
The Politics of Knowledge in Agricultural Research
James Sumberg

The Water-Food-Energy Nexus
Power, Politics and Justice
Jeremy Allouche, Carl Middleton and Dipak Gyawali

The Circular Economy and the Global South
Sustainable Lifestyles and Green Industrial Development
Edited by Patrick Schröder, Manisha Anantharaman, Kartika Anggraeni and Tim Foxon

Water for Food Security, Nutrition and Social Justice
Lyla Mehta, Theib Oweis, Claudia Ringler, Barbara Schreiner and Shiney Varghese

The Politics of Uncertainty: Challenges of Transformation
Edited by Ian Scoones and Andy Stirling

THE POLITICS OF UNCERTAINTY

Challenges of Transformation

Edited by Ian Scoones and Andy Stirling

Routledge
Taylor & Francis Group
LONDON AND NEW YORK

earthscan
from Routledge

First published 2020
by Routledge
2 Park Square, Milton Park, Abingdon, Oxon OX14 4RN

and by Routledge
52 Vanderbilt Avenue, New York, NY 10017

Routledge is an imprint of the Taylor & Francis Group, an informa business

© 2020 selection and editorial matter, Ian Scoones and Andy Stirling;
individual chapters, the contributors

The right of Ian Scoones and Andy Stirling to be identified as the authors
of the editorial material, and of the authors for their individual chapters,
has been asserted in accordance with sections 77 and 78 of the Copyright,
Designs and Patents Act 1988.

British Library Cataloguing-in-Publication Data
A catalogue record for this book is available from the British Library

Library of Congress Cataloging-in-Publication Data
Names: Scoones, Ian, editor. | Stirling, Andy, editor.
Title: The politics of uncertainty: challenges of transformation /
edited by Ian Scoones and Andy Stirling.
Description: Abingdon, Oxon; New York, NY: Routledge, 2020. |
Series: Pathways to sustainability | Includes bibliographical references and index.
Identifiers: LCCN 2020012090 (print) | LCCN 2020012091 (ebook) |
ISBN 9780367903374 (hardback) | ISBN 9780367903350 (paperback) |
ISBN 9781003023845 (ebook)
Subjects: LCSH: Risk–Sociological aspects. | Risk assessment–Political aspects.
Classification: LCC HM1101 .P65 2020 (print) |
LCC HM1101 (ebook) | DDC 302/.12–dc23
LC record available at https://lccn.loc.gov/2020012090
LC ebook record available at https://lccn.loc.gov/2020012091

ISBN: 978-0-367-90337-4 (hbk)
ISBN: 978-0-367-90335-0 (pbk)
ISBN: 978-1-003-02384-5 (ebk)

Typeset in Bembo
by Newgen Publishing UK

CONTENTS

ILLUSTRATIONS

Tables

Figure

Boxes

CONTRIBUTORS

Ian Scoones is a professor at the Institute of Development Studies at the University of Sussex and is co-director of the ESRC STEPS Centre. He currently holds an ERC Advanced Grant and is exploring insights from pastoral systems for wider understandings of uncertainty in policy and practice (www.pastres.org).

Andy Stirling is a professor at the Science Policy Research Unit at the University of Sussex and is co-director of the ESRC STEPS Centre. He researches, teaches and gives policy advice on a wide range of issues around power and uncertainty in science, technology and innovation more widely.

Timo Walter is currently a postdoctoral researcher at the University of Edinburgh, where he works on a project aiming to understand how socio-technical infrastructures help perform 'rational expectations' in financial markets. Publications include 'How Central Bankers Learned to Love Financialisation' (with Leon Wansleben, *Socio-Economic Review*, 2019) and 'Formalising the Future: How Central Banks Set Out to Govern Expectations But Ended Up (En)Trapped in Indicators' (*Historical Social Research* 44.2, 2019).

Leon Wansleben is a research group leader at the Max Planck Institute for the Study of Societies (Cologne) leading a team that works on the sociology of public finances and debt. Among his major publications are: *Cultures of Expertise in Global Currency Markets* (Routledge, 2013), 'How Central Bankers Learned to Love Financialisation' (with Timo Walter, *Socio-Economic Review*, 2019) and 'How Expectations Became Governable: Institutional Change and the Performative Power of Central Banks' (*Theory and Society*, 47.6, 2018).

Leigh Johnson is an assistant professor in the Department of Geography at the University of Oregon. Her research concerns attempts to govern climate and disaster risk through market-based tools, particularly insurance and financial instruments.

Patrick van Zwanenberg is an interdisciplinary researcher working on issues that link science and innovation policy with sustainability. He works at the Fundación Cenit at the University of San Martin, Buenos Aires.

Emery Roe, a policy analyst and researcher, has authored books and articles on large-system policy, management, reliability, risk, environment, complexity and development.

Sobia Ahmad Kaker is a lecturer in urban sociology at Goldsmiths, University of London. Her ongoing interdisciplinary and ethnographic research covers themes such as enclave-making, insecurity, uncertainty, socio-spatial and material inequalities, and dispossession in global South cities.

James Evans is a professor of geography at the University of Manchester. He studies how cities learn to become smarter and more sustainable. He has worked with over 200 organisations around the world to implement collaborative ways of working towards sustainability. James set up the University Living Lab in 2014 and is currently the university lead for sustainability and the Manchester Urban Institute lead for smart cities.

Federico Cugurullo is assistant professor in smart and sustainable urbanism at Trinity College Dublin, where he currently explores how artificial intelligence is reshaping cities.

Matthew Cook researches innovation in and the development of more sustainable urban environments. Working at the intersection of innovation studies and urban studies his current work is concerned with critical perspectives on the governance of smart city innovations, such as urban energy and transport systems, and the policy mobilities that play a profound role in their (re)construction.

Saska Petrova is a senior lecturer in human geography at the University of Manchester. Her research interests focus on the everyday politics of environmental governance, through the lens of precarity and vulnerability.

Lyla Mehta is a professorial fellow at the Institute of Development Studies at the University of Sussex and visiting professor at the Norwegian University of Life Science. She is project leader of the Belmont Forum/Norface/EU/ESRC/JST/RCN/ISC funded project 'Transformation as Praxis: Exploring Socially Just and

Transdisciplinary Pathways to Sustainability in Marginal Environments'TAPESTRY. Her latest co-authored book is *Water for Food Security, Nutrition and Social Justice* (Routledge, 2020).

Shilpi Srivastava is a research fellow at the Institute of Development Studies at the University of Sussex. In her work, she uses the lens of water to understand issues of power and patterns of authority to explore spaces of justice, rights and account-ability. Her current research focuses on the politics of uncertainty and transform-ation; and disaster preparedness, intersectoral collaboration and decision-making under conditions of climatic uncertainty in South Asia.

Hayley MacGregor is a clinically trained medical anthropologist and co-leads the health and nutrition research cluster at the Institute of Development Studies at the University of Sussex. She has worked on the experience and understanding of mental distress and other chronic illness in circumstances of precarity in low-income urban areas in southern Africa, and also co-leads work on epidemic pre-paredness and antimicrobial resistance.

Santiago Ripoll is a postdoctoral researcher and social anthropologist at the Institute of Development Studies at the University of Sussex. He is interested in contrasting people's everyday experiences of social change with conventional models of behav-ioural change and community engagement in humanitarian practice. He co-leads the research and network-building for the Social Science in Humanitarian Action Platform (SSHAP).

Melissa Leach is the director of the Institute of Development Studies at the University of Sussex. A social anthropologist interested in sustainability, equity and health issues in Africa and beyond, she helped establish and lead the Ebola Response Anthropology Platform and is currently co-leading several research and engagement programmes focused on epidemic preparedness and response.

Mark Pelling is professor of geography at King's College London and is a coordin-ating lead author for the Intergovernmental Panel on Climate Change – Impacts, Adaptation and Vulnerability Working Group. He has experience of working on multidisciplinary and interdisciplinary risk reduction projects worldwide.

Detlef Müller-Mahn is professor of development geography at the University of Bonn, Germany, and a spokesperson of the collaborative research centre, Future Rural Africa. His research focuses on political ecology, climate change and rural development in eastern Africa.

John McCloskey is chair of natural hazards science at the University of Edinburgh. He is the lead researcher for the Global Challenges Research Fund Urban Disaster Risk Hub. His research focuses on earthquake geophysics.

Dorte Thorsen is a research fellow at the Institute of Development Studies who has engaged in research in rural West Africa for more than 20 years. Given the prominence of mobility in rural life-worlds, her research has focused on gendered and generational dimensions of labour migration and the intersection with social and cultural transformations. Additionally, she has coordinated research on these topics across Africa and in South and South-East Asia.

Helena Farrand Carrapico is an associate professor in criminology and international relations at Northumbria University, where she is also currently serving as head of subject. Her research focuses on European security governance – in particular, justice and home affairs.

Narzanin Massoumi is a lecturer in criminology and sociology and a British Academy postdoctoral fellow at the University of Exeter. She is the co-editor of *What is Islamophobia? Racism, the State and Social Movements* (Pluto Press, 2017) and the author of *Muslim Women, Social Movements and the War on Terror* (Springer, 2015).

William McGowan is a lecturer at the University of Liverpool in the department of sociology, social policy and criminology. His research interests fall into two broad areas: violence, victimisation and bereavement; and social science methodology. He is currently working on two related projects, the first focusing on survivors of political violence and terrorism and the second exploring the UK funeral industry.

Gabe Mythen is professor of sociology, based at the University of Liverpool. His research is oriented toward engaging in critical analyses of the construction, mobilisation and management of risk and uncertainty across different areas of regulation, including crime, counter-terrorism and the environment.

Nathan Oxley is communications manager for the ESRC STEPS Centre and works at the Institute of Development Studies at the University of Sussex.

PREFACE

Since its establishment in 2006, the ESRC STEPS Centre (www.steps-centre. org) has been deeply concerned with the implications of uncertainty for our understandings of and responses to a complex, turbulent world. Countering the tendencies of a narrow, technocratic approach to sustainability, the 'pathways approach' has argued that considerations of a politics of uncertainty must be central.

As part of the Centre's final phase, the focus of our activities in 2019 was on 'uncertainty', and in particular the politics of uncertainty in transformations to sustainability. It proved timely. In the midst of the Brexit crisis, uncertainties were on everyone's lips across Europe. Disaster hit southern Africa as Cyclone Idai struck with ferocious force, while in the Democratic Republic of Congo another outbreak of Ebola occurred, killing many. While completing this book, the world was gripped by the uncertainties surrounding the spread of the coronavirus (COVID-19) pandemic. Meanwhile, debates about the implications of climate change, the stability of the finance and banking system, the consequences of global migration, the impacts of new technologies and the threats from terrorism continuously filled the news. Uncertainties are everywhere and define our contemporary era.

But how to respond? What are the intellectual, political and practical resources that are needed? Throughout 2019 we convened seminars and talks, commissioned blogs, hosted a major symposium (www.steps-centre.org/uncertainty/) and also wrote a major review paper exploring the diverse literatures on uncertainty (http:// bit.ly/uncertainty-why-does-it-matter). The aim was to encourage interactive debate and synthesis – which were captured in a series of podcasts (http://bit.ly/ uncertainty-podcasts).

This book is a result of this process and draws in particular on the contributions to the symposium. The symposium's themes were: finance and banking; insurance; experimental and adaptive governance; critical infrastructure; technology regulation; cities; infectious diseases; climate change; disasters; migration; crime and terrorism and spirituality and religion. Quite a range!

Each of those leading symposium themes (and now (co-)authors of the chapters in this book) invited a small group to the symposium – mostly academics, but some practitioners and many hybrids – and each theme then joined with two others to debate how uncertainty is understood in different domains, and what we should do about it. We also received some amazing contributions from plenary panels, who explored the political implications of uncertainty, as well as the legacies of Ulrich Beck, in relation to current debates (http://bit.ly/uncertainty-videos). It was an inspiring, intense and productive few days.

The book offers short essays written following the symposium, each reflecting on a theme, while the longer introduction offers an overview that aims to bring some of the strands together, outlining what we mean by a new politics of uncertainty. Taking seriously the many faces of uncertainty – in relation to knowledge, materiality, experience, embodiment and practice – highlights the multi-dimensionality of the concept. Opening up prefigurative spaces for innovation and experimentation, creating a politics of hope, offers a way forward. Yet this requires a form of politics that is rooted in mutuality, conviviality and collective solidarity in order to ensure that such spaces do not exclude the marginalised and are not captured by regressive, authoritarian players.

A focus on uncertainty, we argue, offers a profound challenge and productive focus for a transformational politics of sustainability and development. As a reader of this book, we hope you will reflect on these ideas, exploring areas of work that are unfamiliar and that challenge thinking in your own domain. Across the chapters, there is no unifying consensus either on framing the core ideas or on ways forward. The tensions between different perspectives offer a taste of a rich, ongoing debate. However, all contributors, from different standpoints and across diverse fields, agree that a focus on 'uncertainty' and its politics is essential for both understanding and transforming the contemporary world. In reading the book, we therefore hope that you will join in the practical and political challenges of embracing uncertainty, and thus of rethinking mainstream approaches to addressing sustainability and development.

We would like to thank all those involved in the ongoing intellectual and political project of the ESRC STEPS Centre, and the many people who contributed to the ideas put forward in this book. The introduction draws on discussions held throughout the symposium, both in parallel sessions and plenaries. Not all specific ideas are acknowledged as it was always a free-flowing, cumulative conversation, but certainly our thinking was massively enhanced. We would like to thank the theme leads for not only convening fantastic groups of such diverse and brilliant people – most of whom we had never met – but also leading/facilitating the writing of the chapters. The nine blogposts that followed the symposium allowed for reflections from participants who were not part of the book project, and they are all definitely worth reading (http://bit.ly/uncertainty-blog-posts). The recordings of the plenaries and the overall communications work was ably led by Nathan Oxley, with

Sarah King, while brilliant organisational work was led by Becky Ayre and initial copyediting was undertaken by My Blue Pencil.

Last, but not least, we would like to thank the ESRC (UK Economic and Social Research Council) for its long-term support to the STEPS Centre (steps-centre. org), which has allowed for the development of the ideas in this book over a long time. The symposium and open access publication of the book was co-sponsored by the European Research Council, through an Advanced Grant that supports the Pastoralism, Resilience and Uncertainty: Global Lessons from the Margins (PASTRES) programme (www.pastres.org).

Ian Scoones and Andy Stirling
Co-directors, ESRC STEPS Centre,
IDS and SPRU at the University of Sussex
February 2020

ABBREVIATIONS/ACRONYMS

ARC	African Risk Capacity
BSE	Bovine Spongiform Encephalopathy
DRC	Democratic Republic of Congo
EC	European Commission
EFSA	European Food Safety Agency
ESRC	Economic and Social Research Council
FAST	Families Against Stress and Terror
FEWSNET	Famine Early Warning Systems Network
GE	Genetically engineered
IOM	International Organization for Migration
IPCC	Intergovernmental Panel on Climate Change
MK	Milton Keynes
PEF	Pandemic Emergency Financing Facility
RICU	Research Information and Communications Unit
SSHAP	Social Science in Humanitarian Action Platform
STEPS	Social, Technological and Environmental Pathways to Sustainability
UNFCCC	United Nations Framework Convention on Climate Change
USAID	US Agency for International Development
WHO	World Health Organization

1

UNCERTAINTY AND THE POLITICS OF TRANSFORMATION

Ian Scoones and Andy Stirling

Opening up the politics of uncertainty

Why is the idea of uncertainty so important to politics today?[1] Why is it especially significant for crucial debates about transformations to sustainability? This book tackles these big questions by exploring the politics of uncertainty across a range of domains and diverse case studies.

The book argues that the embracing of uncertainties – as constructions of knowledge, materiality, experience, embodiment and practice – means challenging singular notions of modernity and progress as a hard-wired 'one-track' 'race to the future'. Ideas of development and sustainability are very often associated with a linear perspective on progress, dominated by narrow views of science and economics (Folbre *et al.* 2018). As a result of this, there is often a reliance on simplistic notions of innovation, focusing on those 'lagging behind', who must 'catch up' or 'leapfrog' to where others have reached. In this way, the framing of innovation and progress is reduced to merely how much, how fast, who is ahead and what is the risk of proceeding along an assumed pathway. Such debates too often ignore more important political questions about which way, what direction and who wins and who loses, where issues of uncertainty are central (Stirling 2015). Given diverse uncertainties, there is no single assumed endpoint; no one version of modernity and progress, and so directions chosen in the pursuit of sustainability and development depend on political and social choice (Scoones 2016).

Too often, ideas of transformation and sustainability are framed around particular, expert-defined 'solutions', with uncertainties blanked out. Typically asserted with great confidence, burgeoning notions around, for example, 'smart cities', 'climate-smart agriculture', 'clean development', 'geo-engineering', 'green growth' or 'zero-carbon economies' act to suppress appreciation of many forms of uncertainty. Conceived in narrow, technical terms, informed by relatively homogeneous, specialist views, these core organising ideas for high-level global policy-making typically emphasise aspiring control, asserting romantic visions of visionary leadership, heroic expertise, deterministic systems, orderly values, convergent interests, compliant citizens and expediently predictable futures.

As a consequence, some highly uncertain issues that should remain open for political debate are imagined in circumscribed, biased and one-directional ways. The loudest voices and most powerful interests thus come to enjoy a disproportionate influence in defining what is meant by 'progress'. The contrast could hardly be greater with the potentially open arena for political deliberation constituted by the United Nations' Sustainable Development Goals. Arguably, for the first time in history, these establish a globally-shared discourse enabling the exercise of agency not only over the possibility of progress but also with regard to its direction. The general orientation is clear – towards equality, well-being and ecological integrity; but the particularities of what these values might mean in practice – and how best to go about realising them – remain deeply uncertain.

Why this matters is that a rich and open-ended array of far wider, deeper and more plural kinds of possible societal, cultural and political transformations get obscured (Scoones *et al.* 2015). These many closures of uncertainties in mainstream, global discourses around science, technology and social progress typically serve to suppress the interests of the most marginalised communities, cultures and environments. Such failures to embrace uncertainty can presage perhaps the gravest form of oppression in the world today: the invisible foreclosing of possible futures. As a result, we argue, the opening up of political space to confront radical uncertainty can become as crucial to emancipatory politics as many more direct assertions of neglected interests.

Uncertainties are inevitable in this negotiation of diverse, possible futures concerning different pathways and their consequences (Leach *et al.* 2010). Uncertainties should not be reduced to risk, framed as a zero-sum threat that is in need of taming, controlling and managing, lest innovation is somehow 'held back' (Kearnes and Wynne 2007). In today's complex, turbulent, interconnected, globalised world, uncertainty must be embraced as perhaps more central than ever. We argue that opening up to uncertainty offers opportunity, diversity and a politics of hope. This in turn offers a more plural vision of progress, defined according to different standpoints, with multiple modernities at play.

The hegemonic ideas of linear progress and modernist development that so dominate Western cultures have been exported to the world through waves of colonialism, trade and aid. This 'globalising modernity' (Ahuja 2009; Hobden 2002) is of course not fixed. Indeed, even in the West, past ideas of progress have been framed differently: for example, around cycles of growth and renewal, rather than linear change (Cowen and Shenton 1996). In non-Western cultures, notions of development, progress and modernity often have very different connotations, rooted in subaltern identities and cultural and religious perspectives (Oxley, Chapter 12). This book argues that this globalising version of modernity and progress need not colonise the future in the ways it is presently doing. Instead, a more diverse, plural and contingent perspective can be advocated, involving an appreciation of uncertainty and its diverse framings.

The book reflects on different cases in different settings, each offering narratives about the future, with uncertainty central to the storyline. The chapters focus on banking and finance; insurance systems; the regulation of technology; critical infrastructures; cities; climate change; disease outbreaks; natural disasters; migration flows; crime and terrorism and spirituality and religion. All suggest that the contemporary moment poses fundamental challenges to the *status quo*. Old assumptions of linear, stable systems, amenable to technical risk management and control, do not hold.

This challenges the globalising modernity of (neo)liberal capitalism – with its pretence of stable environments and economies, and assertion of particular cultures of expertise and structures of appropriation and control. Futures are unknown: even when seen from any individual viewpoint, uncertainties are ubiquitous. Diverging interests and perspectives introduce further ambiguities. Underlying all this is the radical, ever-present potentiality of downright ignorance and surprise. Today, financial instability, pandemic disease, climate chaos, recurrent natural disasters and threats to liberal, 'democratic' orders across the world are refashioning the ways policy, politics and governance are thought about. Arguing that uncertainty in all its forms is central, this book suggests a new politics of uncertainty: one that offers opportunities, but also dangers.

The stakes could hardly be higher. On the one hand, the landscape of possible futures for globalising forms of modernity suggest trends towards narrow, technocratic, fearful, risk-focused intensifications of control. On the other hand, subaltern, 'alternative' (Kaup 2012; Gaonkar 1999) and 'minoritarian' modernities (Taraborrelli 2015) – as well as wider emerging 'non-modernities' (Ibarra-Colado 2006) – offer imaginings of new institutions and practices for embracing – even celebrating – uncertainty. It is arguably through more equal engagements between these diverse cultural, political and organisational forms that space can be found for a more plural, mutualistic and hopeful politics of care and conviviality (Stirling 2019b; Arora 2019; cf. Illich 1973).

From framings to practices of uncertainty

Uncertainties are not merely about the absence of knowledge (Walker *et al.* 2003): they can be very concrete – and formatively diverse – in their manifestations. The literatures on uncertainty span many different disciplines, applied to a diversity of domains (Scoones 2019), but a key distinction – highlighted long ago by Frank Knight (1921) – is that between risk and uncertainty. Risk is where we know what the possible outcomes are and can estimate their probabilities. Uncertainty is where we are unsure of the probabilities of particular outcomes. This is important, as there is too often a tendency to 'close down' towards risk (Stirling 2008), pretending to know the probabilities. Yet this is often not realistic in practice, as models and estimates are confounded by uncertainties. In cases where systems are complex, interacting and non-linear, a narrow engineering risk-based approach is inappropriate.

A number of other dimensions of incertitude also arise. These include ambiguities – where there are ongoing disputes about possible outcomes between different groups, reflecting contending social and political worlds (Stirling 1999). Here, for instance, it may be that debates do not mainly concern how likely different outcomes may be, but are about more fundamentally divergent notions of 'benefit' or 'harm', or their distribution across society, or what the alternative options for action may be. There is also the predicament of ignorance, where fundamental indeterminacies of the world and 'non-knowledge' mean we 'don't know what we don't know' (Wynne 1992). And here it is important to remember that surprises can of course be positive as well as negative, depending on who is affected.

Under routine conditions, narrow notions of risk can remain useful in the engineering of closed systems, or where high-frequency, unchanging processes generate long-run comparable statistics. Here, there is no need to throw away the baby with the bathwater. But even where all parameters are well-known, most conditions in the world are uncertain, with specific probabilities and/or outcomes remaining not known or unknowable. And where there is even the possibility of unknown parameters, then ignorance is unavoidable. All these cumulative dilemmas have profound consequences, as the chapters in this book explore. The bottom line, in many circumstances, is that the assumptions of a risk-based approach can be inappropriate, misleading – and even dangerous.

Uncertainties therefore are conditions of knowledge itself – how we understand, frame and construct possible futures – and are not just hard-wired into 'objective' situations. But uncertainties also have other features, beyond these epistemological and ontological implications. Across the chapters of this book, four additional dimensions are discussed:

- Uncertainties have concrete, material features. They are produced from complex, non-linear unpredictable systems (Driebe and McDaniel 2005). They have material origins and effects. For example, the environmental variability of rangelands may be a source of productive advantage for pastoralists as they move across landscapes harvesting nutrients – living with and from uncertainty (Krätli and Schareika 2010). In complex systems, surprises – sudden 'black swan' events – may arise that were never expected (Taleb 2007). Taming and controlling such systems is impossible, but understanding and responding to unpredictable variability is vital (Funtowicz and Ravetz 1990), requiring invention of new forms of science, regulation and management (van Zwanenberg, Chapter 4; Roe, Chapter 5).
- Uncertainties are not experienced in the same way by different people. Knowledges about the present and perspectives on the future are all constructed in particular contexts. Depending on one's situation, uncertainties may be embraced as an opportunity or encountered as a source of dread, fear and anxiety. An experiential, affective stance on uncertainty is therefore

unavoidable. Emotions and feelings matter, as they affect understanding and action. Religious and spiritual beliefs about – and enactment of – relationships between humans and the world may also impinge (Skrimshire 2014; Oxley, Chapter 12), as in Samkhya Hindu philosophy, which offers a plural perspective on understanding, influenced by consciousness, perception and experience.[2] And, in turn, uncertainties are influenced by histories, cultures and identities, as social worlds and historical experiences filter perspectives and condition action (Da Col and Humphrey 2012). Thus, marginalised communities in the global South will experience climate shocks in very different ways to privileged groups in the North, as histories of colonialism and dispossession influence what is possible and how pasts, presents and futures are viewed (Watts and Bohle 1993).

- Perspectives on uncertainties are also embodied, becoming part of who we are, as well as how we think and feel (Csordas and Harwod 1994). Sometimes this is physically reflected in our bodies. For example, men and women, and young and old people, may respond to the uncertainties of climatic or other disasters quite differently, as a result of the consequences of events in their day-to-day lives (Sword-Daniels et al. 2018). School children may find debates about climate change unsettling and anxiety-inducing, especially when 'facts' are unclear,[3] while living with a chronic illness may result in a very different outlook to those of medical professionals and even family members, as both the condition and its treatment are enacted through the body (Mol and Law 2004). Drawing on feminist and queer theory, Wendy Harcourt (2013) argues that the body plays an important – often hidden and contested – role in the ways we encounter the world, and conduct 'development'. As with 'tacit knowledge', embodied uncertainties remain entirely undocumented and even not consciously apprehended by those most intimately affected, making them especially significant when addressing responses to incertitude.

- Finally, our understandings of uncertainty are reflected in practices: how we act, and the type of social imaginaries we construct – or which emerge unintentionally – serve to guide our lives and politics (Arora and Glover 2017; Shove et al. 2012). In response, emerging practices include both controlling forms of 'audit culture' (Power 2004), as well as more flexible, adaptive forms of 'reliability management' (Roe 2013; Roe, Chapter 5). During the financial crisis, it was the practical responses of financial regulators, supervisors and traders that helped avoid total collapse. According to Ilene Grabel, this was due to features of 'productive incoherence' and 'pragmatic innovation' in the financial system (Grabel 2017). A focus on agency, and more distributed possibilities for action, directs attention towards relations of power in responding to uncertainty. Michael Thompson and Michael Warburton, for example, explored power dynamics around deep uncertainties over deforestation and river management in the Himalayas – tracking moves within discourse away from 'what the facts are' towards a focus on what powerful interests 'would like the facts to be'. In this way, the agency of incumbent interests behind major infrastructure proposals was reinforced, while that of less powerful actors – like mountain-dwelling subsistence farmers – was denigrated (Thompson and Gyawali 2007; Thompson and Warburton 1985).

A diverse appreciation of these five dimensions of uncertainty suggests a challenge to the controlling, managerial policy responses that have been the hallmark of technocratic modernity – and, for some, diagnostic of progress. However, as a number of this book's chapters discuss, alternative policy and management approaches have been proposed, ranging from adaptive management (Tompkins and Adger 2004) to experimentalist approaches (Sabel and Zeitlin 2010) to deliberative governance (Dryzek 2012). Central to these are the principles of incremental learning and the negotiation of outcomes along complex, plural pathways. Deliberation, negotiation and inclusive engagement across diverse knowledges and experiences is essential. As the following chapters show through varied examples, this requires an opening up to options and knowledges, and across all aspects of incertitude – including uncertainties in the strict sense, as well as ignorance and ambiguities following our earlier categorisation. Incertitude must therefore be embraced equally in relation to knowledge, materialities, experiences, embodiment and practice.

Yet, as Mary Douglas famously identified, the same apparent 'objective' conditions of uncertainty can be lived in and worked with in very different ways by different people (Douglas 1986). Uncertainties, she argued, are constituted very differently – for instance – in hierarchical or egalitarian social orders, or collectivist or individualist institutional cultures (Thompson *et al.* 1990). Likewise, for the influential German sociologist Niklas Luhmann (1993), it is contrasting practical systems of communication that bring uncertainties to material life. Rather than being seen as external 'states of the world', uncertainties are therefore better understood as the messy gaps, wrinkles and tangles that serve to make societies aware of – and reflexive in relation to – their own conditions of being. And, for the leading theorist of the 'risk society', Ulrich Beck, it is through uncertainties – more than professed knowledge – that contemporary societies most concretely encounter the cumulative contradictions of modernity in which they are embedded (Adam *et al.* 2000; Beck *et al.* 1994; Beck 1992).

Like Beck, the contributors to this book see risk and uncertainty as formative of contemporary politics (Mythen *et al.* 2018). Indeterminacy and non-knowledge fundamentally shape political and managerial possibilities. As discussed further below, the premises of many favoured policy frameworks – from equilibrium economics (Raworth 2017) to audit-based management (Power 2004) to economic regulation (Bronk and Jacoby 2016) to security regimes (Amoore 2013; Dillon 2007) to insurance provision (Ewald 1991) – become incompatible with embracing the full implications of uncertainty. Challenges to such frameworks emerge especially when looking at issues and geographies beyond Beck's original concern with individualised risks associated with accelerating industrial modernity in northern Europe (Caplan 2000). While uncertainties certainly reconfigure politics, they do so in diverse ways. As the various chapters show, class, gender, ethnicity, age and location matter in how uncertainties are understood and responded to (Curran 2018). A focus on uncertainty should therefore not divert attention from long-standing perspectives on social change, but instead highlight new dynamics (Carrapico *et al.*, Chapter 11)

As a challenge to a control-oriented technocratic order of globalising modernity, we argue that a focus on the politics of uncertainty is essential. This confronts the linear assumption that a universalised science creates technologies for singular progress, suggesting instead a more diverse, plural vision, implicating multiple modernities. Indeed, as uncertainties reconfigure politics, we can observe different effects. Uncertainty can create anxiety and fear, and open spaces for rent-seeking, profit-making and forms of populist authoritarianism (Scoones *et al.* 2018), while at the same time it can offer hope – and spaces for experimentation and learning that can lead to an emancipatory politics for the future (Solnit 2016). As the chapters discuss – across a diversity of domains – which directions are taken, and how institutions of science, law and the state respond, are crucial issues for our times (Nowotny 2015).

Topologies of uncertainty

Interweaving through these wider currents are the more specific dimensions of uncertainty explored in the chapters of this book. Just as quantification of any kind is always underlain by qualitative dimensions, so all the different arcane geometries of 'risk' and 'probability' are always shaped by the topologies of uncertainty on which they are built. So, the structures of possibility underpinning commerce, banking and finance are potentially formative of entire wider economies, and deeply influenced by the narratives of economics and the forms of modelling of uncertainty that are deployed (Walter and Wansleben, Chapter 2). Beyond the particular actuarial expediencies, it is the imagined relationships between presents and futures that make insurance so generative of everyday life, and that explain why regarding rigid forms of insurance as routes to social protection becomes problematic under conditions of uncertainty and ignorance (Johnson, Chapter 3; Taylor 2019).

Infrastructures and regulatory orders assert their own materialisations of political imaginations around technology regulation (van Zwanenberg, Chapter 4), the management of critical infrastructures (Roe, Chapter 5) and city planning (Kaker *et al.*, Chapter 6). These chapters highlight how the practices of scientists, regulators and civil society actors can help open up indeterminacies in everything from genetically modified crop technologies to 'smart' cars; they emphasise the importance of everyday practice and network-building in generating reliability in complex critical infrastructures, such as energy systems; and they explore how more effective responses to diverse uncertainties can be nurtured through creating 'experimental spaces' for innovation in urban governance (Evans *et al.* 2016).

Deepening global vulnerabilities around climate (Mehta and Srivastava, Chapter 7), disease (MacGregor *et al.*, Chapter 8) and 'natural disasters' (Pelling *et al.*, Chapter 9) create major political challenges for addressing uncertainties. Too often, there is a closing down towards narrow risk management and securitisation in approaches to early warning, emergency preparedness and disaster risk reduction. Yet, as these chapters show, locating understandings in a more complex appreciation of class, gender, ethnicity and age is essential if those directly affected by outbreaks, emergencies and disasters are to be involved.

The politics of uncertainty in debates over migration (Thorsen, Chapter 10), crime and terrorism (Carrapico *et al.*, Chapter 11) also reflect highly politicised institutional constructions of risk, danger and threat. These may obscure more positive approaches by ignoring alternative framings centred on hope and possibility (Kleist and Thorsen 2016). The knee-jerk, authoritarian response is to control, instil fear, construct borders and subject people to intrusive surveillance. A more encompassing view, on the other hand, would suggest alternatives; for example, focusing on the agency, networks and capacities of migrants themselves in facing uncertainties. How then are the contested meanings and implications of uncertainty negotiated? Underlying cultural, religious and spiritual framings may be underestimated in our rush to assert technocratic orders, as discussed in our final chapter (Oxley, Chapter 12). Religious beliefs involve competing views on destiny, renewal and apocalypse, for instance, and so must continuously grapple with issues of uncertainty as framing human existence, suggesting the need for a wider, more encompassing view.

From calculative control to creative care

A classic insight that arises from non-linear systems understandings – that minor changes can make a big difference – means that simple notions of prediction and control are a myth. Yet even with this acknowledgement widely accepted (if only rhetorically), indeterminacies are too often represented in a controlling, calculative and aggregative register. How often, for example, does discussion of 'tipping points' move from humility in the face of their possibility to hubris in regard to their precise prediction, or misplaced confidence that such complex systems can be subject to 'risk management'? (Lenton *et al.* 2019). As a result, the crucial point about the uncontrollability of uncertainty may paradoxically be most lost when it is apparently most acknowledged.

A number of the book's chapters reflect on a wide range of models. These include the economic forecasting models used by banks (Wansleben 2014); the actuarial and parametric models central to the (re)insurance industry (Johnson 2013); the infectious disease models that predict patterns of spread and impact and the many models that aim to predict the impacts of natural hazards – from floods to volcanoes to earthquakes (Hough 2002). Here as elsewhere, modelling struggles to make sense of uncertain, complex systems, often aiming to predict future patterns. Yet again, these calculative mathematical devices and aggregative practices too often involve attempted reductions of uncertainties to risk (Hastrup and Skrydstrup 2013).

In all these areas, non-linear interactions and disequilibrium dynamics at the heart of complex systems make the necessary simplifications and assumptions of modelling approaches problematic. Offering a sense of certainty where there is none misleads. It may help raise awareness about a particular potential disaster and raise funds for agencies aiming to respond. But this itself may divert attention from diverse lived-with, grounded circumstances, offering instead a headline figure projecting one impending crisis. And these imperatives may also blinker key players against surprise, entrenching ideas that a risk-managed *status quo* will result in stability. Reflecting on the financial crash of 2008, Andy Haldane, chief economist at the Bank of England, observed:

> Securitisation increased the dimensionality, and thus complexity, of the financial network. Nodes grew in size and interconnections between them multiplied. The financial cat's-cradle became dense and opaque. As a result, the precise source and location of underlying claims became anyone's guess (2009: 7).

The resulting crisis, Haldane (2010: 12) argues, was rooted in 'an exaggerated sense of knowledge and control'.

Of course, all models come with lists of provisos, caveats and qualifications, but, even with accuracy thus qualified, a key role persists in governing action. Here, the silences of models are as important as their proclamations. So in the end models are – albeit often quite elaborate – vehicles for telling stories. They equally embody and construct narratives about both present-futures and future-presents, often dressed up with arcane equations and mathematical formulations (Beckert and Bronk 2018). The narratives they relate are socially constructed, becoming accepted through often quite homogenous, uncritical networks of actors (Bronk 2019). Members of such networks all have a vested interest in maintaining an impression of control and giving a sense that collectively they have a capacity to manage complexity and define the future.

While such stories often unravel in the face of real-world events, the incumbent power of professions and their institutions – not surprisingly – soon reinstate the *status quo*. The last crisis is deemed an outlier, models are improved and the fragile performance of control continues in the face of uncertainty. Studies of financiers during and following the 2008 crash are instructive. The psychological imperative to construct 'conviction narratives' and deny uncertainty was evident, as the incentives for promoting positive imaginaries around fictional expectations were huge (Tuckett 2018). In the same way, misplaced concreteness in models at the centre of decision-making can be seen as a defensive mechanism used to displace anxieties around uncertain outcomes (Fenton-O'Creavy 2019).

Exercising huge power in policy processes, this process of storytelling through models is about presenting clear storylines, but also often involves moves to conceal and divert attention. Embedded assumptions typically hide normative, ethical and political positions, but because of the story's form, these appear only obliquely, or are hidden in the footnotes, acknowledgements, sensitivity analyses, funding sources and additional materials. Since models afford less audience interaction than in live storytelling, there is less accountability for the associated fictions and fallacies.

This raises questions about who grants authority to the narrative and how this is mediated; for instance with the media filtering out the headline story and ignoring the detail (Beckert and Bronk 2018).

This combination of rhetorical and market power helps entrench institutional and policy monocultures that in their turn further reinforce the authority given to such partial knowledge (Bronk and Jacoby 2016). Banks, risk management authorities, insurance firms, civil contingency agencies, humanitarian organisations and others require such knowledge that excludes significant dimensions of uncertainty in order to function (Walter and Wansleben, Chapter 2; Johnson, Chapter 3; MacGregor *et al.*, Chapter 8). They have the power to control narratives, stabilise expectations and define the future on their terms. These are classic hegemonic constellations that offer an illusion of control. In economics and finance, for example, commitments to the gold standard, the sanctity of the money supply and the power of equilibrium economics have, at different times, been core to belief systems, each with wide institutional and political commitments. Yet in each case, supported by powerful models with fragile assumptions, they have all been challenged and overturned (Mazzucato 2018).

In order to understand how models – and associated narratives – act to construct and colonise futures in ways that link to a wider political economy of incumbent power, we must understand their social and political lives (Appadurai 1988). This, in particular, means understanding the actors involved and their links across networks (Barthe *et al.* 2009). Insights from science and technology studies show processes through which particular equations and parameters become core to a model, which in turn becomes central to policy thinking. Whether these concern the epidemiologies of disease control (Leach and Scoones 2013) or constructions of financial derivatives (MacKenzie and Spears 2014), the models are not just strings of equations, but are linked to real people, places and problems – and so have social and political origins and consequences. The ways in which complex economies, climate dynamics or disease ecologies are modelled involves deliberate approaches to creating a calculative order (Çalışkan and Callon 2009), part of a performative process of model construction. That models are always tentative and provisional should not be a surprise, but their political role must be interrogated (Morgan 2012). As several chapters in the book show, the hegemonic acceptance of particular models – whether by bankers, auditors, actuaries, corporate risk managers or early warning administrators – remains a political act, even if it is inadvertent and normalised in everyday practice.

Whether in relation to economic or financial collapse, pandemic outbreaks, regulatory responsibilities, earthquake vulnerabilities or climate catastrophe, the dilemmas are highly pressing. How then to go beyond dominant forms of political and market closure – and the ubiquitous analytical monocultures that these engender? This is particularly difficult because prevailing cultures and practices around ever-more-powerful modelling can – through the brittle hubris of their technical disciplines, performative scope and normative sincerity – actually become a core part of the problem, as deadlines are specified, limits and boundaries defined and emergencies declared (Asayama *et al.* 2019; Hulme 2019).

The value of modelling must therefore be recognised as conditional and partial – thus requiring attention to dialogue, deliberation and the practical politics both of conception and application (Christley *et al.* 2013). Models are about different ways of making sense, not definitive ways of asserting precise predictions. Beyond the narrow models that often define a predictive risk paradigm, there are of course alternative cultures of modelling (Lahsen 2005). Here plurality is central – different models tell contrasting stories, and the key for policy is the conversation between them. Models may be derived from different sources of knowledge – from high-end science to more grounded, participatory insights – and so the story must be told as part of an interactive translation between idioms and explanations.

For example, in infectious disease management, analysts may confront uncertainties emerging from process models that examine the underlying population dynamics, from pattern models that explore the spatial dimensions of disease and from participatory models rooted in local people's perspectives, as differentiated by class, age and gender. Only by developing a narrative across all three can a more integrated and effective perspective on disease control emerge (Scoones *et al.* 2017). Similarly, understandings of uncertainties around climate change that are obtained 'from above' – from global circulation models, for example – and 'from below' – such as from those living in flood-prone cities – can encourage a conversation about how to address climate change collectively (Mehta *et al.* 2019). The co-production of knowledge, power and social order (Jasanoff 2004) generates a politics of engagement that is more suited to conditions of uncertainty (Mehta and Srivastava, Chapter 7). An open epistemology is therefore called for, one that follows the well-established traditions of feminist methodology, where plural, partial, situated knowledges are central to emergent understandings and responses (Haraway 1988; Harding 1987).

In embracing uncertainty in modelling practice, the emphasis must therefore shift towards active advocacy of qualities of doubt (rather than certainty), scepticism (rather than credulity) and dissent (rather than conformity) – and so towards creative care rather than calculative control. With indeterminacy thus embraced and irreducible plurality accepted, non-control and ignorance emerge as positive values in any attempt to create narratives for policy under conditions of uncertainty.

Modernities in the mirror

Amid all this complexity, a rather straightforward lesson repeatedly asserts itself: uncertainty (of whatever kind) is by definition not a condition that is simply 'out there' in the world; uncertainty is a property of *relations* between what is known and who is doing the knowing. Uncertainty therefore has at least as much to do with subjective dynamics within processes of knowledge production as the supposedly objective phenomena that are being represented. Whichever view is taken of knowledge itself (from 'objective' to 'subjective'), after all, all uncertainties are always at least to some degree 'subjective' (Kahneman and Tversky 1981). Uncertainties of all kinds are therefore deeply conditioned by the contexts of the subjects of knowledge, and are less reflective of the external objects on which these focus. In short, with uncertainty more a mode of action than a static condition, the phenomenon of being uncertain is perhaps better understood as a relational verb than as a categorical noun (Stirling 2019a).

Why this lesson is inconvenient is that it counters the expedient idea that uncertainties are readily subject to control. And – in the everyday life of institutions around the world – it is claims to be 'in control' of uncertainty that are (as we have discussed) crucial practical political resources for arguments and commitments around modernity and progress (Stirling 2019b). Therefore, for agencies involved in world trade regimes, intergovernmental science assessments, global environmental instruments, (inter)national regulatory standards and corporate risk assessments, for instance, it is claims to be able to control uncertainty that underpin the securing of authority, justification, legitimacy, trust and wider public acceptance (Pielke 2019; Anderson and Jewell 2019). If it were admitted that key uncertainties are not under control, then the roles, identities – as well as legitimacy and authority – of these agencies would be seriously eroded, and their claimed functions of planning, prediction, management and regulation undermined.

Across different kinds of governance structure, then, efforts frequently centre on pretending that uncertainty has been subdued by a series of control measures (Katzenstein and Seybert 2108). This is done in a number of ways. First, as already discussed, many messy, complex, open-ended dimensions of uncertainty are forced into a restrictive straight-jacket of 'risk'. Here, what are held to count as the relevant parameters are simply assumed to take a very few conveniently measurable forms. Values obtained on this basis for 'probabilities' and 'magnitudes' are presumed – as a matter of faith – to take the form of single precise, scalar numbers. And the results of all these highly subjectively situated procedures (often involving various forms of modelling) are then asserted as if they were precisely fixed 'out there' in a supposedly objective world. None of these rhetorics of control are grounded in the more complex and intractable realities of uncertainty, but the resulting performance remains immune to the profound mismatch, because the pretence is so essential to organisational and political functioning.

Hinging on this fallacy of control there emerges a further significant – but often neglected – implication. Reflecting similar confusions between what is 'objective' and what is 'subjective' in the compressions of uncertainty into risk, this concerns modernity itself. For, despite the many flows of creolising diversity discussed earlier, hegemonic forms of modernity also centrally revolve around control. This has been expressed, for example, in processes of individualisation, industrialisation, capitalisation, commoditisation, rationalisation and bureaucratisation, as well as the consolidation of the nation state, the assertive hegemony around science and notions of 'democracy' and – of course – the emergence of European colonialism. All involve their own varieties of fictions, fallacies or fantasies of control (Stirling 2019c).

What is common across the institutions, practices and cultures of globalising modernity, then, is the compulsion to offer performances of control, even if these are a pretence. In this light, the pervasive experience of uncertainty is not so much telling us about the world itself: what we are seeing in anxieties about uncertainty across so many areas are reflections of particular versions of modernity. In this sense, the predicaments of uncertainty are modernities in the mirror.

Yet the modernist institutions of control are patently failing. The performance of 'seeing like a state' (Scott 1998) or 'enclave capital' (Ferguson 2005) is no longer convincing. Challenges to mainstream conceptions of development – and its scientific, bureaucratic and institutional underpinnings – are coming from all directions. The climate crisis, turbulence in global financial institutions, infectious diseases that spread rapidly across continents and migration between nations on a massive scale – to name but a few – all challenge the conventional order. The post-World War II settlement that was overseen by the United Nations and the Bretton Woods institutions (the International Monetary Fund and the World Bank), and later the World Trade Organisation, all underpinned by Western science and technology, is not up to contemporary, intersecting challenges. Visions of modernity and constructions of 'development', established over the last 75 years in the West in particular, are unravelling (Hilgartner *et al.* 2015). Once-accepted parameters of progress – for example, permanent economic growth, an environment without limits, the provision of a welfare state, even parliamentary democracy – are being challenged (Kallis 2019; Mouffe 2018). These are of course not new observations, but it is much less recognised that the deficits of contemporary governance are intimately linked to the cumulative failings on the part of globalising modernities to face up to uncertainty in a complex, turbulent world.

In the face of such challenges, new versions of modernity are in the making. The implications of uncertainty are so profound that they challenge existing hegemonic frameworks and institutions, and drive imaginations of a post-capitalist, sustainable future, rooted in a new politics (Mason 2016; Gibson-Graham 2008). Some may reach out to utopian futures (Levitas 2013) in order to prefigure alternatives and define a new 'common sense', aimed at overturning existing hegemonic forces (Mason 2019). Others may focus on the many experiments in alternative economies, technology prototyping, architecture and design, based on the principles of the commons, community, conviviality and collectivity. While these rarely explicitly emphasise responses to conditions of uncertainty, they certainly reject the dominant modes of control, encouraging creative responses that are rooted in place (Braybrooke and Smith 2018). In turn, through attempting to decolonise the future, a prefigurative politics is imagined (Feola 2019), which defines how a world that embraced uncertainty might look. In *The Way of Ignorance*, the novelist, poet and farmer Wendell Berry (2008: ix–x) makes the case for such an approach:

> Because ignorance is … a part of our creaturely definition, we need an appropriate way: a way of ignorance, which is the way of neighborly love, kindness, caution, care, appropriate scale, thrift, good work, right livelihood … The way of ignorance, therefore, is to be careful, to know the limits and the efficacy of our knowledge. It is to be humble and to work on an appropriate scale.

As Brian Wynne elaborates,[4] to embrace ignorance is to celebrate the pervasive presence of 'the epistemic other' – affirming that there is always space for different ways of knowing any object, no matter how familiar. Surprise is thus not a threat to identity, status or authority, but a source of enriching, unrealised epistemic pluralities. But, rather than nurturing Berry's positive 'way of neighbourly love', reactions can instead emphasise existential threats to a supposed 'natural other', resulting in sometimes brutal reinforcements of control. The challenge then lies in reframing ignorance as an invitation to plural hopes, and respectful recognition of difference, rather than singular fears.

However, as several chapters in the book point out, this more positive vision of the potential of alternative modernities is not without its own challenges. While abandoning the pretence of control can open up space for progressive alternatives, this too can itself also create opportunities for more regressive forces to exploit spaces of uncertainty. Without deliberate efforts at fundamental reinvention of economy, society and politics – in diverse forms, in different contexts – older, regressive tropes and practices can re-emerge. Insecurities and vulnerabilities generated by uncertainties can create a politics of fear and blame (Linke and Smith 2009). Epistemic diversity and a lack of understanding between different races and ethnic groups result in xenophobic exclusions of migrants and fortress mentalities. This entrenches borders, with further erosions of appreciations for diversity resulting in racist attacks and discrimination based on sexualities and identities. Struggles between caring hopes and controlling fears are turbulent.

For across the world today, these political spaces are being encroached on by many forms of populist, nationalist discourse, steeped in authoritarianism and violence – promising reassertions of control in the face of uncertainty (Mudde and Kaltwasser 2018; Scoones *et al.* 2018).[5] The perceived chaos and lack of control that results from the collapse of the mainstream institutions of modernity are therefore breeding grounds for hate and violence and impositions of authoritarian rule. They also open up opportunities for exploitation and profit, in an unregulated, chaos-infused capitalism. Those with privileged positions in structures of appropriation – from national political-military elites to hedge fund managers to land speculators – can make money and gain power from capitalising on expanding conditions of uncertainty.

Across the chapters in this book, we explore how to foster the possibilities of alternative, emancipatory futures, while recognising the perils of embracing uncertainty. We argue that, in a complex, interconnected world, uncertainties are central to our common futures – and to normative ideas of sustainability and development. Through looking in the mirror, we have learned that a globalising, modernist framing of progress will not work, and has failed fundamentally. But how to usher in a more caring, collective, convivial, emancipatory alternative, without opening up to the clear, and sometimes present, dangers?

Uncertainty, vulnerability and precarity

This challenge is especially acute in contexts where people are living in highly vulnerable, uncertain settings. Here, people are necessarily focused on local, immediate, time-dependent life/body challenges, not the long-term future. Vernacular, grounded, everyday uncertainties reflect class, race, age, gender and other dimensions of difference. Therefore, addressing uncertainty means confronting inequality, vulnerability, precarity and the deeply embedded inheritances of history head-on. Uncertainty is never just a technical issue.

As has long been known, there is no such thing as a 'natural' hazard: hazards, and the vulnerabilities arising, are always co-constituted with social, ecological, political and economic contexts (Watts 2015; Blaikie *et al.* 1994). Uncertainties therefore generate place-based political ecologies and economies of vulnerability, raising questions of causal explanation and ethical responsibility (Ribot 2014). For example, the experience of flooding in the outer suburbs of New York City is unavoidably entwined with issues of poverty, housing quality and racial dislocation (Maantay and Maroko 2009). How people approach flood insurance is therefore refracted through these positionalities (Elliot 2018). In the same way, climate change in coastal Bangladesh is very real for those experiencing repeated flooding, yet externally-driven 'adaptation' responses may facilitate dispossession through the creation of alternative, 'modern' livelihoods (Paprocki 2018). The cyclone that struck Mozambique and Zimbabwe in 2019 was one of the most severe on record, but, again, its consequences have to be read politically, just as with Hurricane Katrina, which devastated parts of New Orleans in 2005 (Braun and McCarthy 2005).

Vernacular understandings of those confronting uncertainties and disasters must be the starting point for any analysis (Wynne 1996). For example, as in Mozambique in 2019, the complex effects of a flood – on housing, farming, health, mobility – are often poorly understood by humanitarian agencies and those providing protection (Hope 2019). The logics of local practice are complex, informed by diverse framings of what the risk is and to whom. Thus, in the context of the response to Ebola in West Africa, it was the local people who turned around the epidemic, linked to their located understanding of who was infected and how the disease spread. Interventions in burial ceremonies and movements to markets and between villages were key (Richards 2016). In the case of New York City, residents of the poor, outer suburbs – mostly non-white – reflected not on a technical hazard, nor on uncertainty *per se*, but on 'trouble': a summing up of the challenges of livelihoods linked to debt, poor housing, homelessness, disenfranchisement and lack of faith in the state (Elliot 2018).

Such practical logics and vernacular understandings emerge from place-based experience, as well as histories. People in rural Mozambique, just as suburban New York City, know they are largely on their own. The measures designed to help are palliative and limited. People must therefore respond in ways that are rooted in networked solidarities that get them through a crisis. This draws on deep associations – of religious, racial and ethnic connection – often wrapped up with longer histories and memories. Identity and place are thus inevitably entwined with how responses to uncertainty emerge. For those marginalised in relation to race, for example, people may draw on deep memories of slavery and colonialism where, on the slave ship or in the plantation or in settings subject to colonial rule, ancestors had suffered other uncertainties that resonate with today's experiences (McKittrick 2011). The 'slow violence' of sustained exploitation and recurrent uncertainty (Nixon 2011) contrasts dramatically with a liberal, 'white' vision of open-ended, imagined futures – a luxury created in many respects on the back of sustained exploitation (Anderson et al. 2019; Anderson 2012). In thinking about the constructions of and responses to uncertainty, particularly in contexts with long histories of marginalisation and structural inequality, the framing of ethical choice, issues of temporality and what constitutes the future for whom become critical considerations.

Yet the contemporary institutional paraphernalia of disaster intervention strategies around emergency response, preparedness planning, early warning, civil contingency, disaster risk reduction and so on, frequently fails to take such contexts into account (MacGregor et al., Chapter 8). The risk is tangible, the response is specific and a veritable industry is mobilised around it. The burgeoning institutionalisation of the disaster industry – from the global Sendai framework to local municipal contingency plans – act too often to construct narrow, manageable, technical responses (Cannon and Müller-Mahn 2010; Pelling et al., Chapter 9). Global infectious disease responses, for example, are often medicalised (focusing on a single pathogen, linked to a drugs and vaccine response) and frequently securitised (urging control at source, militarised emergency planning and draconian intervention if needed) (Lakoff 2017; Elbe 2010; MacGregor et al., Chapter 8).

The narratives of 'crisis' and 'emergency' encourage urgency and help mobilise funds, but may act to divert attention from the local and particular, where responses in different forms are being constructed. Emergencies are declared in order that normal democratic rules do not apply, bureaucratic hurdles are jumped and a securitised, post-political technocratic order is imposed (Calhoun 2010). However, the language of crisis can blind those involved to the uncertainties at play, no matter what the urgency. In the complex of responses around disasters and emergencies – from climate change (Mehta and Srivastava, Chapter 7) to disease outbreaks (MacGregor et al., Chapter 8) to terrorism (Carrapico et al., Chapter 11) – a set of technologies and practices act to govern the future.

This style of 'biopolitical' governmentality (Lentzos and Rose 2009) creates forms of control, exerted through a complex of discourse and practice. This in turn results in subjectification of key actors as victims and the reification of particular forms of technical expertise, sometimes resulting in securitised responses. Thus, the uncertainties around, say, biodiversity loss and extinction rates have been fuelling forms of 'militarised conservation' in response to 'emergency' conditions (Duffy et al. 2019). In this and other cases, intersecting modalities of emergency response in turn generate new uncertainties and inequalities, sometimes perpetuating the problem (Samimian-Darash and Rabinow 2015). As the chapters in this book show, such styles of expert-led, technocratic, securitised response are problematic, both practically and politically.

Take infectious disease control responses. From Ebola to avian influenza to COVID-19, a range of agencies have taken on responsibility for disease control within global health bureaucracies. Yet too often, risk is again instrumentalised, resulting in medicalised, securitised responses. This cannot address more complex disease ecologies, or how ill-health is generated through multiple, interacting factors, such as malnutrition, immunodeficiency and marginalisation. Ill-health often emerges from structural inequalities (Farmer 1996), and is lived with, and experienced, by those exposed, generating often quite individualised emotions and bodily responses (Nguyen and Peschard 2003). In such cases, knowledge about outcomes is complex and indeterminate, and so not amenable to a conventional risk response. Instead, responses must be assembled locally by multiple actors (more than singular authorities), be constituted in social relations (more than categories of institutions), be rooted in context (more than universal standards) and deploy practical knowledges from diverse sources (more than elite disciplinary expertise). Effective responses to uncertainties around ill-health are therefore emergent, based on contestation and deliberation, and grounded in everyday practical and emotional experience (MacGregor *et al.* Chapter 8).

However, we must ask: can those living with ill-health or confronting climate change or disasters devote the time and energy to assemble responses in the face of such bewildering, overwhelming uncertainty? Being income- and time-poor, the marginalised are often the last to engage with inclusive, deliberative processes, even if these are offered. Living in conditions of precarity means people do not have the luxury of responding to unknown futures: daily survival is the focus, and stress, anxiety and trauma are common. In such circumstances, time becomes compressed, and it is impossible to contemplate long-term future horizons. It is perhaps such people who most require state protections that are informed by expert judgement. Does passing on the responsibility for managing uncertainties to those experiencing already precarious lives only add to their burden? Who can they trust and rely on to care for their welfare?

Forms of local collective action and mutualism through traditional kin networks, religious congregations, charities, friendly societies or other collectivities have long provided this function, combined with various forms of coping, making-do and improvised resourcefulness.[6] Modern welfare states took this over but have been ravaged by the hollowing out of state functions through neoliberal policies. Meanwhile, social and disaster insurance has recently become a preferred solution, addressing welfare at a distance through the market. Yet none of these models – whether through voluntary association, the state or the market – can easily address the radical uncertainties that people face. Instead, a consideration of uncertainty under conditions of precarity requires a radical rethink of notions of welfare and livelihood support.

As several chapters in this book argue, this suggests the need for a more sensitive, co-produced response that does not impose a technocratic, standardised plan, but at the same time does not load responsibilities wholly onto local people to work out on their own. For example, can insurance approaches be refashioned such that local forms of moral economy and mutual help become supported, rather than side-lined by technocratic, top-down approaches (Johnson, Chapter 3)? Such approaches must encourage 'communities of fate' – those confronting the same uncertainties with the same degree of challenge rooted in historical marginalisation

(Marske 1991) – to come together around shared solidarities and mobilise around demanding new terms, and different approaches to insurance provision and welfare support (Elliot 2018).

Alongside welfare and livelihood support, a focus on uncertainty also requires us to re-imagine the institutions surrounding preparedness planning, contingency measures and early warning systems. As discussed above, expert-led, technocratic impositions premised on risk do not work. But what might? Can an inclusive early warning system for, say, drought or disease outbreaks be imagined, where burdens are shared, multiple knowledges brought together, networks of trust built and negotiation around interpretations facilitated? Could this be based around an improvised, experimental approach across sites, but linked to and informed by climate data, disease monitoring or disaster/hazard mapping? As Chapters 7 and 8 show, knowledge intermediaries and brokers become crucial for such initiatives, facilitating deliberation and negotiation, and offsetting rumour, speculation and concealment, which often result in expert-led systems being rejected. Who such intermediaries are would depend on the context, but trust across social differences and hierarchies is essential. Such an approach would move beyond assignations of risk and cultures of blame to a common, shared goal of navigating uncertainty together.

In sum, a new politics of uncertainty must challenge the biopolitical framings and governmentalities of conventional technocratic approaches that define populations or geographic areas as 'at risk'. Instead, the intersections of uncertainty, vulnerability, precarity and marginalisation must be taken seriously, alongside a commitment to 'cognitive justice' (Visvanathan 2005). This suggests a very different type of approach, centred on shared understandings, negotiation of outcomes and collective solidarity and mobilisation. It must be rooted in what we have earlier identified as a politics of care and conviviality, rejecting a simple reliance on state protection, standardised welfare and market-based insurance.

Asking questions about whose crisis, catastrophe or emergency it is, and how it is experienced, is not a denial of the importance of the event, or the roles for expertise in defining key aspects. Instead, it is a recognition that climate change, disease, earthquakes – or other uncertain events – will look different from the standpoint of those living in conditions of precarity and vulnerability. This means recasting responses, moving away from ones that are forged through externally-imposed, expert-led governmentality towards forms of 'response-ability' (Haraway 1997), with located capabilities and horizontal accountabilities at the core. As we discuss further in the next section, this has profound implications, including a need to reject all kinds of authoritarian control – technocratic as much as autocratic – in order to foster opportunities for more caring forms of political relations and action under conditions of uncertainty.

Uncertainty and the politics of responsibility

Uncertainties create cultures of blame, but also a politics of responsibility and accountability. Who is in charge? Who owns what risk? Who is responsible for mitigation? Where does epistemic, cognitive justice lie? The rise of a marketised form of risk governmentality, typified by the promotion of various forms of insurance (Johnson, Chapter 3), has generated a particular style of politics, where risks are redistributed through market mechanisms. These approaches often overshadow other approaches to the redistribution of risk and the allocation of responsibility.

In particular, the less obvious forms of social solidarity and mutualism, based on collective forms of protection against risk and uncertainty, are too often ignored. But, if uncertainties are indeterminate and non-knowledge is central, then ways of life are simply not insurable in any conventional sense, and alternative, 'moral economy' responses are required. As a result, very different types of governance must emerge, associated with new roles for citizens confronting uncertainty. To respond to complex uncertainties, citizens cannot just be customers of standardised insurance products, nor passive citizens of supposedly benevolent technocratic states – they must take on new roles, as part of collectivities that are based on the principle of solidarity, where care and collaboration are central (Bollier and Helfrich 2014; Gibson-Graham 2008).

If openness is encouraged, challenges will necessarily arise around 'regulatory arbitrage' – deciding which version counts in commitments to negotiated outcomes. We must ask: who is the bearer of risk and uncertainty of last resort, and what is the role of the state in the context of a less hierarchical, more citizen-led approach to governance? Responsibilities must be shared, fostering horizontal and vertical accountabilities as embedded politically vibrant relationships, not as part of simple auditable accounting (Gaventa 2002). And such relationships need to be sustained over time, since the addressing of one source of uncertainty inevitably raises new ones. Processes must be continuous and recursive, based on experimentation, learning, evaluation and adaptation (Guijt 2019). This requires new styles of expertise, legal mediation and state regulation that are more flexible and open, requiring a radical reconfiguration of professional and institutional approaches in planning and regulation (van Zwanenberg, Chapter 4; Kaker *et al.,* Chapter 6).

The sort of deliberative, adaptive, experimental forms of governance that accepting uncertainty demands already happen, of course – but often without recognition. So, for example, in relation to the governance of energy infrastructure in Europe, experiments have taken place around the transport and supply of electricity, allowed for by the European Union's decentralised policy regime, and guided by the principle of subsidiarity (Rangoni 2019). Learning among companies and regulators has taken place, and substantial shifts have occurred in regimes over time, without directed intervention. Similarly, in complex, dispersed supply chains for high-tech manufacturing, where networks spread across the world between large and small companies, collaborative negotiations around contracts occur incrementally. No one player is in a position to impose, and the technological and market conditions are highly uncertain, but cooperation is essential if the products are to be delivered (Dodgson 2018). This is not just *ad hoc* 'muddling through' (Lindblom 1959), but a form of networked collective action based on inclusion, conversation and collaboration.

These 'new commons', frequently facilitated by easy digital connection, allow for a whole range of collaborative approaches to inclusive innovation and shared economic activity – from hacker and maker spaces to urban gardening and food sovereignty to community energy supply systems to urban development in 'transition towns' (Kirwan *et al.* 2016). In different ways, these create both a new form of community-based wealth-building, but also – crucially – a different route to addressing uncertainty through a more collective, shared approach. A key feature of all these initiatives – from global technology supply chains to small community gardens – is the movement towards an expected norm of permanent adaptability, as part of a process shared within a collective or network. Thus, equality and democracy – locally and across networks – become intrinsic to addressing uncertainties (Rayner and Cantor 1987).

Debates about the governance of risk and uncertainty must therefore go beyond the rigidities of the allocation and distribution of responsibility through insurance liability, legal claims or regulatory fiat, and move to a more open, co-produced, negotiated approach, where relationships and trust are central. Some profound challenges are presented to discourses on trust itself. By contrast to conventional emphases on relations of trust flowing up power gradients (from those who are governed to those doing the governing), trust becomes recognisable as an intrinsically reciprocal and symmetrical social process (Stirling 2015). And, of course, the political implications here concern not just relations within structures, but the constituting of such structures themselves. In moving beyond cultures of control to ones of care and conviviality, hierarchy, inequality and appropriation are seen as problematic as the modes of calculation, standardisation and aggregation discussed earlier.

As we have already observed, this creates a momentum for a fundamental rethinking of existing relationships between state protection, technical expertise and deliberative citizenship under uncertainty. And this, in turn, requires a newly pluralised, inclusive politics of responsibility, where states, corporations, legal systems and science all have different, new roles. In moving from control to care and conviviality, the only meaningful ways to achieve robustness and reconciliation in the face of burgeoning uncertainties involve justice, equality and plurality.

Rethinking the politics of uncertainty: the challenges of transformation

As we have seen, uncertainties can create fear, anxiety and closure, and can be linked to the rise of regressive, authoritarian populisms, profit- and rent-seeking capital and capture by elites. But uncertainties can also generate hope, creativity, curiosity, entrepreneurship, discovery, innovation and epistemic humility – and so possibilities for emancipatory democratic transformation. Diverse questions therefore emerge around facilitating these progressive transformations. What methods, processes and mobilisations can tilt the balance towards more positive outcomes? How can alternatives be prefigured to reinforce this new politics? Who is centred in transformatory spaces, and who is to the side? And what solidarities, ethics and styles of reflexivity are required for this new politics of uncertainty?

It is in relation to such questions that the balance between control and care/ conviviality comes to the fore. As we have suggested, open discussion of contrasts between risk and uncertainty can profoundly challenge the failures, fallacies and fictions of control. By interrogating what uncertainties are – and how we understand, feel and respond to them – we can both help to destabilise, but also rebalance and reinvent, the institutions and practices of globalising modernity. This helps resist the 'closing down' effects of individualisation, commodification, financialisation, bureaucratisation, audit and securitisation. And beyond this deconstruction, this book attempts a reflection on the politics of uncertainty across different areas of political life – highlighting both possibilities and limits for the opening up of new forms of transformation.

Again, uncertainties can be generative of diverse, imagined alternatives. By opening up spaces to re-imagine futures, to dream and to construct alternatives, uncertainties can be confronted in positive ways: not as threats or sources of fear, but as sources of hope and possibility. As Rebecca Solnit (2016: xii) argues:

> Hope locates itself in the premises that we don't know what will happen and that in the spaciousness of uncertainty is room to act. When you recognize uncertainty, you recognize that you may be able to influence the outcomes – you alone or you in concert with a few dozen or several million others. Hope is an embrace of the unknown and knowable, an alternative to the certainty of both optimists and pessimists.

As she says, this requires a mobilisation of future-making among different actors. Eschewing grand visions and stylised expert scenarios, these unofficial futures emerge in intersecting uncertainties from the ground up, in everyday, 'quotidian utopias of experience' (Mahony and Beck 2019). In relation to climate change, this is perhaps already happening through the arguments of the youth climate strikers addressing 'system change' not just climate change, or the demand from Extinction Rebellion for 'citizens' assemblies' to deliberate on alternatives (Bain and Bongiorno 2019). While often framed problematically in sometimes authoritarian and controlling terms of 'urgent action' and 'impending emergency', and with frequently misplaced deference to narrow forms of expert science and singular targets (Asayama *et al.* 2019), these mobilisations can nevertheless help to open up spaces that demonstrate, explore and experiment with alternatives.

It is essential to bring into these conversations, the diverse implications of uncertainty. One recurrent theme running through this book is that open and accountable engagements with the politics of uncertainty are more imperative now than ever. For it is through such politics that the mainstream science and institutions of climate change must grapple with issues such as intergenerational justice and alternative perspectives on 'limits' or 'growth' (Kallis 2019), and so challenge the standard integrated assessment models that have guided the work of the International Panel on Climate Change and others to date (Beck and Mahony 2017). All this requires uncertain futures to be central to debates about climate change, environmental justice and sustainability.

Yet we must recognise that the socio-technical imaginaries that guide policy and politics are deeply resistant to change (Jasanoff and Kim 2015). Policy narratives routinely get stuck because they serve professional and institutional interests, and become convenient myths that are taken for granted (Keeley and Scoones 2003). Disrupting the comfortable *status quo* and confronting incumbent privilege and hegemonic power can be difficult. Mobilisations, such as those we are seeing around climate change, are important, but must extend across domains, as the chapters that follow argue. As with climate change, rethinking migration policy, city planning, infectious disease responses, critical infrastructure design, the regulation of technology, and finance and banking practice, among others, is hugely challenging, given the power and authority of incumbent regimes. The argument of this book is that appreciations of uncertainty provide the golden thread that connects these issues. Given the consistent failures of mainstream modernist, technocratic institutions, it is vital to embed the imagining of transformative change in a vibrant politics of uncertainty.

This is not going to happen by itself. The lesson of the emergent, networked climate movement – as with others around food sovereignty, housing and land rights, energy poverty or commoning approaches – is that new solidarities are essential. Confronting uncertainty becomes central; not as separate and additional to resistance to inequality, injustice and poverty, but as simultaneous and inseparable from it. This requires imagining very different futures that challenge deeply entrenched power and authority. In forging progressive alliances for re-imagining the future, the potential exclusions of both knowledges and people must be acknowledged, as we have discussed. Who has the luxury to create such alternatives? Whose jobs and livelihoods are threatened by alternative pathways? How can contingent privileges be harnessed to flatten encompassing gradients of power that restrict inclusion?

For many living precarious lives, uncertainties that threaten existence on a daily basis are created through histories of oppression and marginalisation. While the uncertainties of climate change may be affecting us all, the fossil fuel dependency of the global economy only emerged through unequal patterns of development linked to historical processes of exploitation. Those digging coal in hazardous working conditions, perhaps in the global South, are also facing uncertainties of a more immediate kind. The debate about uncertainty and transformations to sustainability therefore must create forms of solidarity and alternative pathways that appreciate longer histories in the politics of uncertainty.

All this involves actively supporting alternatives emerging in experimentation and action, especially in marginalised settings. And, in this way, these new politics of uncertainty chime with the long-standing politics of emancipation and decolonisation. For the resulting transformative aspirations are essentially the same: in moving from institutions of control to cultures of care and conviviality, familiar values come to the fore – of equality, solidarity, collectivity and mutuality. Each draws on moral economies of hope, rather than fear. And it is through embracing uncertainties in their many forms – and challenging the pervasive kinds of controlling apparatus that work to deny and obscure them – that a positive, progressive potential emerges at a time of crisis for democratic struggle. Now is therefore the moment for such pluralised, diversified, distributed and egalitarian processes of action and transformation. Just as knowledges are co-produced with social orders, so may the more explicit embracing of uncertainties help to open up recalcitrant political structures and decolonise our unfolding futures.

Notes

1 The global COVID-19 pandemic was unfolding as this book went to press. Whilst this chapter therefore does not address this issue directly, the discussion is nonetheless relevant throughout.
2 See comments by Dipak Gyawali at *The Politics of Uncertainty* symposium, July 2019, www. buff.ly/35D5RSI (accessed, 7 February 2020).
3 See podcast, 'Youth Transformations and Global Warming', November 2019, www. transformineducation.org/podcasts/youth-transformations-global-warming (accessed 7 February 2020).
4 In comments by Brian Wynne at *The Politics of Uncertainty* symposium, July 2019, and elaborated in subsequent very helpful personal communications.
5 See materials from the Emancipatory Rural Politics Initiative, www.opendemocracy.net/ en/authoritarian-populism-and-rural-world/ (accessed 7 February 2020).
6 In the Democratic Republic of Congo this is referred to as '*débrouillardise*', which is seen as a national trait that is vital for survival under conditions of war and economic collapse (Jourdan 2013).

References

Adam, B., Beck, U. and Van Loon, J. (eds) (2000) *The Risk Society and Beyond: Critical Issues for Social Theory*, London: Sage

Ahuja, R. (2009) *Pathways of Empire: Circulation, 'Public Works' and Social Space in Colonial Orissa, c. 1780 1914 (New Perspectives in South Asian History)*, Hyderabad: Orient Black Swan

Amoore, L. (2013) *The Politics of Possibility: Risk and Security Beyond Probability*, Durham NC and London: Duke University Press

Anderson, B. (2012) 'Preemption, Precaution, Preparedness: Anticipatory Action and Future Geographies', *Progress in Human Geography* 34.6: 777–798

Anderson, B., Grove, K., Rickards, L. and Kearnes, M. (2019) 'Slow Emergencies: Temporality and the Racialized Biopolitics of Emergency Governance', *Progress in Human Geography*, May 2019, DOI: 10.1177/0309 132519849263

Anderson, K. and Jewell, J. (2019) 'Debating the Bedrock of Climate-Change Mitigation Scenarios', *Nature*, 16 September 2019, www.nature.com/articles/d41586-019-02744-9 (accessed 25 October 2019)

Appadurai, A. (ed) (1988) *The Social Life of Things: Commodities in Cultural Perspective*, Cambridge: Cambridge University Press

Arora, S. (2019) 'Admitting Uncertainty, Transforming Engagement: Towards Caring Practices for Sustainability Beyond Climate Change', *Regional Environmental Change* 19.6: 1571–1584

Arora, S. and Glover, D. (2017) *Power in Practice: Insights from Technography and Actor-Network Theory for Agricultural Sustainability*, STEPS Working Paper 100, Brighton: STEPS Centre

Asayama, S., Bellamy, R., Geden, O., Pearce, W. and Hulme, M. (2019) 'Why Setting a Climate Deadline is Dangerous', *Nature Climate Change* 9.8: 570–572

Bain, P.G. and Bongiorno, R. (2019) 'It's Not Too Late to do the Right Thing: Moral Motivations for Climate Change Action', *Wiley Interdisciplinary Reviews: Climate Change* 11: 615

Barthe, Y., Callon, M. and Lascoumes, P. (2009) *Acting in an Uncertain World: An Essay on Technical Democracy*, Cambridge MA: MIT Press

Beck, S. and Mahony, M. (2017) 'The IPCC and the Politics of Anticipation' *Nature Climate Change* 7: 311–313

Beck, U. (1992) *Risk Society: Towards a New Modernity*, London: Sage

Beck, U., Giddens, A. and Lash, S. (1994) *Reflexive Modernization: Politics, Tradition and Aesthetics in the Modern Social Order*, Stanford CA: Stanford University Press

Beckert, J. and Bronk, R. (eds) (2018) *Uncertain Futures: Imaginaries, Narratives and Calculation in the Economy*, Oxford: Oxford University Press

Berry, W. (2008) 'The Way of Ignorance', in W. Jackson and B. Vitek (eds) *The Virtues of Ignorance: Complexity, Sustainability, and the Limits of Knowledge*, Kentucky: The University Press of Kentucky

Blaikie, P., Cannon, T., Davis, I. and Wisner, B. (eds) (1994) *At Risk: Natural Hazards, People's Vulnerability and Disasters*, London: Routledge

Bollier, D. and Helfrich, S. (eds) (2014) *The Wealth of the Commons: A World Beyond Market and State*, Amhurst: Levellers Press

Braun, B. and McCarthy, J. (2005) 'Hurricane Katrina and Abandoned Being', *Environmental and Planning D: Society and Space* 23.6: 802–809

Braybrooke, K. and Smith, A. (2018) 'Introduction: Liberatory Technologies for Whom? Exploring a New Generation of Makerspaces Defined by Institutional Encounters', *Journal of Peer Production* 2.12: 1–13

Bronk, R. (2019) '*Uncertain Futures and the Politics of Uncertainty*', STEPS Centre Blog, 3 September 2019, https://steps-centre.org/blog/uncertain-futures-and-the-politics-of-uncertainty/ (accessed 7 February 2020)

Bronk, R. and Jacoby, W. (2016) *Uncertainty and the Dangers of Monocultures in Regulation, Analysis, and Practice*, MPIFG Discussion Paper 16/6, Cologne: Max Planck Institute for Studying Societies

Calhoun, C. (2010) 'The Idea of Emergency: Humanitarian Action and Global (Dis)order', in D. Fassin and M. Pandolfi (eds) *Contemporary States of Emergency: the Politics of Military and Humanitarian Interventions*, New York: Zone Books

Çalışkan, K. and Callon, M. (2009) 'Economization, Part 1: Shifting Attention from the Economy Towards Processes of Economization', *Economy and Society* 38.3: 69–398

Cannon, T. and Müller-Mahn, D. (2010) 'Vulnerability, Resilience and Development Discourses in Context of Climate Change', *Natural Hazards* 55.3: 621–635

Caplan, P. (ed) (2000) *Risk Revisited*, London: Pluto Press

Christley, R.M., Mort, M., Wynne, B., Wastling, J.M., Heathwaite, A.L., Pickup, R., Austin, Z. and Latham, S.M. (2013) '"Wrong, but Useful": Negotiating Uncertainty in Infectious Disease Modelling', *PLOS One* 8.10e76277

Cowen, M. and Shenton, D. (1996) *Doctrines of Development*, London: Routledge

Csordas, T.J. and Harwood, A. (eds) (1994) *Embodiment and Experience: The Existential Ground of Culture and Self*, Cambridge: Cambridge University Press

Curran, D. (2018) 'Beck's Creative Challenge to Class Analysis: From the Rejection of Class to the Discovery of Risk-Class', *Journal of Risk Research* 21.1: 29–40

Da Col, G. and Humphrey, C. (2012) 'Introduction: Subjects of Luck-Contingency, Morality, and the Anticipation of Everyday Life', *Social Analysis* 56.2: 1–25

Dillon, M. (2007) 'Governing through Contingency: the Security of Biopolitical Governance', *Political Geography* 26.1: 41–47

Dodgson, M. (2018) *Technological Collaboration in Industry: Strategy, Policy and Internationalization in Innovation*, London: Routledge

Douglas, M. (1986) *Risk Acceptability According to the Social Sciences*, New York: Russell Sage Foundation

Driebe, D. and McDaniel, R.R. (2005) 'Complexity, Uncertainty and Surprise: An Integrated View', in R.R. McDaniel and D.J. Driebe (eds) *Uncertainty and Surprise in Complex Systems*, Berlin and Heidelberg: Springer

Dryzek, J.S. (2012) *Foundations and Frontiers of Deliberative Governance*, Oxford: Oxford University Press

Duffy, R., Massé, F., Smidt, E., Marijnen, E., Büscher, B., Verweijen, J., Ramutsindela, M., Simlai, T., Joanny, L. and Lunstrum, E. (2019) 'Why We Must Question the Militarisation of Conservation', *Biological Conservation* 232: 66–73

Elbe, S. (2010) *Security and Global Health*, Cambridge: Polity

Elliott, R. (2018) '"Scarier than Another Storm": Values at Risk in the Mapping and Insuring of US Floodplains', *The British Journal of Sociology* 70.3: 1067–1090

Evans, J., Karvonen, A. and Raven, R. (eds) (2016) *The Experimental City*, London: Routledge

Ewald, F. (1991) 'Insurance and Risk', in G. Burchell, C. Gordon and P. Miller (eds) *The Foucault Effect: Studies in Governmentality*, Chicago: Chicago University Press

Farmer, P. (1996) 'On Suffering and Structural Violence: A View from Below', *Daedalus* 125.1: 261–283

Fenton-O'Creevy, M. (2019) *Solidarity, Insurance, Emotions and Uncertainty*, STEPS Centre blog, 19 September https://steps-centre.org/blog/solidarity-insurance-emotions-and-uncertainty/ (accessed 7 February 2020)

Feola, G. (2019) 'Degrowth and the Unmaking of Capitalism Beyond "Decolonization of the Imaginary"', *ACME: An International Journal for Critical Geographies* 18.4: 977–997

Ferguson, J. (2005) 'Seeing like an Oil Company: Space, Security, and Global Capital in Neoliberal Africa', *American Anthropologist* 107.3: 377–382

Folbre, N., Olin Wright, E., Andersson, J., Hearn, J., Himmelweit, S. and Sterling, A. (2018) 'The Multiple Directions of Social Progress: Ways Forward', in International Panel on Social Progress (ed) *Rethinking Society for the 21st Century: Report of the International Panel on Social Progress*, Cambridge: Cambridge University Press

Funtowicz, S.O. and Ravetz, J.R. (1990) *Uncertainty and Quality in Science for Policy*, New York: Springer

Gaonkar, D.P. (1999) 'On Alternative Modernities', *Public Culture* 11.1: 1–18

Gaventa, J. (2002) 'Exploring Citizenship, Participation and Accountability', *IDS Bulletin* 33.2: 1

Gibson-Graham, J.K. (2008) 'Diverse Economies: Performative Practices for Other Worlds', *Progress in Human Geography* 32.5: 613–632

Grabel, I. (2017) *When Things Don't Fall Apart: Global Financial Governance and Developmental Finance in an Age of Productive Incoherence*, Cambridge, MA: MIT Press

Guijt, I. (2019) 'How Can NGOs Feel at Home with Uncertainty?', STEPS Centre blog, 19 November, https://steps-centre.org/blog/how-can-ngos-feel-at-home-with-uncertainty/ (accessed 7 February 2020)

Haldane, A. (2010) 'The $100 Billion Question', available at: www.bankofengland.co.uk/speech/2010/the-100-billion-question-speech-by-andy-haldane (accessed 7 February 2020)

—— (2009) 'Rethinking the Financial Network', available at: www.bankofengland.co.uk/speech/2009/rethinking-the-financial-network (accessed 7 February 2020)

Haraway, D. (1988) 'Situated Knowledges: The Science Question in Feminism and the Privilege of Partial Perspective', *Feminist Studies* 14.3: 575–599

Haraway, D. (1997) *Modest_Witness@ Second_Millennium. FemaleMan_Meets_OncoMouse: Feminism and Technoscience*, London: Routledge

Harcourt, W. (2013) *Body Politics in Development: Critical Debates in Gender and Development*, London: Zed Books

Harding, S.G. (1987) *Feminism and Methodology: Social Science Issues*, Bloomington: Indiana University Press

Hastrup, K. and Skrydstrup, M. (eds) (2013) *The Social Life of Climate Change Models: Anticipating Nature*, London: Routledge

Hilgartner, S., Miller, C.A. and Hagendijk, R. (eds) (2015) *Science and Democracy: Making Knowledge and Making Power in the Biosciences and Beyond*, London: Routledge

Hobden, S. (2002) *Historical Sociology of International Relations*, Cambridge: Cambridge University Press

Hope, M. (2019) 'Cyclones in Mozambique May Reveal Humanitarian Challenges of Responding to a New Climate Reality', *The Lancet Planetary Health* 3.8: e338–e339

Hough, S.E. (2002) *Earthshaking Science: What We Know (and Don't Know) About Earthquakes*, Princeton: Princeton University Press

Hulme, M. (2019) 'Climate Emergency Politics is Dangerous', *Issues in Science and Technology* Fall 2019, 23–25

Ibarra-Colado, E. (2006) 'Organization Studies and Epistemic Coloniality in Latin America: Thinking Otherness from the Margins', *Organization* 13: 463–488

Illich, I. (1973) *Tools for Conviviality*, New York: Harper & Row

Jasanoff, S. (ed) (2004) *States of Knowledge: The Co-Production of Science and the Social Order*, London: Routledge

Jasanoff, S. and Kim, S.H. (eds) (2015) *Dreamscapes of Modernity: Sociotechnical Imaginaries and the Fabrication of Power*, Chicago and London: University of Chicago Press

Johnson, L. (2013) 'Index Insurance and the Articulation of Risk-Bearing Subjects', *Environment and Planning A* 45.11: 2663–2681

Jourdan, L. (2013) 'From Humanitarian to Anthropologist: Writing at the Margins of Ethnographic Research in the Democratic Republic of Congo', in S. Thomson, A. Ansoms and J. Murison (eds) *Emotional and Ethical Challenges for Field Research in Africa*, London: Palgrave Macmillan

Kahneman, D. and Tversky, A. (1981) *Variants of Uncertainty*, Stanford: Stanford University Press

Kallis, G. (2019) *Limits: Why Malthus was Wrong and Why Environmentalists Should Care*, Stanford: Stanford University Press

Katzenstein, P.J. and Seybert, L.A. (eds) (2018) *Protean Power: Exploring the Uncertain and Unexpected in World Politics*, Cambridge: Cambridge University Press

Kaup, M. (2012) *Neobaroque in the Americas: Alternative Modernities in Literature, Visual Art and Film*, Charlottesville: University of Virginia Press

Kearnes, M. and Wynne, B. (2007) 'On Nanotechnology and Ambivalence: The Politics of Enthusiasm', *NanoEthics* 1: 131–142

Keeley, J. and Scoones, I. (2003) *Understanding Environmental Policy Processes: Cases from Africa*, London: Routledge

Kirwan, S., Dawney, S. and Brigstocke, J. (eds) (2016) *Space, Power and the Commons: The Struggle for Alternative Futures*, London: Routledge

Kleist, N. and Thorsen, D. (eds) (2016) *Hope and Uncertainty in Contemporary African Migration*, London: Routledge

Knight, F.H. (1921) *Risk, Uncertainty and Profit*, New York: Courier Corporation

Krätli, S. and Schareika, N. (2010) 'Living off Uncertainty: The Intelligent Animal Production of Dryland Pastoralists', *The European Journal of Development Research* 22: 605–622

Lahsen, M (2005) 'Seductive Simulations? Uncertainty Distribution around Climate Models', *Social Studies of Science* 35: 895–922

Lakoff, A. (2017) *Unprepared: Global Health in a Time of Emergency*, Oakland: University of California Press

Leach, M. and Scoones, I. (2013) 'The Social and Political Lives of Zoonotic Disease Models: Narratives, Science and Policy', *Social Science and Medicine* 88: 10–17

Leach, M., Stirling, A.C. and Scoones, I. (2010) *Dynamic Sustainabilities: Technology, Environment, Social Justice*, London: Earthscan Routledge

Lenton, T.M., Rockström, J., Gaffney, O., Rahmstorf, S., Richardson, K., Steffen, W. and Schellnhuber, H.J. (2019) 'Climate Tipping Points—Too Risky to Bet Against', *Nature* 575: 592–595

Lentzos, F. and Rose, N. (2009) 'Governing Insecurity: Contingency Planning, Protection, Resilience', *Economy and Society* 38.2: 230–254

Levitas, R. (2013) *Utopia as Method: The Imaginary Reconstitution of Society*, London: Palgrave Macmillan

Lindblom, C.E. (1959) 'The Science of Muddling Through', *Public Administration Review* 19.2: 79–88

Linke, U. and Smith, D.T. (eds) (2009) *Cultures of Fear: A Critical Reader*, London: Pluto Press

Luhmann, N. (1993) *Risk: A Sociological Theory*, R. Barrett (trans.), New York: W. de Gruyter

Maantay, J. and Maroko, A. (2009) 'Mapping Urban Risk: Flood Hazards, Race and Environmental Justice in New York', *Applied Geography* 29.1: 111–124

MacKenzie, D. and Spears, T. (2014) 'The Formula that Killed Wall Street': The Gaussian Copula and Modelling Practices in Investment Banking', *Social Studies of Science* 44.3: 393–417

Mahony, M. and Beck, S. (2019) 'Infrastructures of the Imagination: Uncertainty and the Politics of Prefiguration', STEPS Centre blog, 1 October, https://steps-centre.org/blog/infrastructures-of-the-imagination-uncertainty-and-the-politics-of-prefiguration/ (accessed 7 February 2020)

Marske, C.E. (ed) (1991) *Communities of Fate: Readings in the Social Organization of Risk*, Maryland: University Press of America

Mason, P. (2019) *Clear Bright Future: A Radical Defence of the Human Being*, London: Penguin

—— (2016) *Post-Capitalism: A Guide to Our Future*, London: Macmillan

Mazzucato M (2018) *The Value of Everything: Making and Taking in a Global Economy*, London: Allen Lane

McKittrick, K. (2011) 'On Plantations, Prisons, and a Black Sense of Place', *Social & Cultural Geography* 12.8: 947–963

Mehta, L., Srivastava, S., Adam, H.N., Alankar, Bose, S., Ghosh, U. and Kumar, V. (2019) 'Climate Change and Uncertainty from "Above" and "Below": Perspectives from India', *Regional Environmental Change* 19.6: 1533–1547

Mol, A. and Law, J. (2004) 'Embodied Action, Enacted Bodies: The Example of Hypoglycaemia', *Body and Society* 10.2–3: 43–62

Morgan, M.S. (2012) *The World in The Model: How Economists Work and Think*, Cambridge: Cambridge University Press

Mouffe, C. (2018) *For a Left Populism*, London: Verso Books

Mudde, C. and Rovira Kaltwasser, C. (2018) 'Studying Populism in Comparative Perspective: Reflections on the Contemporary and Future Research Agenda', *Comparative Political Studies* 51(13): 1667–1693

Mythen, G., Burgess, A. and Wardman, J.K. (2018) 'The Prophecy of Ulrich Beck: Signposts for the Social Sciences', *Journal of Risk Research* 21.1: 96–100

Nguyen, V.K. and Peschard, K. (2003) 'Anthropology, Inequality, and Disease: A Review', *Annual Review of Anthropology* 32.1: 447–474

Nixon, R. (2011) *Slow Violence and the Environmentalism of the Poor*, Cambridge MA: Harvard University Press

Nowotny, H. (2015) *The Cunning of Uncertainty*, Chichester: John Wiley and Sons

Paprocki, K. (2018) 'Threatening Dystopias: Development and Adaptation Regimes in Bangladesh', *Annals of the American Association of Geographers* 108.4: 955–973

Pielke, R. (2019) 'If Climate Scenarios Are Wrong For 2020, Can They Get 2100 Right?' *Forbes Magazine*, 21 October 2019, www.forbes.com/sites/rogerpielke/2019/10/21/ if-climate-scenarios-are-wrong-for-2020-can-they-get-2100-right/#4773cf502c7f (accessed 7 February 2020)

Power, M. (2004) *The Risk Management of Everything: Rethinking The Politics of Uncertainty*, London: Demos

Rangoni, B. (2019) 'Architecture and Policy-Making: Comparing Experimentalist and Hierarchical Governance in EU Energy Regulation', *Journal of European Public Policy* 26.1: 63–82

Raworth, K. (2017) *Doughnut Economics: Seven Ways to Think like a 21st-Century Economist*, Vermont: Chelsea Green Publishing

Rayner, S. and Cantor, R. (1987) 'How Fair is Safe Enough? The Cultural Approach to Societal Technology Choice', *Risk Analysis* 7.1: 3–9

Ribot, J. (2014) 'Cause and Response: Vulnerability and Climate in the Anthropocene', *Journal of Peasant Studies* 41.5: 667–705

Richards, P. (2016) *Ebola: How a People's Science Helped End an Epidemic*, London: Zed Books

Roe, E. (2013) *Making the Most of Mess: Reliability and Policy in Today's Management Challenges*, Durham NC: Duke University Press

Sabel, C.F. and Zeitlin, J. (eds) (2010) *Experimentalist Governance in the European Union: Towards a New Architecture*, Oxford: Oxford University Press

Samimian-Darash, L. and Rabinow, P. (eds) (2015) *Modes of Uncertainty: Anthropological Cases*, Chicago: University of Chicago Press

Scoones, I. (2019) *What is Uncertainty and Why Does it Matter?*, STEPS Working Paper 105, Brighton: STEPS Centre

—— (2016) 'The Politics of Sustainability and Development', *Annual Review of Environment and Resources* 41: 293–319

Scoones, I., Edelman, M., Borras Jr, S.M., Hall, R., Wolford, W. and White, B. (2018) 'Emancipatory Rural Politics: Confronting Authoritarian Populism', *The Journal of Peasant Studies* 45.1: 1–20

Scoones, I., Jones, K., Lo Iacono, G., Redding, D.W., Wilkinson, A. and Wood, J.L.N. (2017) 'Integrative Modelling for One Health: Pattern, Process and Participation', *Philosophical Transactions of the Royal Society B: Biological Sciences* 372: 1725

Scoones, I., Newell, P. and Leach, M. (eds) (2015) *The Politics of Green Transformations*, London: Routledge

Scoones, I., Stirling, A., Abrol, D., Atela, J., Charli-Joseph, L., Eakin, H., Ely, A., Olsson, P., Pereira, L., Priya, R. and van Zwanenberg, P. (2018) *Transformations to Sustainability*, STEPS Working Paper 104, Brighton: STEPS Centre

Scott, J.C. (1998) *Seeing Like a State: How Certain Schemes to Improve the Human Condition Have Failed*, New Haven: Yale University Press

Shove, E., Pantzar, M. and Watson, M. (2012) *The Dynamics of Social Practice: Everyday Life and How it Changes*, London: Sage

Skrimshire, S. (2014) 'Climate Change and Apocalyptic Faith', *Wiley Interdisciplinary Reviews: Climate Change* 5.2: 233–246

Solnit, R. (2016) *Hope in the Dark: Untold Histories, Wild Possibilities*, London: Haymarket Books

Stirling, A. (2019a) 'How Deep is Incumbency? A "Configuring Fields" Approach to Redistributing and Reorienting Power in Socio-material Change', *Energy Research and Social Science* 58: 101239

—— (2019b) 'Engineering and Sustainability: Control and Care in Unfoldings of Modernity', in D.P. Michelfelder and N. Doorn (eds) *Routledge Companion to the Philosophy of Engineering*, Routledge: London

—— (2019c) 'Sustainability and the Politics of Transformations: From Control to Care in Moving Beyond Modernity', in J. Meadowcroft, D. Banister, E. Holden, O. Langhelle, K. Linnerud and G. Gilpin (eds) *What Next for Sustainable Development?*, Cheltenham: Edward Elgar Publishing

—— (2015) 'Emancipating Transformations: from Controlling "the Transition" to Culturing Plural Radical Progress', in I. Scoones, M. Leach and P. Newell (eds) *The Politics of Green Transformations*, London: Routledge

—— (2008) '"Opening Up" and "Closing Down" Power, Participation and Pluralism in the Social Appraisal of Technology', *Science, Technology and Human Values* 33.2: 262–294

—— (1999) 'On "Precautionary" and "Science Based" Approaches to Risk Assessment and Environmental Appraisal', in A. Klinke, O. Renn, A. Rip, A. Salo and A. Stirling (eds) *On Science and Precaution in the Management of Technological Risk. Vol. II, Case Studies*, Sevilla: European Science and Technology Observatory, report EUR 19056/EN/2, European Commission Joint Research Centre

Sword-Daniels, V., Eriksen, C., Hudson-Doyle, E.E., Alaniz, R., Adler, C., Schenk, T. and Vallance, S. (2018) 'Embodied Uncertainty: Living with Complexity and Natural Hazards', *Journal of Risk Research* 21.3: 290–307

Taleb, N.N. (2007) *The Black Swan: The Impact of the Highly Improbable*, New York: Random House

Taraborrelli, A. (2015) *Contemporary Cosmopolitanism*, London: Bloomsbury

Taylor, N. (2019) 'Whose Risk? Whose Responsibility? The Politics and Financialisation of Uncertainty', STEPS blog, 25 September, https://steps-centre.org/blog/whose-risk-whose-responsibility-the-politics-and-financialisation-of-uncertainty/ (accessed 7 February 2020)

Thompson, M. and Gyawali, D. (2007) 'Uncertainty Revisited or the Triumph of Hype Over Experience. New Introduction', in M. Thompson, M. Warburton and T. Hatley, *Uncertainty on a Himalayan Scale*, Kathmandhu: Himal Press

Thompson, M. and Warburton, M. (1985) 'Uncertainty on a Himalayan Scale', *Mountain Research and Development* 5.2: 115–135

Thompson, M., Ellis, R. and Wildavsky, A. (1990) *Cultural Theory*, London: Routledge

Tompkins, E. and Adger, W.N. (2004) 'Does Adaptive Management of Natural Resources Enhance Resilience to Climate Change?', *Ecology and Society* 9.2: 10

Tuckett, D. (2018) 'Conviction Narrative Theory', in R. Beckert and R. Bronk (eds) *Uncertain Futures: Imaginaries, Narratives, and Calculation in the Economy*, Oxford: Oxford University Press

Visvanathan, S. (2005) 'Knowledge, Justice and Democracy', in M. Leach, I. Scoones and B. Wynne (eds) *Science and Citizens: Globalization and the Challenge of Engagement*, London: Zed Books

Walker, W.E., Harremoës, P., Rotmans, J., van der Sluijs, J.P., van Asselt, M.B.A., Janssen, P. and Krayer von Krauss, M.P. (2003) 'Defining Uncertainty: A Conceptual Basis for Uncertainty Management in Model-Based Decision Support', *Integrated Assessment* 4.1: 5–17

Wansleben, L. (2014) 'Consistent Forecasting vs. Anchoring of Market Stories: Two Cultures of Modeling and Model Use in a Bank', *Science in Context* 27.4: 605–630

Watts, M. (2015) 'Now and Then: The Origins of Political Ecology and the Rebirth of Adaptation as a Form of Thought', in T. Perreault, G. Bridge and J. McCarthy (eds) *The Routledge Handbook of Political Ecology*, London: Routledge

Watts, M.J. and Bohle, H.G. (1993) 'The Space of Vulnerability: The Causal Structure of Hunger and Famine' *Progress in Human Geography* 17.1: 43–67

Wynne, B. (1996) 'May the Sheep Safely Graze. A Reflexive View of the Expert-Lay Knowledge Divide', in S. Lash, B. Szerszynski and B. Wynne (eds) *Risk, Environment and Modernity: Towards a New Ecology*, London: Sage

—— (1992) 'Uncertainty and Environmental Learning: Reconceiving Science and Policy in the Preventive Paradigm', *Global Environmental Change* 2.2: 111–127

2

THE ASSAULT OF FINANCIAL FUTURES ON THE REST OF TIME

Timo Walter and Leon Wansleben

Introduction

In Alexander Kluge's movie *Der Angriff der Gegenwart auf die übrige Zeit* (The Assault of the Present on the Rest of Time), people live in a 'distended present' (Kluge *et al.* 1990: passim): faced with uncertain – personal and societal – futures, they are unable to make lasting decisions and remain trapped in an unending present. In this contribution, we discuss another 'assault on the rest of time' that was just in the making when Kluge's film appeared in 1985 – namely, the ways in which finance shapes and formats the politics of the future. Our central tenet is that, far from providing an engine for imagining substantive futures that guide (collective) actions, finance 'consumes' forecasts, plans or visions. They serve as mere signals (Langenohl and Wetzel 2011), fuelling an increasingly short-term (Montagne 2009), febrile hunt for novelties from which profit can be generated by beating others to it.

In (economic) theory, prices will oscillate – more or less – evenly around the expected 'intrinsic' value in response to incoming signals, so that 'the time average of an observable [is] equal to its expectation value' (Peters 2019: 1216). Based on this statistical premise of 'ergodicity', there can be no fundamental discontinuity between future, on the one hand, and past and present, on the other – so that *rational* inter-temporal calculation and expectations become possible (Beckert and Bronk 2018: 18–20).[1] As the formal models and calculative devices through which economic agents project and imagine the future are built on these assumptions, the ergodic continuity between past, present and future effectively becomes part of the background frame within which signals *about the future* are given meaning and translated *in the present*. We thus suggest that the temporality of contemporary finance is at odds with modernist conceptions of futurity as involving an epistemic 'back and forth' between a given present and an open future, out of which emerge contingency, freedom and choice (Esposito 2004; Luhmann 1976). The 'future' towards which finance is oriented (Arrow 1978) is constantly collapsed into the present through an ongoing process of 'pricing in' the future and rendering it calculable according to an a-temporal space of possibilities. For modern finance, the future has become a useful means of acting *in the present*, rather than an onto-logically distinct state that we imagine and construct based on joint imaginations as we proceed towards it *from the present*. We develop this point by discussing the case of derivatives markets. We show how derivatives markets depend directly on the assumption of a 'synchronicity' of present and future, built directly into the central valuation device on which the functioning of these markets depends – the so-called Black-Scholes-Merton formula. We extend this argument in the second part of our contribution, where we describe how central banks have developed a finance-oriented and finance-based 'governmentality' (Foucault 2007[1978]). Under this regime, central banks really do *not* govern future inflation, but present *expectations* of future inflation as expressed in the 'yield curve' and built into interest rate derivatives. We suggest that the use of rational expectations models that construe the future as 'conserved' within an ergodic, a-temporal world allows central banks to ignore possible 'random' fluctuations in *actual* inflation and concentrate on the internal calibration of present expectations of future inflation as the sole criterion for monetary policy success. We show that this 'assault' of present expectations on a future that never becomes actualised was an important factor in the run-up to the crisis of 2007–2009. Central banks have facilitated forms of financial valuation that rely on key fictions of an ergodic world (in particular the 'natural' interest rate), by stabilising the expectational parameters which manifest these fictions, and have thus helped to black-box uncertainties. The crisis itself, and post-crisis interventions, have not led to a 'reckoning' with a different temporality, but have activated various support mechanisms and new policy tools (e.g. 'forward guidance') that shield and maintain this 'practical fiction' and the 'infrastructure' (Star and Ruhleder 1996) of an ergodic world for contemporary finance. What has become clearer, though, is that the particular constellations of policy institutions and financial markets found in contemporary capitalism do not support economic prosperity and sustainability for society as a whole.

The ergodic world of 'quantitative' finance

Compared to the embedded, 'boring finance' of the period from the 1950s to the 1980s, in the contemporary financial system the contingency of all financial activity with regard to the future has become much more visible. In particular, the 'openness of the future' (Beckert 2015: 35ff), and the problem that an open future is neces-sarily contingent and therefore 'fundamentally uncertain' (Knight 1921) has moved centre-stage in discussions about contemporary finance. Whereas, in the 'golden age of capitalism' (Marglin and Schor 2000), finance lived well by the '3-6-3' rule (charge a 3 per cent mark-up on credit over the 3 per cent interest paid out on deposits and be off to the golf course at 3pm) (Walter 2006), the de-regulation and financial innovation that started in the 1970s (Helleiner 1994) has turned the future into an explicit epistemic problem. As a result, financial (and economic) activity has become much more directly dependent on the elaboration of 'imagined futures' and calculative 'instruments of imagination' for the coordination of expectations (Beckert 2016: 216ff.). Since the liquidity and stability of markets hinge directly on the continuity of valuations (and the knowledge underpinning them) (Carruthers and Stinchcombe 1999) this means that these epistemic practices and calculative instruments – and the joint expectations of the futures that they help construct – have become central to the functioning of contemporary finance.

It has therefore become common for both practitioners and observers to understand contemporary finance as revolving around the problem of mitigating the fundamental epistemic uncertainty of a future that is open and contingent. In this view, finance has become a primary site for 'acting in an uncertain world' (Callon *et al.* 2009), where market participants learn to forecast and imagine such futures through calculative devices and/or hedge against uncertainties using various financial tools. The crucial significance of finance in modern society thus stems from its role as an institution that allows social actors to cope, manage and live with an uncertain future, and to render this open future as a space of possibilities – for speculation, investment, hedging, insurance, betting etc.

There is, however, some reason to be cautious about the notion that uncertainty in finance is – primarily – a function of the irreducible gap between *present futures* and actual *future presents*. The historian Reinhart Koselleck (1989) has theorised this gap as being a result of historical experiences that have led actors to distinguish these two distinct forms of 'future': the future as imagined in the present ('present future') and future presents, i.e. future states of the world when they (have) become present, or actualised. However, this decidedly modern form of temporality is not the one that reigns in contemporary finance.

To argue this point, we need to look at precisely how epistemic accuracy of expectations about the future present matters in finance. As John Maynard Keynes and Hyman Minsky pointed out long ago, the openness of the future manifests itself as an 'economic survival constraint': false or inaccurate present futures are costly, or even life-threatening, to economic units, if investments fail. For that reason, Keynes and Minsky thought that as uncertainty is more directly and intensively felt, economic units will avoid tying down their wealth in risky investments and will protect themselves against adverse risks by stocking up on liquid reserves.

The key characteristic of this uncertainty – the uncertainty of having enough liquid means to meet upcoming obligations – is that it cannot readily be made measurable: it depends on the behaviour of various other actors (e.g. money market lenders) and the various feedback processes by which one's own and others' decisions (e.g. asset sales) affect the state of the financial system as a whole. However, as central banks have encouraged and supported financial markets' reliance on 'ergodic fictions' for valuation and risk management, this uncertainty has ceased to feature in the regular calculations and strategies of financial actors and in the structures of the financial system, giving way to a world in which actors act most of the time as if market liquidity and stable asset prices will be maintained indefinitely.

To understand how and why, we need to decipher the role played by rational expectations (as both a category of practice and a theory) in contemporary finance. Discounting expected future returns to calculate an asset's present value requires knowledge of the future development of macroeconomic variables (such as growth, interest rates or inflation, etc.) which, in models and formulas derived from rational expectations economics, shape this present value, as joint expectations about such parameters become widely embedded in valuations (Bryan and Rafferty 2006). Such parameters come to define a 'normality' as background to and a condition of asset valuations, with market actors closely tracking any anomalies that might affect asset values (Christophers 2017; Zaloom 2009). This 'normality' has become an intrinsic background for the joint structures of knowledge that secure the continuity of valuations and market transactions, and thus undergird the liquidity and stability of 'market-based finance' (Hardie and Howarth 2013). This background establishes a (calculative and epistemic) continuity between the present and the future, built directly into the fabric of financial markets, against which more narrow present futures can be elaborated, processed, adopted or discarded. The intense concern with the future in contemporary finance is thus made possible by this 'synchronist' (Langenohl 2018) background, which anchors the impressive array of instruments of imagination in an a-temporal skeletal structure upon which the validity of any calculation of present futures depends.

This ergodic conception of time (Kirstein 2015) is important for contemporary finance particularly in those contexts in which the respective parameters are directly incorporated into the markets' valuation devices. A case in point are the derivatives markets, which do not value and trade normal financial assets (such as stocks or currencies) but which are based on contracts through which parties directly wager on future prices of underlying assets in relation to specific future events. Derivatives thus express imagined futures and the valuations they imply (through discounting), without the need to possess or actually trade underlying assets. This might suggest that, if anywhere, it is in the derivatives markets that actors care about whether their present futures actually become future presents at some point in time. But this is not how valuation and pricing works in these markets, which are based on the common valuation infrastructure that relies on the Black-Scholes-Merton formula (Watson 2007; MacKenzie and Millo 2003; Black and Scholes 1973). With this formula, traders no longer focus on particular events and future presents as they arrive but instead trade what is called 'volatility' – a measure of the variability of prices over time that is dependent on such variation remaining ergodic (Davidson 1982). Using this calculative tool, participants thus engage in a market process in which particular events and risks are subsumed with regards to a 'synchronic' background system of valuation and pricing.

The validity and applicability of the Black-Scholes-Merton formula is thus premised on this assumption of a fundamentally static and continuous world that does not undergo any fundamental substantive changes. In this world, present futures are nothing but short-lived inputs or signals that generate possibilities for arbitrage, but do *not* affect the static background continuity that undergirds the system. However, in the case of 'black swan' events (Taleb 2007) – that is, when highly improbable 'tail-end' events in a probability distribution occur – a system of valuations premised on ergodicity becomes incoherent, leading markets to freeze. As Donald MacKenzie (2004; MacKenzie and Millo 2003) has shown, the 1987 stock market crash drove home the limits of this ergodic depiction of temporality, and practitioners adjusted their Black-Scholes-Merton pricing *ad hoc* and modified the price curve for options so that longer-termed options now include an uncertainty premium (the so-called 'volatility smile' or 'skew') on top of their 'ergodic' price.

Derivatives markets thus highlight particularly clearly how the synchronist background against which financial valuation operates mitigates uncertainty, not by encouraging actors to reckon with an uncertain future but by excluding the possibility that the future might be discontinuous with the present (in aggregate terms) in any radical sense. For the continuous functioning of financial markets, it is more important to uphold a stable background of expectations than to know the future accurately. The synchronist frame operatively decouples actions taken in reaction to and in terms of present futures from the actual future present(s) that come to pass.

Many observers and practitioners have noted how this separation from this calculative background has made the sequential processing of transitory present futures at the 'surface' of the market almost ritualistic (e.g. LiPuma 2017; Ayache 2016). The unfolding of present futures is largely irrelevant to, and does not feed into, the static expectations about the future encoded in this background, which are re-asserted or 'performed' anew with every transaction that makes use of instruments of valuation or calculation derived from rational expectations models (cf. LiPuma 2017). Derivatives markets thus form the extreme end of a continuum but highlight the logical conditions of why the liquidity and stability of modern financial markets depends on this calculative background. They illustrate why the *accuracy* of expectations is not actually put to the test (or at least only idiosyncratically, for individual traders) as long as markets can *operatively* hold on to this 'useful' fiction of a continuous, normal and ergodic world. As a result, for modern finance the future itself is continuously 'ontologically absent' (Law and Urry 2004): it is a horizon of possibilities that provides inputs for arbitrage, but must remain invisible at the level of the constitutive fiction of the never-changing future on which market stability rests.

The modern financial system is thus based on 'wilful' or 'strategic ignorance' (McGoey 2012) of the future present as a constitutive principle: excluding the possibility of substantive discontinuities between present and future is what enables the 'transformation of uncertainty into risk' (Carruthers 2013) and secures the possibility of rational calculation and action in markets in the present. As market coordination increasingly depends on the construction, projection and diffusion of 'commensurable' (Espeland and Stevens 1998) present futures, this common background has gained in importance. It allows translating present futures into numeric prices, and thus is central to securing the congruence of expectations (about present and future prices) in markets. The financial system's ability to process information about the future thus depends on the continuous operative denial of the openness of this very future. Whatever individual actors might think privately, at the level of the market public, uncertainty must not be allowed to manifest itself, but must continuously be absorbed and neutralised – as a precondition for the system's ability to process any signals about the future that might entail (limited) re-valuations and price changes at all.

Evidently, excluding the possibility of a fundamental discontinuity of the economic present and future mathematically does not protect financial actors from suffering the consequences of being (collectively) wrong. However, Minsky has shown, with his now famous 'financial instability hypothesis' (Minsky 1980), that if central banks are actively working to protect markets from a breakdown of the fictional continuity and the 'normal market conditions' it enables, they are effectively removing the survival constraint on financial institutions. In other words, they protect market actors from ever having to face fundamental discontinuity, allowing them instead to continue processing present futures without concerning themselves with their accuracy. As Minsky pointed out, by continuously neutralising the effects of fundamental dissonances about the future, and shoring up 'normal' assumptions about the future in order to secure the 'normal' operations of the system, one also abolishes any incentives to look out for, and be prepared for, the possibility of fundamentally different futures, blanking out underlying systemic uncertainties.

The more market actors are assured that normal market conditions will continue (indefinitely) into the future, the more the future becomes a 'useful fiction', that is continuously presupposed but must never actually affect the normal operations of the system. As we shall see in the next section, central banks' efforts to gain 'infrastructural power' (Walter and Wansleben 2019; Braun and Gabor 2019; Braun 2018a), by seeking to develop technologies for influencing financial markets (and the economy) by 'governing through expectations' (Wansleben 2018; Braun 2015), have become directly complicit with this specific temporality of modern finance.

Hegemonic futures in financialised capitalism

The role of an ergodic world as a calculative background for market coordination has gained increased general societal and economic importance through processes of financialisation. Financialisation can be used as a descriptive term to depict how the size of finance has grown compared to the rest of the economy (Stockhammer 2008), how corporations shift their sources of profit from production to financial activities (Krippner 2005) and/or how households in Western economies have become increasingly entangled in financial markets, as mortgage holders, employees with private pension plans, owners of life insurance products and the like (van der Zwan 2014; Davis 2009). We use the concept here in a related but somewhat different sense. Our interest is in how the logics of coordination that are reliant on particular conceptions of futurity become dominant in regard to the ways in which capitalist democracies are rendered governable. We are thus interested in reconstructing a particular 'governmentality' that is not exhaustively described with regards to shareholder value, speculative identities or even particularistic elite interests, but that concerns the fundamental ways in which capitalism is stabilised as a social system. This sounds like a rather grand claim but we believe there is strong evidence for the rise of finance as a new governmentality, which is closely associated with the emergence of central banks as the most powerful governors in advanced capitalist states.

The specific proposition that we make is that central banks have contributed to transcending the role of contemporary finance by tying their own practices of macroeconomic policy-making to this particular realm (Krippner 2011). We will here limit this discussion to the symbolic-communicative dimension of central banks' governing – a topic that has raised much interest in sociological (Braun 2015) and anthropological (Holmes 2013) research. The innovation identified by these scholars is that central bankers have learned to govern monetary developments by communicating their intentions and planned interventions; the markets, reacting to such signals, then are thought to adapt accordingly, performatively bringing about the effects that the central banks intended to obtain. The point that we want to elaborate on here is that such 'performative' central banking should not be considered as a neutral strategy for achieving legitimate political objectives like low inflation and stable growth. The respective practices of governing rather require that central banks align their interventions with the structure of financial markets, and with the particular mechanisms through which these markets project their 'present futures'.

This firstly entails a subtle, but important, shift in the very object of governing. The sociological argument underlying the idea of 'expectational governance' is that central banks can control price-setting in the economy by influencing the expectations that economic actors have with regard to changes in the inflation rate (Beckert 2016). When these actors – like wage bargainers – expect inflation to remain stable, they will be more moderate with their wage claims and their mark-up pricing, and thereby *produce* the low inflation rates that they assume will prevail. This self-confirmatory logic is intuitive. But surveys have shown time and again that the general public's expectations are relatively fickle and that inflation rates can be influenced by various factors, not all of which are expectational (Lombardelli and Saleheen 2003). Central bankers have resolved these uncertainties and problems by redefining what they actually control: *not inflation itself but inflation expectations, as incorporated into financial markets' calculations and operations.* The assumption is that, as long as these specific expectations remain stable, it does not matter that prices actually fluctuate somewhat, or that most people do not have a good understanding of how inflation will evolve. As a consequence, cognitive and normative expectations inherent in markets, rather than the demands, claims and ideas from the broader economy, become the linchpin for assessing central bankers' success, and for orienting their macroeconomic policies. Financial market expectations thus have become central banks' primary objects of governing: all that matters is that financial market prices – primarily long-term interest rates – reflect expectations that inflation will remain stable and low.

This reorientation to markets was well articulated by Ben Bernanke – an architect of inflation targeting – who claimed that 'monetary policy is a cooperative game. *The whole point is to get financial markets on our side* and for them to do some of our work for us' (cited in Mallaby 2017: 612, our emphasis). In other words, central banks rely on financial markets to assume a hegemonic role in defining economic futures more generally, and they reinforce this hegemony by aligning their communications with the specific logics of these markets.

This brings us to a second dimension of such finance-oriented expectation coordination – the fictitious elimination of radical uncertainty and the simulation of an ergodic socio-economic system with stable parameters within which financial expansion can unfold. To illustrate this point, let us imagine a central bank that has some expertise in finance and the economy, but that only imprecisely and 'with uncertainty' knows how the economy will evolve going forward – what the level of employment will be, how much output is going to be produced, how the employment level and output are going to relate to the productive capacities of the economy, how such interactions will affect the price level – not to speak of the uncertainties arising from developments in asset and credit markets that affect banking, household wealth, productive facilities, consumer spending etc. Such a semi-knowledgeable, semi-ignorant central bank would decide on interest rates in somewhat unpredictable ways, and there may be many occasions in which markets are taken by surprise.

However, with the introduction of inflation targeting since the late 1980s, it became imperative to create far more predictability between central banks and markets. This made it necessary to render invisible these fundamental uncertainties faced by policy-makers (Walter and Wansleben 2019). Accordingly, central bankers increasingly drew on a model of the economy in which uncertainty was in fact not an important factor (Woodford 2009). Equilibrium output, the non-inflationary rate of employment and the natural rate of interest were all assumed to be knowable variables that could orient policy-making and its coordination with financial markets. Accordingly, there were fewer and 'fewer occasions on which the authorities' decisions – as opposed to the underlying economic developments – cause[d] uncertainty in the markets' (Butler and Clews 1997: 48) – which was perceived as a *virtue* of the inflation targeting regime.

In other words, the tools and techniques of macroeconomic policy championed by central banks have enhanced and strengthened the 'normality expectations' undergirding valuations in financial markets. This has then reinforced the expansionary dynamics of finance, leading to a proliferation of contracts (e.g. of securitised assets), market relations and balance sheets that presuppose an unchanging macroeconomic background structure upon which financialisation rests (Nesvetailova 2015; Mehrling 2011). Particular features of financialisation, such as the interrelated expansion of asset and money markets, rely on these normality expectations, and more generally on the notion that central banks will maintain stability in regard to all major macroeconomic variables (inflation, interest rates) that are relevant for financial markets. However, as the transatlantic financial crisis of 2007–2009 has brought home, the 'success' of central banks' coordination with finance should *not* be confused with the development of reliable and sustainable ways of governing capitalist democracies. Indeed, the events in these years rather demonstrated that the self-validation between policy-makers and market actors had become dissociated from the actual socio-economic structures – precarious labour market situations, debt pyramids etc. – to which their macroeconomic models and valuation practices purported to refer (e.g. Fligstein *et al.* 2017). However, this has not led to a fundamental questioning of the governmentality regime associated with financialisation. Rather, central banks' 'unconventional' expansionary monetary policies since 2009 reflect a reinforcement of finance-oriented and finance-centred policy-making (Braun 2018b). The central aim of post-crisis policy has been to reinstate confidence within finance about the indefinite continuity of 'normal' patterns of output, inflation, interest rates etc., with the intended effect of inducing market actors to re-engage in investments and credit provision, which are believed to generate growth. Finance thus remains at the centre of macroeconomic governance and thus maintains its privileged role in 'mature' capitalism.

To be fair, there has been some critical discussion among expert economists about the adverse consequences of such regimes. For instance, Tobias Adrian and Nelly Liang write that:

> Monetary policy works though financial conditions on expected economic outcomes, but risks to financial stability involve potential tail risks. The tail risks to future macroeconomic outcomes manifest only in some states of the world, when adverse shocks are realized. These dimensions are important because they greatly complicate efforts to incorporate financial stability in the determination of monetary policy. Policy makers would need to look beyond expected conditions for downside risks that arise with uncertain probability in the future (2016: 4).

Yet there seems to be little appetite among policy-makers to take seriously these adverse financial stability effects, not to speak of the broader societal problems, which arise from the current finance-oriented governance regime.

Conclusion

Up until now the highly problematic 'politics of the future' entailed by the characteristic temporality of modern finance, and its widening implications due to financialisation, have by-and-large passed under the radar (but see, Adkins 2018; Langenohl 2018; 2007). While our focus in this chapter has been on how technological, epistemic and political infrastructures make this temporality more durable and lend it a degree of invisibility, the concerns we would like to raise are related to these – for the most part sociological and anthropological – 'diagnostics of the present'.

To be sure, the fragilities in the financial system that result from the continuous need to stabilise the 'discounted' fictive future values in the present have been widely noted (Mehrling 2011; Nesvetailova 2007), but they have only rarely been linked to the peculiar temporalities of modern finance (but see LiPuma 2017). More commonly, financial fragility is instead interpreted as an issue of *complexity* – to be addressed by increasing the transparency of markets, and in particular by reducing the epistemic uncertainty that this complexity generates with regard to the system's own future (Gräbner and Kapeller 2015; Cooper 2011).

Following from our argument, the present attempts, through regulation and monetary policy, to manage and contain the complexity of contemporary finance may, paradoxically, contribute to instability if the main aim remains to stabilise the working fiction of an ergodic, 'timeless' temporality on which financial markets are premised. This ergodic normality has become the very foundation of the calculability of financial values (Peters 2019), its commensurability across assets and markets, and thus the liquidity and stability of those markets themselves. This is all the more the case as there has been a marked, global trend towards market-based finance (Murau 2017; Gabor 2016) in which the ability to shift assets in markets has become the basis of liquidity (Mehrling 2011), increasing the systemic risk entailed by disruptions to this frame of calculability. The need to protect this temporality, the frame of calculability and structure of valuations it undergirds, forces central banks into continuing their role of reinsurer of systemic risk and market-maker of last resort that contributed to the 2007–2009 crisis, backstopping the value of a widening pool of – only seemingly – 'liquid' assets (Mehrling 2011; Borio and White 2004). The 'unconventional' monetary policies of quantitative easing pursued by central banks around the world since 2008 are even named so as to evoke their rationale of restoring and safeguarding the technical presuppositions of 'normal' or 'conventional' forms of governability. Likewise, the 'macro-prudential' financial regulation that has come to dominate regulatory debates (Coombs 2017; Baker 2013) attempts to correct the fragilities created by the 'distended present' of modern finance by increasing the transparency of risks (e.g., through stress tests), creating resiliences and facilitating 'efficient' risk-sharing within the financial system. Despite some undeniable innovations at the level of technical frameworks and instruments at its disposal since 2008–2009, monetary policy thus continues to be geared towards ergodicity as its operative framework. 'Macro-pru' and unconventional policies aim, first and foremost, at restoring and protecting *normal conditions* in financial markets, as a platform for effective monetary policy. This *normality* is conceived of in ergodic terms and observed through (mathematical) models that are premised on ergodicity. Deviations from normality thus become an impediment to be neutralised in order to secure the inter-temporal consistency and effectiveness of monetary policy – rather than being seen as (potentially) indicative of (fundamental) uncertainties of which market actors (and central banks!) would need to take heed, and which might require adjustments to their calculative strategies. Instead, central banks proactively seek to restore 'quasi-ergodic' conditions in financial markets, by reducing what they perceive as market imperfections that prevent the even inter-temporal dissemination of monetary policy signals. However, in combating manifestations of uncertainty as *anomalies* that stand in the way of monetary policy operations premised on the ergodicity of finance and the economy, central banks are sterilising the very signs that the future may indeed substantively differ from past and present. Their interventions provide financial markets with a working fiction of an ergodic world, and, rather than *removing* vulnerabilities, they counteract the very processes through which collective sense-making could solidify into effectively constraining price signals – until, that is, the next crisis…

Note

1 In technical terms, '[e]rgodicity is fulfilled, if the time average of a system or process equals its ensemble average. The time average is the average of one observed trajectory or realisation of a process (one time series). The ensemble average is the average over every possible state of a system' (Kirstein 2015: 1). The assumption of ergodicity is crucial for predominant formalisations of economic dynamics as 'the ergodic case is much easier to handle mathematically', although in principle 'non-ergodicity is a necessary property of a mathematical model, if the model is supposed to describe trajectory occurrences of endogenous novelties and change' (*ibid.*).

References

Adkins, L. (2018) *The Time of Money. Currencies*, Stanford, California: Stanford University Press

Adrian, T. and Liang, N. (2016) *Monetary Policy, Financial Conditions, and Financial Stability*, Federal Reserve Bank of New York Staff Reports No. 690

Arrow, K.J. (1978) 'The Future and the Present in Economic Life', *Economic Inquiry* 16.2: 157–169

Ayache, E. (2016) *The Medium of Contingency: An Inverse View of the Market*, Basingstoke: Palgrave Macmillan

Baker, A. (2013) 'The New Political Economy of the Macroprudential Ideational Shift', *New Political Economy* 18.1: 112–139

Beckert, J. (2016) *Imagined Futures: Fictional Expectations and Capitalist Dynamics*, Cambridge, MA: Harvard University Press

—— (2015) 'Re-Imagining Capitalist Dynamics. Fictional Expectations and the Openness of Economic Futures', in P. Aspers and N. Dodd (eds) *Re-Imagining Economic Sociology*, Oxford: Oxford University Press: 57–78

Beckert, J. and Bronk, R. (2018) 'An Introduction to Uncertain Futures', in J. Beckert and R. Bronk, *Uncertain Futures: Imaginaries, Narratives, and Calculation in the Economy*, Oxford: Oxford University Press: 1–36

Black, F. and Scholes, M. (1973) 'The Pricing of Options and Corporate Liabilities', *Journal of Political Economy* 81.3: 637–654

Borio, C. and White, W.R. (2004) *Whither Monetary and Financial Stability? The Implications of Evolving Policy Regimes*, BIS Working Papers 147, Basel: Bank for International Settlements

Braun, B. (2018a) 'Central Banking and the Infrastructural Power of Finance: The Case of ECB Support for Repo and Securitization Markets', *Socio-Economic Review*, February, https://doi.org/10.1093/ser/mwy008

—— (2018b) 'Central Bank Planning? Unconventional Monetary Policy and the Price of Bending the Yield Curve', in J. Beckert and R. Bronk (eds) *Uncertain Futures: Imaginaries, Narratives, and Calculation in the Economy*, Oxford: Oxford University Press: 31–37

—— (2015) 'Governing the Future: The European Central Bank's Expectation Management during the Great Moderation', *Economy and Society* 44.3: 367–391

Braun, B. and Gabor, D. (2019) 'Central Banking, Shadow Banking, and Infrastructural Power', Preprint. *SocArXiv* https://doi.org/10.31235/osf.io/nf9ms

Bryan, D. and Rafferty, M. (2006) *Capitalism with Derivatives: A Political Economy of Financial Derivatives, Capital and Class*, Basingstoke and New York: Palgrave Macmillan

Butler, C. and Clews, R. (1997) *Money Market Operations in the United Kingdom*, BIS Conference Papers 3 (Implementation and Tactics of Monetary Policy), Basel: Bank for International Settlements 45–70

Callon, M., Lascoumes, P. and Barthe, Y. (2009) *Acting in an Uncertain World: An Essay on Technical Democracy*, Inside Technology. Cambridge, MA: MIT Press

Carruthers, B.G. (2013) 'From Uncertainty Towards Risk: The Case of Credit Ratings', *Socio-Economic Review* 11.3: 525–551

Carruthers, B.G. and Stinchcombe, A.L. (1999) 'The Social Structure of Liquidity: Flexibility, Markets, and States', *Theory and Society* 28.3: 353–382

Christophers, B. (2017) 'The Performativity of the Yield Curve', *Journal of Cultural Economy* 10.1: 63–80

Coombs, N. (2017) 'Macroprudential Versus Monetary Blueprints for Financial Reform', *Journal of Cultural Economy* 10.2: 207–216

Cooper, M. (2011) 'Complexity Theory After the Financial Crisis: The Death of Neoliberalism or the Triumph of Hayek?' *Journal of Cultural Economy* 4.4: 371–385

Davidson, P. (1982) 'Rational Expectations: A Fallacious Foundation for Studying Crucial Decision-Making Processes', *Journal of Post Keynesian Economics* 5.2: 182–198

Davis, G.F. (2009) *Managed by the Markets: How Finance Reshaped America*, New York: Oxford University Press

Espeland, W.N. and Stevens, M.L. (1998) 'Commensuration as a Social Process', *Annual Review of Sociology* 24.1: 313–343

Esposito, E. (2004) 'The Arts of Contingency', *Critical Inquiry* 31.1: 7–25

Fligstein, N., Brundage, J.S. and Schultz, M. (2017) 'Seeing Like the Fed: Culture, Cognition, and Framing in the Failure to Anticipate the Financial Crisis of 2008', *American Sociological Review* 82.5: 879–909

Foucault, M. (2007)[1978] *Security, Territory Population: Lectures at the Collège de France, 1977–78*, Basingstoke and New York: Palgrave Macmillan

Gabor, D. (2016) 'The (Impossible) Repo Trinity: The Political Economy of Repo Markets', *Review of International Political Economy* 23.6: 967–1000

Gräbner, C. and Kapeller, J. (2015) 'New Perspectives on Institutionalist Pattern Modeling: Systemism, Complexity, and Agent-Based Modeling', *Journal of Economic Issues* 49.2: 433–440

Hardie, I. and Howarth, D.J. (eds) (2013) *Market-Based Banking and the International Financial Crisis*, 1st edition, Oxford: Oxford University Press

Helleiner, E. (1994) *States and the Reemergence of Global Finance: From Bretton Woods to the 1990s*, Ithaca NY: Cornell University Press

Holmes, D.R. (2013) *Economy of Words: Communicative Imperatives in Central Banks*, Chicago: University of Chicago Press

Kirstein, M. (2015) 'From the Ergodic Hypothesis in Physics to the Ergodic Axiom in Economics', in Diskussionspapier 7. Wintertagung ICAE, Linz, 4–5 December 2015

Kluge, A., Evans, T. and Liebman, S. (1990) 'The Assault of the Present on the Rest of Time', *New German Critique* 49 (Winter): 11–22

Knight, F.H. (1921) *Risk, Uncertainty and Profit,* Boston and New York: Houghton Mifflin

Koselleck, R. (1989) *Vergangene Zukunft*, Frankfurt am Main: Suhrkamp

Krippner, G.R. (2011) Capitalizing on Crisis: The Political Origins of the Rise of Finance, Cambridge, MA: Harvard University Press

—— (2005) 'The Financialization of the American Economy', *Socioeconomic Review* 3.2: 173–208

Langenohl, A. (2018) 'Sources of Financial Synchronism: Arbitrage Theory and the Promise of Risk-Free Profit', *Finance and Society* 4.1: 26–40

—— (2007) *Finanzmarkt Und Temporalität: Imaginäre Zeit Und Die Kulturelle Repräsentation Der Gesellschaft*, Qualitative Soziologie, Stuttgart: Lucius & Lucius

Langenohl, A. and Wetzel, D.J. (2011) 'Finanzmärkte Und Ihre Sinnformen: Handlungskoord ination Und Signalkommunikation', *Berliner Journal Für Soziologie* 21: 539–559

Law, J. and Urry, J. (2004) 'Enacting the Social', *Economy and Society* 33.3: 390–410

LiPuma, E. (2017) *The Social Life of Financial Derivatives: Markets, Risk, and Time*, Durham: Duke University Press

Lombardelli, C. and Saleheen, J. (2003) 'Public Expectations of UK Inflation', *Bank of England Quarterly Bulletin*, Autumn 2003: 281–290

Luhmann, N. (1976) 'The Future Cannot Begin: Temporal Structures in Modern Society', *Social Research* 43.1: 130–152

MacKenzie, D. (2004) 'The Big, Bad Wolf and the Rational Market: Portfolio Insurance, the 1987 Crash and the Performativity of Economics', *Economy and Society* 33.3: 303–334

MacKenzie, D. and Millo, Y. (2003) 'Constructing a Market, Performing Theory: The Historical Sociology of a Financial Derivatives Exchange', *American Journal of Sociology* 109.1: 107–145

Mallaby, S. (2017) *The Man Who Knew: The Life and Times of Alan Greenspan*, London: Bloomsbury

Marglin, S.A. and Schor, J.B. (eds) (2000) *The Golden Age of Capitalism: Reinterpreting the Postwar Experience,* reprinted, WIDER Studies in Development Economics, Oxford: Clarendon Press

McGoey, L. (2012) 'Strategic Unknowns: Towards a Sociology of Ignorance', *Economy and Society* 41.1: 1–16

Mehrling, P. (2011) *The New Lombard Street: How the Fed Became the Dealer of Last Resort*, Princeton, NJ: Princeton University Press

Minsky, H. (1980) 'Capitalist Financial Processes and the Instability of Capitalism', *Journal of Economic Issues* 14.2: 505–523

Montagne, S. (2009) 'Short-Termism as a Rule: The Effects of Portfolio Management Delegation', *Revue d'économie Financière* 9 (Hors-Série: Sovereign Wealth Funds): 381–395

Murau, S. (2017) 'Shadow Money and the Public Money Supply: The Impact of the 2007–2009 Financial Crisis on the Monetary System', *Review of International Political Economy* 24.5: 802–838

Nesvetailova, A. (2015) 'A Crisis of the Overcrowded Future: Shadow Banking and the Political Economy of Financial Innovation', *New Political Economy* 20.3: 431–453

—— (2007) *Fragile Finance: Debt, Speculation and Crisis in the Age of Global Credit*, Basingstoke and New York: Palgrave Macmillan

Peters, O. (2019) 'The Ergodicity Problem in Economics', *Nature Physics* 15.12: 1216–1221

Star, S.L. and Ruhleder, K. (1996) 'Steps Toward an Ecology of Infrastructure: Design and Access for Large Information Spaces', *Information Systems Research* 7.1: 111–134

Stockhammer, E. (2008) 'Some Stylized Facts on the Finance-Dominated Accumulation Regime', *Competition & Change* 12.2: 184–202

Taleb, N.N. (2007) *The Black Swan: The Impact of the Highly Improbable*, 1st edition, New York: Random House

van der Zwan, N. (2014) 'Making Sense of Financialization', *Socio-Economic Review* 12.1: 99–129

Walter, J.R. (2006) 'The 3-6-3 Rule: An Urban Myth?' *Economic Quarterly* 92.1: 51–78

Walter, T. and Wansleben, L. (2019) 'How Central Bankers Learned to Love Financialization: The Fed, the Bank, and the Enlisting of Unfettered Markets in the Conduct of Monetary Policy', *Socio-Economic Review*, March, https://doi.org/10.1093/ser/mwz011

Wansleben, L. (2018) 'How Expectations Became Governable: Institutional Change and the Performative Power of Central Banks', *Theory and Society* 47.6: 773–803

Watson, M. (2007) 'Searching for the Kuhnian Moment: The Black-Scholes-Merton Formula and the Evolution of Modern Finance Theory', *Economy and Society* 36.2: 325–337

Woodford, M. (2009) 'Convergence in Macroeconomics: Elements of the New Synthesis', *American Economic Journal: Macroeconomics* 1.1: 267–279

Zaloom, C. (2009) 'How to Read the Future: The Yield Curve, Affect, and Financial Prediction', *Public Culture* 21.2: 245–268

3

SHARING RISKS OR PROLIFERATING UNCERTAINTIES?

Insurance, disaster and development

Leigh Johnson

Introduction

Today, anyone who is under the impression that insurance is a luxury that is only available in wealthy countries of the global North is faced with a multitude of examples to the contrary. Not only are traditional lines of insurance business, like life and health insurance, growing rapidly in much of the global South, new forms of insurance harnessing powerful geospatial monitoring and modelling technologies are increasingly being deployed to offer Southern governments insurance for hazards such as droughts, floods, cyclones and diseases. It is hoped that such coverage will secure development gains. But has the growth of such tools actually reduced uncertainties? So far, the evidence is mixed.

The actuarial technologies of the insurance industry have long been central to the development of methods to assess uncertainty. These methods yield quantifiable – and thus priceable and transferable – risk. Amid the proliferating uncertainties of climate change and the growing cost of disasters, the impulse to insure across more geographic and hazard domains has grown. Insurers and multilateral institutions now explicitly seek to narrow what they call the 'global protection gap' – the difference between total economic losses and insured losses (Lloyd's 2018; Swiss Reinsurance 2015). Development institutions and insurers have advanced several strategies to occupy this protection gap, which is widest in countries of the global South. They have advocated insurance-linked tools such as catastrophe bonds, promoted the application of insurance-based logic to new domains like pandemic diseases and launched insurance pools at new multi-country scales.

Yet almost none of these instruments look like what we imagine as traditional insurance arrangements. The large majority of these instruments are 'parametric' products, in which payouts are triggered by measured or modelled environmental variables. This chapter first explores why parametric insurance and related risk transfer tools are increasingly popular responses in development practice. It then argues that this embrace can paradoxically proliferate uncertainties when insurance contracts fail to pay out, illustrated with reference to drought insurance in Malawi and pandemic insurance in the Democratic Republic of Congo. The chapter closes by envisioning how insurance might be refashioned from a 'technology of hubris' to a 'technology of humility' (Jasanoff 2003), suggesting some principles for more relational deployments of insurance that could begin to recuperate its promise as a technique of mutual solidarity and sustainable risk-sharing.

The impulse to insure

There are both economic and political reasons why insurance – and disaster risk finance more broadly – have become major domains for development intervention. Given that many Southern countries have long since been compelled to remove social safety nets and market controls as a condition for continuing to receive loans from international institutions, there is often little to cushion their populations, leaving them especially vulnerable to shocks. An early World Bank piece advancing the framework of weather risk management identified the processual link between micro and macro: 'Ultimately, the precariousness of farmers and producers translates into macroeconomic vulnerability' (Hess *et al.* 2002: 296). Multilateral institutions now identify disaster shocks as a major impediment to a country's macroeconomic stability and its ability to maintain the welfare of its citizens (Cummins and Mahul 2009). Disasters constitute a fiscal 'squeeze': while a government's unbudgeted relief expenditures rise, its future revenue-raising capacity deteriorates as household assets are lost and incomes decline. Declining revenues impair a government's capacity to pay off existing loans or issue bonds, forcing it to take on more emergency debt. Such dynamics are not just the concern of international financial institutions: activist organisations such as the Jubilee Debt Campaign have recently argued that climate change is intensifying these patterns, warning of 'climate debt traps' resulting from post-disaster emergency borrowing, such as the loan Mozambique took following Cyclone Idai in 2019 (Sauer 2019).

Insurance – and particularly the global insurance industry – occupies pride of place in the push to move from *ex post* to *ex ante* financing arrangements. This is partly a result of scalar relations. The difficulty of some of the thorniest problems in the field of development – large 'natural' disasters, climate change impacts and pandemic disease among them – is that they are spatially and temporally covariant. While everyday coping systems might work to buffer people from quotidian individual shocks, they are overwhelmed when many people in a region suffer from the same event at the same time. Likewise, government funds, if they exist at all, are quickly exhausted, particularly in countries with small economies. For instance, the Solomon Islands has no disaster reserves, and average annual disaster losses consume 6.5 per cent of Vanuatu's GDP (World Bank 2015: 9).

In these contexts, the large and globally diversified pools of capital held by the reinsurance industry have become a virtually indispensable element of the development sector's approach. In the absence of a multilateral development insurer,[1] it is the reinsurance industry that can quickly dispatch the quantities of post-disaster liquidity required. This industry has also systematically cultivated actuarial and modelling expertise and positioned itself as a consummate provider of risk management solutions. Its operational framework dovetails with Western donors' mandates to make aid more auditable and economically efficient, and to deploy market-based solutions and private sector capital to bridge financing gaps (Mawdsley 2015).

Since the mid-2010s, cash-strapped humanitarian and aid agencies have faced ballooning numbers of crisis-affected populations, exacerbated by ongoing conflict, extreme weather events linked to climate change and increasingly uncertain funding streams from isolationist Western donors. This precarious situation has driven an emphasis on the dollar-for-dollar efficiency of aid and objective criteria for its disbursement. This aligns with an insurance-based approach to modelling, pricing and contractually managing risks. Formal insurance or insurance-like instruments require contractual specifications that delineate who is responsible for post-disaster transfers, for what and in what circumstances. Such specificity holds obvious appeal for improving welfare given the delays and chaos of ordinary humanitarian response – what Dunn (2012) terms 'adhocracy'.

In theory, the process of deciding what insurance coverage to purchase should encourage pre-disaster risk assessment, management and response planning. The pre-defined terms of insurance contracts should secure funding for response and delineate post-disaster responsibilities (Clarke and Dercon 2016). In turn, the automaticity of payouts based on environmental measures should secure timely financing for urgent needs and facilitate disbursement from a distance, while transparency about payout conditions should reduce perennial donor concerns about aid leakage and corruption. This, at least, is the vision.

In practice, many applications of insurance technologies have demonstrated the hazards of what science studies scholar Sheila Jasanoff (2003: 238) calls 'technologies of hubris'. By this, she refers to technologies that leverage science 'to facilitate management and control even in areas of high uncertainty … [which] achieve their power through claims of objectivity and a disciplined approach to analysis' (*ibid.*). Despite the power of these technologies, their advocates are often overconfident of their accuracy and rigour, and blind to forms of uncertainty that fall outside their framing assumptions. They tend to invoke the objectivity of their expertise in order to avoid political debate and calls for social accountability. The cases of drought and pandemic insurance, to which the chapter turns next, suggest that parametric insurance is no stranger to the hazards of technological hubris.

The political economy of basis risk: blame and liability

To understand how uncertainty becomes a transferred political and economic object we need to grasp the logic of assembly behind parametric insurance tools. In ordinary *indemnity-based* insurance contracts, losses are inspected and the monetary payout made is at least ostensibly proportional to that loss. But indemnification is expensive, and requires constant work with regards to surveillance and data gathering. In contrast, most disaster risk insurance contracts now on offer are built on *parametric* logic. In parametric contracts, payouts are determined by the value of one or more measured environmental variable – a parameter like rainfall or pasture greenness – that can be monitored at a distance. Parametric logic posits scalar correspondence between selected variables at easily observed scales, and actual losses at less easily observed scales. Contract designers inevitably make tremendous simplifications and exclusions when postulating this correspondence.

By definition, parametric contracts must abstract from contextual conditions, setting standardised proxies that can be efficiently applied to determine payouts. These technical processes of simplification, exclusion and decontextualisation have allowed insurance to be offered for places and perils previously deemed too unremunerative and risky for traditional insurance to operate. But these abstractions have generated their own new sets of uncertainties.

Most prominently, parametric design inevitably leaves those insured holding 'basis risk'. This refers to the risk of a discrepancy between the measures and models that determine payouts, on the one hand, and events on the ground, on the other. Even traditional indemnity insurance carries some basis risk: those insured typically have some 'deductible' amount of losses they must self-fund first, and claims can be denied if losses were caused by a contractually-excluded event (Muir-Wood 2017). Indeed, traditional insurers regularly make legal recourse to carefully constructed contractual definitions of harm and limits to liability in order to avoid paying indemnities (e.g. Baker 1994).

But basis risk for parametric insurance is of a different nature. One-to-one indemnification for losses is never promised. Payout determinations can be made without the insurer conducting any on-the-ground loss assessment with insured parties. A great deal then rests on the accuracy of the measures and models selected as proxies. Yet insured parties are rarely familiar with how well these proxies correspond to their experience (or not), and often lack the actuarial skills to assess a contract's reliability. Compounding the problem of proxy accuracy, catastrophe insurance coverage poses a more general problem. Unlike insurance for more quotidian events, catastrophe insurance is a 'credence good', where the irregular and infrequent temporality of loss events makes it difficult for buyers to assess the quality of the product before purchase. Learning takes place after premiums have been paid, when those insured see how an actual contract performs in comparison to their expectations (Clarke and Wren-Lewis 2013).

Drought insurance

Several countries insured by the African Risk Capacity[2] drought insurance programme have learned retrospectively about the limitations of the coverage they purchased. Organisationally housed within the African Union, ARC brings sovereign nations into a mutual insurance pool for drought protection, with backstopping by global reinsurers. ARC's design is routinely championed as a path-breaking example, leveraging satellite data and regional solidarity to finance drought disaster response (UNFCCC 2017). The risk pool is capitalised by participating countries' premiums, alongside interest-free equity from the UK and German development agencies. Payouts are triggered based on estimates of the number of drought-vulnerable people requiring relief, as modelled by ARC's proprietary software, Africa RiskView. If triggered, ARC payouts must be used to fund the member's pre-approved contingency plan for relief operations.

A great deal rests on the accuracy of the model's estimated number of drought-vulnerable people. Africa RiskView constructs a complex causal chain to arrive at this number. It feeds satellite-based rainfall estimates into agronomic models of reference crops; shortfalls are then compared with pre-existing analyses of food security and population vulnerability to generate an estimate of the maximum number of people affected by a drought event. Member countries customise their insurance contracts to trigger a payout when a certain threshold number is reached.

In 2015, Malawi became the first southern African country to join the ARC pool of seven total members, paying US$4.7 million in premiums from its treasury for drought insurance cover. In March 2016, the Malawian government declared a drought emergency. Rains had failed at a critical time for the staple maize crop, and the stress was compounded by extremely high temperatures. Households' food stores and assets were already depleted by the previous season's droughts, floods and high food prices, stemming partly from an ongoing El Niño event (e-Pact 2017). In June, ARC announced that Malawi's drought insurance contract had not triggered a payout. Its model estimated the size of the drought-affected population at just 21,000 people. Meanwhile, a joint assessment by the government and aid organisations put the number at 6.5 million people (ActionAid 2017).

Though the biggest drivers of this staggering discrepancy are still subject to debate, poor data and poor model specification both played a part. Initially, ARC blamed the underestimate on the fact that Malawi had selected a long-cycle maize variety as the model's agronomic reference crop, while the majority of Malawi's farmers had recently switched to planting a short-cycle hybrid variety that was catastrophically damaged by cessation of rains after planting. Because the reference crop was chosen by government teams presumed to be knowledgeable about their country's agricultural sector and its vulnerabilities, ARC deflected responsibility for the discrepancy to the Malawian government. Yet a later ground-based survey and model assessment found that both short- and long-maturing varieties of maize suffered similar drought impacts, suggesting that the model would have performed poorly even with the correct reference crop (e-Pact 2017: 33–34). The likely greater problems lay in the model's parameters: it did not account for the impacts of high temperatures on plant evapotranspiration and water stress, or the timing of dry spells during a crop's growth cycle (*ibid.*). After seven months of consultations, donor pressure and international media scrutiny, ARC's Board of Directors formally approved a policy exception and agreed to disburse US$8.1 million to resolve the 'Malawi crisis' (ARC Agency 2016). Nine months after the government's emergency declaration, Malawians finally received ARC-funded relief in the form of legumes for household consumption.

Though ARC adjusted its model following the Malawi crisis, its problems did not end there. Africa RiskView again did not trigger a payout for a 2017 drought in Mauritania, despite dire conditions on the ground. A ground-truthing team suggested the discrepancy stemmed from inaccurate rainfall data, poor assumptions in the agronomic model and the strikingly invalid assumption that farmers would have the resources to replant following failed rains (ARC Agency 2017). Again ARC's board approved an exception and made an extra-contractual payout (ARC Agency 2018).

Pandemic bonds

No such exceptions to policy were possible when the World Bank's first pandemic bond failed to trigger a payout in July 2019. That month, the World Health Organization declared the Ebola virus outbreak that began in 2018 in the eastern DRC a 'Public Health Emergency of International Concern' (WHO 2019). By this time, it was already the second largest Ebola outbreak in recorded history, responsible for more than 1,500 deaths.

Following donors' abysmally slow response to the 2014–2016 Ebola outbreak in West Africa, the World Bank developed the Pandemic Emergency Financing Facility in consultation with the WHO. The PEF is intended to disburse surge financing to enable rapid responses to 'infectious disease outbreaks before they take on pandemic proportions' (World Bank 2018a: 4).[3] Unlike ARC, where countries must self-select into the risk pool and pay an insurance premium, the PEF coverage automatically applies to all countries eligible for assistance from the World Bank's International Development Association lending arm, without requiring any premium payment.[4] While it includes a 'cash window' for early donor support, the PEF's signal innovation is an 'insurance window' that draws down private investments made in a US$425 million catastrophe bond (Erikson 2019). An insurance payout for relief efforts is triggered if three major conditions are met: reports from the WHO confirm at least 250 total deaths; a third-party model deems rates of disease transmission to be growing over a sustained period and the disease spreads across borders resulting in at least 20 deaths in a second country (World Bank 2018a).

The requirement for geographical spread disqualified the Ebola epidemic in the DRC from triggering PEF's insurance window. Though several Ebola deaths were confirmed in Uganda and feared in Rwanda and Tanzania, the count never reached 20 in a second country. As medical anthropologist Susan Erikson (2019) notes, the PEF's emphasis on the transparency and exactitude of disease counts ignores the vastly uncertain conditions under which disease data are collected: often by freelance enumerators and irregularly paid health workers hired to travel vast distances in dangerous conditions, and possibly denied access to villages. Recent violent attacks on health workers in the DRC underscore the ongoing precarity of the counting enterprise. Nonetheless, so far, no one has alleged that the insurance window trigger conditions were actually met in the DRC and neighbouring countries, or that an error of measurement prevented a payout. Rather, the contractual criteria set a high enough bar – confirmed deaths *and* cross-border spread *and* growth rate – that it may well be the case that not all were met at the same time. It is impossible to know. Meanwhile, investors in the PEF catastrophe bond lost none of their principal, and continued to receive interest payments. Critics have heaped opprobrium on the World Bank for its role in designing the unscathed bond (Garrett 2019; Jonas 2019), and public health scholars suggested its conditions would have generated a payout for only two events since 2006 (Brim and Wenham 2019). Indeed the PEF bond did not trigger its US$195 million payout for COVID-19 until late April 2020, when this chapter was already in press (World Bank 2020).

Uncertain liability

ARC's and PEF's recent experiences suggest new domains of uncertainty introduced by insurance tools. In Malawi, bad data and poor model specifications led ARC to underestimate the actual extent of drought and its impact on farmers. Rather than introducing automaticity and timeliness to drought relief funding, the ARC contract gave rise to dispute, blame and delay. In the DRC, the bond's activation criteria legally prevented the World Bank from drawing down investors' funds despite the raging epidemic (Erikson and Johnson 2020). Rather than delivering capital market funds for public health emergencies, the coverage gave rise to befuddlement and recrimination.

In both cases there is a political economy of basis risk and liability. Contractual structures designed to preserve tight control over payouts are necessary in order to secure reinsurance cover or capital market investments. Both reinsurers and investors demand surety that their capital will only be depleted under specific conditions. Firms model the likelihood of these conditions transpiring in order to price contracts, estimate total exposures and hedge portfolios. When basis risk events occur, reinsurers and investors are largely unaffected – although reinsurers may suffer reputational damage from being associated with a product that did not pay out when public opinion deems it should have.

Who then *is* liable? In Malawi and Mauritania, ARC's governing board eventually approved exceptions to policy to allow the compensatory payouts. In both cases, ARC's reinsurers did not object, because the payouts (US$8.1 million and US$2.1 million, respectively) were small enough that the reinsurance coverage was not activated. The funds came out of ARC's risk pool, co-owned by German and British government aid agencies and ARC's African member states. Ultimately, it was governments and their taxpayers who shouldered the exceptional payments.

Unlike ARC, PEF's catastrophe bond cannot permit *post hoc* exceptions, as it is legally bound by the terms of the prospectus circulated to investors. If an epidemic does not meet the bond's activation criteria, but still meets minimum epidemiological thresholds, governments or responding humanitarian agencies can request funds from the PEF's 'cash window', funded by German and Australian development aid (World Bank 2018b). It was this window that disbursed US$50 million for the 2019 Ebola epidemic in the DRC, and was empty by the time COVID-19 emerged as a new threat in 2020. Again, it was governments and their taxpayers who shouldered the cash payments.

Indeed, there is a good argument to be made for wealthy governments bearing such costs. But this reflects a different political economy of liability than one in which capital from private reinsurers and investors is truly leveraged to narrow the 'global protection gap'. In the cases of ARC and PEF, the reinsurer and investor capital underwriting these products remained intact in the midst of severe droughts and a historic epidemic.

There are some cases when parametric tools fortunately work as advertised, such as a US\$22 million ARC payout to Senegal in November 2019. Yet models and triggers for sovereign parametric products thus far appear biased in favour of insurers. If basis risk errors were random, the number of 'downside' basis risk events should roughly equal the number of 'upside' events (when an index suggests conditions on the ground are worse than they actually are, potentially triggering an excessive payout). Yet there is little evidence of upside events. The number and variety of cases in which contracts misfire suggest that the turn towards parametric insurance products is not consistently reducing uncertainty for Southern governments, or reliably transferring it to the private sector. Rather, it may be redistributing the undesirable components of uncertainty as basis risk both to those insured and to donor governments, who bear the costs when parametric products fail to deliver protection.

While parametrics promise Southern government decision-makers coverage for a stated hazard, they also expose them to a new kind of risk. This, in the words of a senior risk modelling executive, is 'the toxic politics of basis risk' (Muir-Wood 2017). This is the political liability of spending scarce treasury funds to purchase a policy that does not pay out when the government expects it to, or when angry citizens think it should. If fear of basis risk drives enough decision-makers to remove their countries from a risk pool – as occurred with ARC following the Malawi crisis – this creates cascading doubts for other members about the long-term viability of the pool itself. Uncertainty proliferates.

Technologies of humility?

Given these challenges, one might ask whether it is possible to rescue the promise of insurance as a technique of mutual solidarity and sustainable risk-sharing. Can parametric insurance arrangements ever reliably *reduce* uncertainties and secure financing for disaster liabilities, as proponents hope? Or are they bound simply to pass uncertainties around?

It is possible to imagine insurance otherwise. Here, we might begin our re-envisioning with Jasanoff's (2003) proposal for new 'technologies of humility' in policy-making that complement and correct the hazards of technologies of hubris. Technologies of humility are 'institutionalized habits of thought that try to come to grips with the ragged fringes of human understanding – the unknown, the uncertain, the ambiguous, and the uncontrollable' (*ibid.:* 227). These habits of thought acknowledge areas of fundamental uncertainty, the possibility of unforeseen consequences and the need for plural viewpoints and collective learning. This epistemological disposition is a crucial corrective to technically complex modelling, which by its nature tends to minimise the significance of whatever falls outside its field of vision, and overstate the importance of whatever falls within it (*ibid.*: 239). Approaching parametric insurance products from the disposition of technological humility yields some unconventional ideas for re-imagining their design and function.

Jasanoff suggests four focusing questions we might use to cultivate technologies of humility. These are questions that technologies of hubris persistently avoid. Is the scope of the problem appropriately *framed*? Who is *vulnerable*? What are the *distributive* implications? And how should we *learn* from failure? Let us consider each in turn.

Framing: The framing of the 'global protection gap' suggests both a problem and a solution. If the problem is uninsured losses then the solution that follows is extending the reach of insurance tools to new hazards, new geographies and new domains of the economy. But, as the law of the instrument holds, 'to someone with a hammer, everything looks like a nail'. If the problems of uninsured losses and unassigned contingent liabilities are instead reframed as missing safety nets and absent social contracts, the fields of play suddenly become much larger. Questions of social protection and democratic governance come into view. Insurance can be put into perspective as only a modest and partial solution. Parametric products may or may not fulfil a need.

Attention to framing might also lead us to consider whether calling parametric products 'insurance' is cognitively useful, or instead misleading. Language shapes expectations. The term 'insurance' connotes a relationship of security and indemnification that parametric products expressly avoid. Calling parametric products 'insurance' may downplay the inevitable uncertainty and basis risk they contain. Describing them rather as 'derivatives' – financial products whose value is based on the behaviour of another underlying variable – would make these uncertainties more evident. At first glance, this might seem a counterintuitive suggestion: derivatives were notoriously implicated in the accumulation, packaging and trade of massive mortgage debts culminating in the global financial crisis of 2007–2010. Yet this experience arguably raised media and political awareness of their prevalence and the risks of their use. Unless or until parametric insurance products are systematically quality-controlled to track and ensure correspondence between indices and losses, they are essentially weather and environmental derivatives. Describing them as such might signal their limitations and prompt a healthy new degree of scrutiny over their use.

Vulnerability: We have already seen how the design of parametric products sometimes leaves those insured holding large basis risk. This is the chance that they will pay an insurance premium, experience a catastrophic event and then receive no payout according to contractual terms. Though basis risk can be reduced through careful design, it can never be eliminated. It must be accepted as a corollary of extending insurance arrangements to populations and locales not traditionally deemed insurable.

Who, then, is particularly vulnerable to such basis risk? Countries whose governments are willing to experiment with the imperfect coverage of parametric sovereign insurance contracts tend to be those whose marginal position in the global political economy compels them to accept a compromise on terms set by global insurers, investors and development banks. Those with limited technical and actuarial training are especially vulnerable, as they may not be able to assess fully the terms of the coverage offered, and thus may remain unaware of the basis risk their treasuries will retain. Building technologies of humility to address such vulnerability would minimally require transparent technical and actuarial analysis of competing options, advocacy on countries' behalf with insurance providers, and cultivation of regional or country-based networks of expertise. It is critical that such a data analytics-intensive technical role be played by parties without any financial or operational interests in a country's ultimate risk management choices, unlike in today's model, in which technical expertise flows from reinsurers, reinsurance brokers and the World Bank.

Distribution: An obvious question often monitored by donor institutions concerns the distribution of insurance payouts. This is in essence a question of auditing who receives payouts from insurance policies, and tracking the cost to distribute each dollar of aid via this channel as opposed to another, such as cash transfers (Jensen *et al.* 2017). Although it is indeed critical to understand this, a deeper question of distribution remains: where does the bulk of donor funds put into parametric insurance ultimately accrue? What is the likelihood of a given donor dollar being distributed (in cash or kind) to a vulnerable person, or being retained by an insurer or intermediary? When would a contract have paid out for past historical events? While historical calibration is often conducted for the purposes of pricing insurance contracts, this information is rarely made public, nor are payout frequencies (and their relative costs and trade-offs) subject to public deliberation. An approach promoting humility could mandate the standardised disclosure of these distributional arrangements and facilitate debates over the minimum criteria for publicly-subsidised coverage.

Learning: When technological innovations in insurance fail to live up to the expectations heaped upon them – as so many technologies inevitably do – a crucial question concerns what and how we can learn from these experiences. When predictive models misfire, blame and recrimination typically follow. The opacity or transparency with which insurance institutions review and revise models and data sources is a critical determinant for (re)building credibility among those insured and the public. But there will always be some degree of causal ambiguity, and competing explanations for failure will depend on actors' positions within the insurance relationship.

A better question, then, is not what institutions learn about the shortcomings of their models, but rather how basis risk events could galvanise the development of different fora for decision-making that would make parametric insurance more adaptive, context-dependent and responsive. This would require letting go of some of the persistent impulses towards control that led to the embrace of parametric insurance tools in the first place. We might imagine, for instance, fora for participatory deliberation among mutually insured parties about what should constitute a basis risk event, or what criteria should be used to reallocate inevitably limited indemnification funds to such cases. Such fora would need to be animated by a different model of trust than the asymmetric one that characterises typical insurer–insured relations, in which those who are insured are asked to place their trust in an insurer who expressly doubts the trustworthiness (or wisdom) of those being insured. Within participating countries, fora could be established in which civil servants, civil society organisations and beneficiaries themselves could deliberate over the inevitable trade-offs involved in their country's selection of particular contractual terms and triggers.

Some will object that this reorientation would undermine the entire ontological framework of insurance, based as it is on probabilistic calculation and objective payout criteria. Yet the history of insurance in mutuals, friendly societies (Van Leeuwen 2016; Ismay 2015) – and even commercial reinsurance (Jarzabkowski *et al.* 2015) – demonstrates that more relational and contextual deployments of insurance are possible, and indeed were the norm for centuries. But these have typically been built on more extensive interpersonal ties and expectations of longer-enduring relationships, both between members of the risk pool and between insurer and insured.

Despite their promise to extend insurance security to new geographies and hazard domains, parametric insurance and 'insurance-like products' currently suffer from a legitimacy deficit due to the basis risk they transfer to those insured. Basis risk needs to be understood not simply as a problem of poor design, but as an existential political challenge to the framework of parametric insurance. If we are to salvage the value of parametric insurance as a solidaristic tool for coping with uncertainties, then we must approach the technology with a dose of humility. Parametric insurance could become a far more democratic tool of risk governance, building 'on people's legitimate expectations of equality, representation, fairness and public accountability' (Jasanoff 2010: 29). But this requires a radical openness to re-imagining its design and the constituencies to which it is accountable – and a willingness to relinquish the illusions of objective control at a distance.

Notes

1 The likes of which are proposed by Clarke and Dercon (2019).
2 www.africanriskcapacity.org.
3 However, anthropological accounts of Ebola's spread in West Africa suggest that funding shortfalls were far from the most significant factor in preventing the disease's containment (Erikson 2016; Wilkinson and Leach 2015).
4 In 2020, this included 76 countries, 39 of which were in Africa (http://ida.worldbank.org/about/borrowing-countries).

References

ActionAid (2017) *The Wrong Model for Resilience: How G7-Backed Drought Insurance Failed Malawi, and What We Must Learn From it*, Johannesburg: ActionAid

African Risk Capacity Agency (2018) 'Report of the Sixth Session of the Conference of the Parties of the African Risk Capacity Agency, Nouakchott, Mauritania', ARC/COP6/D043.0103_18

―― (2017) *Technical Analysis of the Africa RiskView 2017 Customization for Mauritania*, Johannesburg: African Risk Capacity Agency

―― (2016) 'Malawi to Receive USD 8M Insurance Payout from African Risk Capacity', press release 14 November, Johannesburg: African Risk Capacity Agency

Baker, T. (1994) 'Constructing the Insurance Relationship: Sales Stories, Claims Stories, and Insurance Contract Damages', *Texas Law Review* 72: 1395–1433

Brim, B. and Wenham, C. (2019) 'Pandemic Emergency Financing Facility: Struggling to Deliver on its Innovative Promise', *The British Medical Journal* 367: l5719

Clarke, D. and Dercon, S. (2019) *Beyond Banking: Crisis Risk Finance and Development Insurance in IDA19*, London: Center for Disaster Protection

―― (2016) *Dull Disasters: How Planning Ahead Will Make a Difference*, Oxford: Oxford University Press

Clarke, D. and Wren-Lewis, L. (2013) *Learning from Lemons: The Role of Government in Index Insurance for Individuals*, Paris: Fondation pour les Études et Recherches sur le Développement International

Cummins, J.D. and Mahul, O. (2009) *Catastrophe Risk Financing in Developing Countries: Principles for Public Intervention*, Washington, DC: The World Bank

Dunn, E.C. (2012) 'The Chaos of Humanitarian Aid: Adhocracy in the Republic of Georgia', *Humanity: An International Journal of Human Rights, Humanitarianism, and Development* 3.1: 1–23

e-Pact (2017) 'Independent Evaluation of the African Risk Capacity (ARC) Formative Phase 1 Report', Oxford: e-Pact Consortium: Oxford Policy Management and Itad

Erikson, S. (2019) 'Global Health Futures? Reckoning with a Pandemic Bond', *Medicine Anthropology Theory* 6.3: 77–108

―― (2016) 'Money Matters: Ebola Bonds and Other Migrating Models of Humanitarian Finance', in M. Böckenförde, N. Krupke and P. Michaelis (eds) *Reflections on Global Cooperation and Migration*, Duisberg: Käte Hamburger Kolleg/Centre for Global Cooperation Research

Erikson, S. and Johnson, L. (2020) 'Will Financial Innovation Transform Pandemic Response?', *The Lancet Infections Diseases* 20.5: 529-530

Garrett, L. (2019) 'The World Bank has the Money to Fight Ebola but Won't Use It', *Foreign Policy*, 22 July

Hess, U., Richter, K. and Stoppa, A. (2002) 'Weather Risk Management for Agriculture and Agri-Business In Developing Countries', in R. Dischel (ed) *Climate Risk and the Weather Market: Financial Risk Management with Weather Hedges*, London: Risk Books

Ismay, P. (2015) 'Between Providence and Risk: Odd Fellows, Benevolence and the Social Limits of Actuarial Science, 1820s–1880s', *Past & Present* 226.1: 115–147

Jarzabkowski, P., Bednarek, R. and Spee, P. (2015) *Making a Market for Acts of God: The Practice of Risk-Trading in The Global Reinsurance Industry*, Oxford: Oxford University Press

Jasanoff, S. (2010) 'Beyond Calculation: A Democratic Response to Risk', in A. Lakoff (ed) *Disaster and the Politics of Intervention*, New York: Columbia/Social Science Research Council: 14–40

—— (2003) 'Technologies of Humility: Citizen Participation in Governing Science', *Minerva* 41: 223–244

Jensen, N.D., Barrett, C.B. and Mude, A.G. (2017) 'Cash Transfers and Index Insurance: A Comparative Impact Analysis from Northern Kenya', *Journal of Development Economics* 129: 14–28

Jonas, O. (2019) 'Pandemic Bonds: Designed to Fail in Ebola', *Nature* 572: 285

Lloyd's (2018) *A World at Risk: Closing the Insurance Gap*, London: Lloyd's of London

Mawdsley, E. (2015) 'DFID, the Private Sector and the Re-Centring of an Economic Growth Agenda in International Development', *Global Society* 29.3: 339–358

Muir-Wood, R. (2017) 'The Politics of Basis Risk', *RMS Blog*, Newark: Risk Management Solutions

Sauer, N. (2019) 'Mozambique "Faces Climate Debt Trap" as Cyclone Kenneth Follows Idai', *Climate Home News*, 26 April

Swiss Reinsurance (2015) *Underinsurance of Property Risks: Closing the Gap*, Sigma 5/2015, Zürich: Swiss Reinsurance

UN Framework Convention on Climate Change (2017) *Compendium on Comprehensive Risk Management Approaches*, Bonn: UN Framework Convention on Climate Change

Van Leeuwen, M.H. (2016) *Mutual Insurance 1550–2015: From Guild Welfare and Friendly Societies to Contemporary Micro-Insurers*, London: Palgrave Macmillan

Wilkinson, A. and Leach, M. (2015) 'Briefing: Ebola – Myths, Realities, and Structural Violence', *African Affairs* 114.454: 136–148

World Bank (2018a) *Pandemic Emergency Financing Facility Operations Manual*, Washington, DC: The World Bank Group

—— (2018b) 'World Bank Group's Pandemic Emergency Financing Facility Welcomes Australia as New Donor', press release 21 June, Washington, DC: The World Bank Group

—— (2015) 'Pacific Catastrophe Risk Insurance Pilot: From Design to Implementation – Some Lessons Learned', Washington, DC: The World Bank Group

—— (2020) 'PEF Allocates US$195 Million to More than 60 Countries to Fight COVID-19', press release 27 April, Washington, DC: The World Bank Group

World Health Organization (2019) 'Ebola Outbreak in the Democratic Republic of the Congo Declared a Public Health Emergency of International Concern', press release 17 July, Geneva: World Health Organization

4

THE UNRAVELLING OF TECHNOCRATIC ORTHODOXY?

Contemporary knowledge politics in technology regulation

Patrick van Zwanenberg

Introduction

Technology regulation has long been an area of governance where the problematic nature of officially sanctioned knowledge regularly spills over into wider political and public settings. From clashes over atmospheric nuclear testing in the 1950s to more recent disputes over the commercialisation of agricultural genetic engineering, virtually all technology-related controversies of the last 70 years have pivoted around conflicts over the knowledge claims that regulatory institutions invoke to inform and justify policy decisions. Critics have long argued that officially sanctioned knowledge claims reflect a particular, usually very narrow, framing of what are generally profoundly ambiguous issues (Wynne 1975), and frequently provide a false precision in regard to what are often arbitrary and highly uncertain judgements and assessments (National Research Council 1983). They have also stressed that the precise ways in which these forms of knowledge 'closure' occur are invariably shaped by the political commitments and policy preferences of incumbent state and industrial actors, whether intentionally or inadvertently (Jasanoff and Wynne 1998). Any form of closure will, in turn, delimit the kinds of policy and technological options that decision-makers even contemplate, and prefigure the choices made about those options that are subject to consideration (Felt *et al.* 2007). As a consequence, regulatory decisions are often strongly influenced, even determined, by the political values and policy preferences of states and regulated industries, but those values and preferences are disguised in apparently logical and rational language (Stirling 2008a; Mayer and Stirling 2004; Jasanoff and Wynne 1998).

The evident tensions have been exacerbated by a long-standing historical tendency on the part of scientific and policy institutions everywhere to insist that there are, in fact, no political or normative dimensions to the knowledge claims that inform and justify policy decisions. This has been achieved firstly by depicting technology regulation as concerned only with addressing the safety of individual technologies, as if this were *logically* the only legitimate grounds for social concern about technology, and secondly by treating issues of safety as if they were fully comprehendible and predictable *ex ante* as a problem of calculable risk, or at least as a resolvable technical uncertainty.

In this portrayal, technological change is assumed to reflect the inevitable unfolding of scientific progress, rather than human choice, while the business of understanding potential harm is a rational scientific problem that can be solved in an impartial and objective way. Technology policy therefore becomes a technocratic exercise of calculating risks to human and environmental health and diminishing them to a socially acceptable level, in order to 'optimise' singular, apparently inevitable pathways of technological change.

It is not difficult to see why this depiction is expedient, at least for some actors, but it is wishful thinking. The world has experienced a long series of major unexpected problems with technologies, from the huge human toll from the use of asbestos, to the effects of chlorofluorocarbons on ozone depletion, to major industrial accidents such as at Chernobyl and Fukushima. These have shown how very serious harm often comes as a complete surprise, or despite very low official estimations of the chances of it occurring or at a magnitude far greater than predicted (Pfotenhauer *et al.* 2012; Harremoës *et al.* 2001). Furthermore, the utter failures, at least in some jurisdictions, to secure legitimacy for politically contentious technologies such as civil nuclear power and agricultural genetic engineering have torpedoed the implicit assumption that safety is the only meaningful public issue at stake in relation to the ways in which our technological futures unfold (Wynne 1983).

Policy institutions and jurisdictions have responded very slowly and unevenly, if at all, to these kinds of problems, and to an important critique of orthodox regulation, led by both the environmental and public health movements and by natural and social scientists (e.g. Stirling 2008b; Global Environmental Change Programme 1999; Santillo *et al.* 1998; Wynne 1982). Even where events and acute crises have made it overwhelmingly clear that at least some aspects of claims to science-based objectivity in regulatory decision-making are highly normative, the traditional depiction of regulation as a singularly rational technocratic endeavour has proved remarkably resilient in many institutions.

In this chapter I reflect on this conundrum through a brief discussion of two areas of contemporary European technology regulation, which I suggest have wider resonance: the cultivation of transgenic plant varieties and efforts to reform pesticide regulation. Both cases illustrate how unfolding events, campaigning and contextual issues and processes can sometimes force a partial 'opening up' of otherwise routine or opaque processes of knowledge closure, potentially heralding a broadening of technology regulation, for example so that policy addresses a wider set of potential vulnerabilities, or compares the pros and cons of different technological practices. Yet both cases also show how a more intellectually honest appreciation of, and response to, the uncertain, contested and provisional nature of much regulatory knowledge is politically very challenging for many institutions and the industries they regulate, and how many regulatory agencies and industry bodies have responded, and are responding, to such 'opening up' dynamics by trying aggressively to reassert an orthodox technocratic depiction of regulation, and in doing so shut down the rationale for more ambitious regulatory experimentation.

The more general phenomenon here is that political contexts and processes mediate a dynamic, perhaps dialectic, tension in much contemporary technology regulation – between the long-standing tradition of framing technology regulation around a control-based vision of risk management, supported by government-industry knowledge claims, and countervailing pressures to challenge the power embodied in such reductionist framings and to broaden out questions about technological vulnerability, and ultimately technological choice, for wider deliberation and collective decision-making. How such tensions play out in any specific area of regulation and whether a more emancipatory knowledge politics – and in turn transformative technology policy – can be fostered remain open questions. I argue that the emerging sustainability transformation agenda holds considerable potential to help foster such a shift, given that it invites a framing of the ways we think about technological vulnerabilities, and about socio-technical futures, that is fundamentally incompatible with orthodox regulatory approaches.

Transgenic crop regulation and the intractability of 'incertitude'

More than two decades of protracted conflict and regulatory paralysis in Europe in regard to the cultivation of genetically engineered (GE) crops illustrate very well how different dimensions of what Stirling (2008b) calls 'incertitude' – an unpacking of the broad, colloquial notion of 'uncertainty' (see Box 4.1) – affect and sometimes complicate knowledge production and regulatory decision-making.

In the early 1990s, the brand new European transgenic crop regulatory regime was typical of most areas of technology regulation: its remit was to anticipate and avoid 'adverse effects' on human health and the environment from individual technological artefacts, in this case transgenic crop varieties. The need for, and the potential benefits of, the new technology did not form part of the assessment, but were effectively assumed. Assessment focused, at least initially, on anticipating relatively direct forms of (practically measurable or estimable proxies for) potential harm, which were then evaluated against the benchmark of damage already caused by prevailing technological practice, in this case intensive agriculture. Scientific and regulatory conclusions about the potential 'risks' posed by the new crop technology were reported as if they were derived from an objective assessment of the scientific facts, with little if any acknowledgement of uncertainties, subjective assumptions or limits to what scientists could practically anticipate. This way of analytically defining, conducting and representing technology regulation was not inevitable, but rather followed the practice that had been established almost everywhere in the post-war period (Stirling 2010; Millstone and van Zwanenberg 2002).

BOX 4.1 DIFFERENT DIMENSIONS OF INCERTITUDE

Risk – possible outcomes and their likelihoods can be reliably estimated

Uncertainty – possible outcomes are clear, but there is no basis for assigning probabilities

Ignorance – neither outcomes nor their probabilities can be fully characterised

Ambiguity – probabilities can in principle be characterised, but there is no agreement over how to define the possible outcomes – for example, in terms of what the problem is, how the object of regulatory attention is bounded and which questions to address

Source: Stirling (2008b)

Right from the outset the new European regime ran into difficulties. The European single market meant that regulations had to be consistent across member states, so the new regime was based on the expectation that authorisation of a new transgenic crop in one member state would apply across Europe. In practice, unanimity proved impossible to obtain.

In the early 1990s, several biotechnology firms applied to release novel GE varieties. Regulators in the countries where the applications had been made accepted the firms' claims, based on field trial data, that adverse effects were unlikely. However, several other countries immediately dissented, claiming that a broader range of plausible potential adverse effects should have been taken into consideration. For example, Denmark and Austria objected to the approval in the UK of herbicide-tolerant canola (also known as oil seed rape) on the grounds that commercial cultivation of that variety might result in an increase in overall herbicide usage and, via hybridisation with wild relatives, might create herbicide-tolerant weeds, requiring additional herbicides to be used. These effects had been acknowledged as possible during the initial approval process in the UK but had been discounted, not on the grounds that they were unlikely but because any increase in herbicide usage would be a result of crop management practices, and not a *direct* harmful effect of the transgenic variety itself, and because the emergence of herbicide-tolerant weeds would be an 'agricultural problem' rather than a cause of 'environmental harm' (Levidow 2001). This was *not* a disagreement about how evidence should be interpreted but rather reflected *ambiguities* regarding how 'harm' should be defined and what precisely the potential 'problem' was that regulation ought to be addressing, and therefore what issues should properly fall within the boundary of any assessment. The reasons why the objectors dissented had to do with their own particular agricultural priorities and contexts. Denmark, for example, was trying to reduce agrochemical contamination of groundwater, which it relied on for drinking water.

The European Commission overruled these kinds of objections and approved the new transgenic varieties. Yet the refusal to recognise the validity of these objections, and subsequently many others about the scope and analytical framing of assessment, eventually provoked several countries unilaterally to ban crop varieties that had already secured Europe-wide approval. As the decade wore on and GE crops and food became increasingly contentious, a range of broader concerns about the 'problem' posed by transgenic crops began to find expression in public debates. For example, the Italian parliament emphasised the risks of dependence on multi-national firms and the threat to traditional crop varieties (Levidow 2009). But these were not issues that regulators were permitted to consider.

The more familiar issue of technical *uncertainty* was also utterly pervasive. Consider, for example, the potential problem described above of the hybridisation of transgenic canola with wild relatives, creating herbicide-tolerant weeds. Although we know that transfer of canola genes to weedy relatives can occur, measurements of pollen flow at 100 metres from transgenic canola have varied across different data sets by nine orders of magnitude (Meyer *et al.* 2005). Estimates of the frequency of gene transfer will also depend heavily on contingent management practice, and the development of resistant weeds by selection will also depend on herbicide use practices by farmers, which are also highly variable. As Meyer and colleagues put it: 'obvious problematic effects … can be identified. To what extent they should be regarded as harmful to the environment is a matter of interpretation. Credible probability calculations cannot be made' (Meyer *et al.* 2005: 237).

In such circumstances, subjective judgements have to be invoked if the conclusions of assessments are not to remain chronically open-ended. For example, what kinds and qualities of evidence are *sufficient* to conclude that herbicide-tolerant weeds will emerge as, say, a serious environmental problem? Regulatory institutions' responses to such uncertainties were contentious, but not only because the necessarily subjective judgements deployed were invariably represented as flowing from the scientific 'facts'.

In addition, several critics argued that such judgements were deployed inconsistently, with evidence suggestive of harm assumed to be 'insufficient' far more readily than evidence indicative of the absence of harm (Hilbeck *et al.* 2012; Levidow 2001). In the late 1990s, for instance, a laboratory study on the ecological effects of transgenic insecticidal maize reported significant mortality among lacewing butterfly larvae (a beneficial predator insect often found in maize fields) that had been fed on another species of caterpillar that was first raised on GE maize leaves. UK advisers did not challenge these experimental findings but argued that the laboratory study was not a realistic representation of the field situation – for example, because the larvae would have had a more varied diet in real-world conditions, and would therefore have been exposed to less GE maize (Wynne 2006). Critics pointed out that 'although such hypotheses were not unreasonable' they were almost exclusively made about studies that indicated potential harm: laboratory-based observations that suggested there was no harm from new transgenic plant varieties were routinely taken to be an adequate representation of real field situations (Wynne 2006; Levidow 2001).

Ignorance about the consequences of cultivating GE crops was an even more formidable problem, but it was barely recognised as such, and its implications were neglected. By definition, ignorance cannot be identified except after the fact, but it is interesting to observe how scientists and regulators sometimes diminished earlier states of 'institutional ignorance', in the sense that categories of adverse effect or causal pathways of harm that were not initially recognised by regulators (and so were not made the subject of questioning) were later discovered. The above example of the lacewing butterfly larvae study illustrates this point. Early regulatory-scientific studies of the possible effects of insecticidal GE maize on 'non-target harm' were based on investigating the *direct* effects of the insecticidal toxin expressed in GE maize varieties on beneficial insects (Levidow 2003). Those tests had found no additional harm from the GE maize. However, experimental tests were later performed by a university on carnivorous insects (i.e., the lacewing larvae study) further along the food chain in what is called a tri-trophic test (i.e., involving the plant, a pest and a predator). This more *indirect* causal pathway did indicate harm, in ways that had not been previously recognised or considered.

This example of institutional ignorance is entirely normal. Anticipatory regulatory knowledge about the consequences of commercially growing GE plants, based on small numbers of field trials and laboratory studies, has no chance of adequately capturing the complexity, contingency and variety of the conditions of actual commercial use. In part this is because of a host of practical constraints on what can be practically explored, but it is also because of normal scientific and regulatory commitments to particular kinds of theoretical models, testing methods and assumptions (Wynne 1992). Such commitments *are* sometimes questioned and enlarged, as part of a normal healthy process of scientific learning, as in the above example – although it is telling that in that case the prevailing experimental design was only re-examined by a non-regulatory-scientific institution in a context of intense public concern about the new crop technology.

A window of opportunity?

Intra-European disputes over the licensing of GE crops, particularly in relation to competing understandings as to what precisely the potential 'problem' was with the new crop technology, and therefore what kinds of questions ought to be explored, but also over what should count as adequate or sufficient evidence of safety, posed a serious challenge to the prospects of arriving at common regulatory decisions. One response would have been to recognise the challenges of incertitude, which were increasingly obvious, and which social scientists, NGOs and some protagonists had helped highlight. Taking those challenges seriously would have entailed making explicit and justifying – and if necessary renegotiating – the inevitable normative assumptions that are part and parcel of regulatory-scientific assessment. This would have entailed, for example, debating what burdens of proof were appropriate in particular situations of technical uncertainty, or what the relevant scientific questions to ask should be, given ambiguity over the potential problems posed by GE crop technology. Taking ignorance seriously might have involved adopting a less hubristic representation of what anticipatory assessment can achieve, and might have involved trying to nurture a learning culture within regulatory institutions.

Initially, it appeared that something approaching these kinds of responses might be forthcoming. By the late 1990s, concerns about the safety and acceptability of GE crops had exploded as a public issue across Europe. Environment ministers from several member states refused to support any more applications for new crop varieties until substantial revisions to the legislation were made. Ministers demanded that a wider range of potential risks be considered in applications – in particular, indirect effects that arise from the changed agricultural practices associated with a GE crop. They also wanted an obligation to monitor crops after approval, the rationale being to check for any adverse consequences that had not been discovered in experimental field trials, and for food and animal feed produced using GE plants to be traceable throughout the product chain, in order to ensure that food could be withdrawn if new evidence emerged regarding unknown health hazards (Levidow *et al.* 2005). Interestingly, these latter proposed revisions showed a recognition of ignorance about the potential consequences of agricultural biotechnology commercialisation, and an institutional attempt to try to diminish our vulnerability to such 'unknown-unknowns' (Wynne 1992).

New legislation incorporating all of these demands came into force in 2001. This occurred in the wake of the BSE or 'mad cow' crisis of 1996, shortly after which it became clear that profound uncertainty about whether the cattle disease might be transmitted to humans had been entirely glossed over by ministers and officials, in both the UK and within the European Commission. In the wake of the BSE crisis many regulatory institutions began to emphasise how important it was from now on that the institutions responsible for the assessment of scientific evidence should be 'independent' and that scientists should ensure that levels of uncertainty should be explicitly identified and communicated in plain language to decision-makers, and that any assumptions should be explicitly documented (OST 2005). A key driver of these reforms was the actions of government chief scientists, who had been alarmed not only by the potential catastrophe of BSE but also by the way in which 'science' had been used as political cover for ministers and officials throughout the saga (van Zwanenberg and Millstone 2005).

Reasserting orthodoxy at the European Commission

In practice, however, a more intellectually honest treatment of incertitude was not forthcoming. Instead, the Commission and its advisers attempted to reassert a modified version of the orthodox, technocratic depiction of regulation, although – in a partial concession – regulation was now split into two distinctive parts: 'risk assessment', which was represented as a policy-free, objective scientific endeavour, and 'risk management', which involved some normative decisions (Millstone 2009). Levidow (2017) notes how many senior people at the Commission had diagnosed the conflicts over GE crop assessment and decision-making over the previous decade as arising from national politics interfering with the proper scientific basis of risk regulation. New legislation introduced a centralised procedure of authorisation by the European Commission (Dolezel *et al.* 2011), and the idea was that the new

European Food Safety Agency (EFSA) would now play a more central role in scientific assessment of GE crops, while risk management would be the responsibility of the European Commission. As Directorate-General for Health and Consumers Commissioner David Byrne put it in 2002:

> [EFSA's] independence will ensure that scientific risk assessment work is not swayed by policy or other external considerations. ... [The development of EFSA's reputation for independence and excellence] will put an end to competition in such matters among national authorities in the Member States. We have seen evidence of this in the past and I hope that it will over time become a thing of the past (Byrne 2002: 3–4).

However, the new role for EFSA only exacerbated intra-European disputes. After several new transgenic crop varieties were approved by the Commission in the 2000s, Germany, France, Austria and Italy declared national prohibitions on their cultivation, which they were permitted to do under a 'safeguard clause' if new scientific information demonstrated a risk to human health or the environment. EFSA concluded that all the prohibitions lacked sufficient scientific evidentiary support and the Commission ruled that the bans were illegal – although none of the member states concerned backed down.

The unilateral bans had been made for the same kinds of reasons that had underpinned disputes in the previous decade: disagreements over which effects should count as 'adverse', and over what should count as meaningful or adequate or relevant evidence for a risk assessment (Levidow 2017; Wickson and Wynne 2012). EFSA's role was thus critical in facilitating the continuing impasse. For the Agency there was only one relevant framing of the scientific-regulatory problem and only one plausible interpretation of the evidence, namely its own. Its own scientific guidelines required Agency staff to make all assumptions explicit (EFSA 2009), but in practice it had ignored normative judgements within science, or represented them as scientific considerations (Levidow 2017).

For some analysts, the Commission and EFSA's 'normative-free' sound science representation of transgenic crop assessment reflects an entrenched institutional commitment to the European single market, which in turn requires a single regulatory system and therefore a centralised, standardised risk assessment (Wynne 2006). For others it is more an attempt by the Commission and EFSA to disguise a pro-biotech agenda – the Commission sees biotech as essential for future growth and competitiveness – under the guise of unitary science (Levidow 2015; Dolezel *et al.* 2011). Yet others point to naive beliefs in the political neutrality and universality of regulatory science on the part of some scientists and officials, and in particular in the scientistic assumption that science ought to define the human meaning of issues such as GE crop innovation. In this reading, any concerns other than those identified by officially sanctioned scientific institutions must be illegitimate 'hidden interests' and 'anti-scientific', especially if they are not exclusively about public or environment health but extend to cover public concerns about the political-economic effects, or drivers, of GE crop innovation (Wynne 2014).

Additional explanations are not necessarily incompatible with any of the above. For example, Commission officials may have concluded that it was too politically risky to acknowledge openly the contingent and highly uncertain nature of regulatory-scientific knowledge because it could then become very difficult to draw a line and prevent further, endless deconstruction of whatever claims were officially sanctioned. The political risk here is not just that institutions are unable to pretend that contentious policy decisions can be justified solely by recourse to evidence, but that events may quickly spiral out of control. An explicit acknowledgement that we cannot predict future impacts might lead logically to demands for expensive or burdensome controls, or to politically problematic questions being posed, such as 'why then are we supporting this technology?', 'what and whose needs is it designed to satisfy?' and 'what are the alternatives?' It is far easier politically, perhaps, to insist that knowledge claims are universal and complete. British officials often made this kind of political calculation during the BSE saga, for instance (van Zwanenberg and Millstone 2005).

Pesticide regulation and the sustainability transformation agenda

In attempting to impose a singular meaning of 'risk', and a single analytical treatment of it, on multiple European countries with diverse sets of concerns and agricultural priorities, European GE crop regulation has scuppered any prospect of common regulatory decisions. By contrast, in the field of pesticide regulation standard approaches to risk regulation have been stretched to accommodate a much wider analytical framing. A significant factor influencing this is the emerging sustainability transformation agenda, which has challenged some long-held orthodoxies in pesticide regulation.

In 2011, two new pieces of European legislation on pesticide approval and pesticide use came into force (EC 2009a; 2009b). The new legislation contained four novel regulatory measures that drive a coach and horses through the traditional analytical treatment of pesticide regulation. These are to:

- use *hazard-based cut-off criteria* to prohibit all pesticides that exhibit the intrinsic potential of serious toxicity or persistence;
- use *comparative hazard assessment* to substitute authorised chemical pesticide uses for the least hazardous alternatives, including non-chemical techniques;
- promote *non-chemical pest management*, specifically organic farming and
- establish *integrated pest management* in all agricultural practice (in which biological, agronomic and physical forms of insect, weed and fungal control are given priority over chemical control).

The new measures represent a profound challenge to the central regulatory tenet that anticipatory risk assessment provides a sufficiently reliable and complete basis upon which to anticipate and control potential harm from the commercial use of a technology. Consider, for example, the new hazard-based cut-off criteria measure, which means that the intrinsic toxic potential or persistence of a compound becomes grounds for prohibition. The traditional risk-based approach would also involve estimating the likely exposure to the compound under different conditions of use and to different populations; it would model and estimate dose–response relationships based on experimental rodent studies, and then derive estimates of the magnitude of potential harm to humans under different use scenarios, as the basis upon which regulatory decisions are taken. That orthodox approach is, however, afflicted by persistent uncertainties because numerical estimates of the magnitude of harm at different levels of exposure (or more typically the derivation of a threshold level of exposure that constitutes 'no harm') are usually impossible to derive without deploying a series of cumulative, entirely subjective assumptions (Bailar and Bailar 1999). They are also vulnerable to ignorance – for example, because relevant exposure pathways may be entirely unknown (Wynne 1992).

The adoption of a hazard-based approach (long advocated in the literature on precautionary forms of appraisal, see Lofstedt 2011 and Harremoës *et al.* 2001) does not avoid vulnerability to incertitude. Important forms of toxicity may be unknown and therefore remain untested. Yet it substantially diminishes such vulnerability, for the reasons provided above. It errs on the side of caution, on the grounds that we are unlikely to be able reliably to identify thresholds of safe exposure to compounds that are, for instance, carcinogens or endocrine disruptors, or to ensure that actual use of such compounds will conform to regulatory assumptions about working practice.

The particular formulation of the measure on comparative hazard assessment under these new pieces of European legislation – in which non-chemical techniques of pest control must be included as a comparator – also demolishes another orthodox regulatory tenet: the traditional bounding of the 'object' of regulatory scrutiny as only involving individual technological artefacts. Yet that bounding is ambiguous. There is no scientific reason why, instead, the object of regulatory attention should not extend to multiple artefacts (and their synergies and interactions), or an entire technological system or technological trajectory or, as in the new European legislation, an artefact assessed by comparison with alternative technological or policy means of obtaining the same social goal. Indeed, since the greater scope of specificity of such a comparative approach would be more scientifically rigorous, the real reason for restricting attention in the conventional approach must be recognised instead as expediency, in favour of the privileged interests whose particular innovations receive such singular treatment.

More generally, the combination of the four new measures under the new legislation – which both increase regulatory pressure to withdraw existing chemical technologies and support the creation of non-chemical alternatives – effectively defines the entire system of chemical pesticide-based crop production itself as a source of vulnerability, even though that system is based on approved pesticides. The purpose of regulation is no longer the orthodox one of 'optimising' supposedly self-unfolding pathways of chemical pesticide-based agricultural production, but rather of redirecting those pathways and transforming agricultural production.

What, then, prompted this much wider analytical framing of pesticide regulation? The novel assessment measures were drafted by Green Party Members of the European Parliament on the European Parliament's Environment, Public Health and Food Safety Committee, and then steered through the legislative process with the support of some of the smaller EU states (Bozzini 2017; Panke 2012). The measures were strongly informed by ideas about precautionary forms of technology appraisal, and specifically long-standing concerns about the failure of orthodox pesticide regulation to anticipate and control threats to human health and the environment (Bozzini 2017: 66). In 2019, the committee emphasised the central role of pesticides in the collapse in insect species, farmland birds and other biodiversity, and argued that current dependence on pesticides was 'incompatible with sustainable agriculture' (European Parliament 2019: 3). It described the new legislation as 'a prerequisite for … accomplishing a transition towards sustainable agriculture' (*ibid.*: 11). Here, then, we see a new political context, shaped by the rise of precautionary thinking, and by the emerging 'sustainability transformation' agenda, and which, in response to existential environmental threats, seeks to reframe the traditional regulatory focus, moving from the management of individual technologies to fostering transformative socio-technical change (cf. Intergovernmental Science-Policy Platform on Biodiversity and Ecosystem Services 2019).

A reassertion of orthodoxy?

Unsurprisingly, the new measures were heavily criticised by many governments and by the chemical pesticide industry, both before and after the legislation came into force. In 2008, for example, the UK's Pesticide Safety Directorate objected to the then proposed hazard-based cut-off criteria, insisting that 'no meaningful benefits to public health protection from any criteria, beyond those delivered by the existing risk assessment arrangements, have been demonstrated' (cited in Bozzini 2017: 71). Those remarks are a defence of the fundamental orthodox regulatory assumption that asserted risk parameters, and their supposed means for definitive quantification, provide an entirely adequate basis for control – an assumption that, of course, the new legislative measures fatally undermine.

Tellingly, the UK government has interpreted the legislative obligation to establish integrated pest management in all agricultural practice as an issue of economic optimisation, rather than as a means of reducing harm, on the basis that risk-based regulatory approval of pesticides already adequately manages safety (Department for Environment, Food and Rural Affairs 2012). It has therefore made minimal efforts to support the adoption of integrated pest management, suggesting instead that this should be a voluntary option for utility-maximising farmers. As with GE crop regulation, explicit recognition of the challenges of incertitude, and the implications this logically entails for broadening the scope and ambition of regulatory decision-making, has prompted a reaction on the part of some jurisdictions to reassert an orthodox technocratic depiction of regulation.

It remains unclear how this will play out. The European Parliament has described how, in the eight years since the new legislation came into force, implementation has become bogged down in arguments about the desirability, precise meaning and practical implications of many of the proposed new objectives (European Parliament 2019; 2018). The introduction of the hazard-based 'cut-off' assessment of substances was delayed to 2014, and five years later had resulted in the prohibition of only one pesticide active ingredient; meanwhile several member states and the agro-chemical industry have been lobbying to drop the use of the hazard-based cut-off assessment altogether. Comparative assessment began in 2015, but so far no compounds have been substituted for safer alternatives. Little progress, in most member states, has been made on encouraging the use of alternative pest control techniques or the adoption of integrated pest management. Instead, there has been an increase in the overall volume of chemical pesticide use across the EU as a whole (*ibid.*).

Conclusion

This chapter has argued that the contemporary politics of technology regulation play out through a key tension: between an established narrow framing of what is at stake in technology regulation, namely the optimisation of singular pathways of technological progress based on a control-based vision of risk management, and countervailing pressures to challenge those reductionist framings and open up questions about technological vulnerability, and ultimately technological choice, to wider deliberation and collective decision-making.

The experience of European regulation of transgenic plant varieties shows how a key moment of 'opening up' was associated with processes of regulatory harmonisation, following the creation of the European single market, and the fallout from the BSE crisis. In the case of pesticide regulation, new, emergent political processes associated with ideas about precaution and the 'sustainability transformation' agenda have challenged established approaches to assessment. Both cases illustrate how contestation over knowledge can unsettle established regulatory practice and prompt a broadening of the scope of regulation – radically so in the pesticides case. They also illustrate how some institutions and industry bodies have responded by trying to reassert an orthodox depiction of knowledge and regulation, thus undermining a rationale for more ambitious, potentially transformative, forms of policy.

The pesticides case suggests that the sustainability transformation agenda may be a particularly significant, emerging aspect of the political contexts that mediate the tensions described in this chapter. Propelled onto policy agendas by the twin crises of climate breakdown and biodiversity collapse, the significance of the transformation agenda is that it invites a framing of the ways we think about technological vulnerabilities and of socio-technical futures that is fundamentally incompatible with orthodox regulatory approaches. That agenda focuses policy attention on the vulnerabilities posed by entire trajectories of linked socio-technical change, rather than the threats presented by individual artefacts; on questions about what kinds of futures we want, rather than the assumption that there is a single deterministic pathway of progress and on questions about the multiple contending pathways involved in getting there, and so the importance of appreciating plural knowledge and deliberating among different options, rather than denial of ambiguity. Above all, it undermines the orthodox assumption that regulation can adequately anticipate and control the vulnerabilities posed by our unfolding technological futures. If that were so, why is there an urgent need to transform established socio-technical practice?

References

Bailar, J.C. and Bailar, A.J. (1999) 'Risk Assessment-the Mother of All Uncertainties: Disciplinary Perspectives on Uncertainty in Risk Assessment', *Annals of the New York Academy of Sciences* 895: 273–285

Bozzini, E. (2017) *Pesticide Policy and Politics in the European Union. Regulatory Assessment, Implementation and Enforcement*, London: Palgrave Macmillan

Byrne, D. (2002) 'EFSA: Excellence, Integrity and Openness', speech at inaugural meeting of the European Food Safety Agency Management Board, Parma, Italy: EFSA, https://ec.europa.eu/commission/presscorner/detail/en/SPEECH_02_405

Department for Environment, Food and Rural Affairs (2012) *UK National Action Plan for the Sustainable Use of Pesticides (Plant Protection Products)*, London: UK Department for Environment, Food and Rural Affairs

Dolezel, M., Miklau, M., Hilbeck, A. *et al.* (2011) 'Scrutinizing the Current Practice of the Environmental Risk Assessment of GM Maize Applications for Cultivation in the EU', *Environmental Sciences Europe* 23: 33

European Commission (2009a) Regulation (EC) No 1107/2009 of the European Parliament and of the Council of 21 October 2009 Concerning the Placing of Plant Protection Products on the Market and Repealing Council Directives 79/117/EEC and 91/414/EEC

—— (2009b) Directive 2009/128/EC of the European Parliament and of the Council of 21 October 2009 Establishing a Framework for Community Action to Achieve the Sustainable Use of Pesticides

European Food Safety Agency (2009) 'Guidance on Transparency in the Scientific Aspects of Risk Assessment Carried out by EFSA, Part 2: General Principles', *EFSA Journal* 1051: 1–22

European Parliament (2019) 'Report on the Implementation of Directive 2009/128/EC on the sustainable Use of Pesticides (2017/2284(INI))', A8-0045/2019

—— (2018) 'Report on the Union's Authorisation Procedure for Pesticides (2018/2153(INI))', A8-0475/2018

Felt, U. *et al.* (2007) 'Science and Governance: Taking the European Knowledge Society Seriously', Report of the Expert Group on Science and Governance to the Science, Economy and Society Directorate, Directorate-General for Research, European Commission

Global Environmental Change Programme (1999) *The Politics of GM food: Risk, Science and Public Trust*, Brighton: ESRC Global Environmental Change Programme, Special Briefing No. 5

Harremoës, P., Gee, D., MacGarvin, M., Stirling, A., Keys, J., Vaz, S.G. and Wynne, B. (eds) (2001) *Late Lessons from Early Warnings: The Precautionary Principle 1896–2000*, Brussels: European Environment Agency: Environmental Issue Report 22

Hilbeck, A., Meier, M. and Trtikova, M. (2012) 'Underlying Reasons of the Controversy over Adverse Effects of Bt Toxins on Lady Beetle and Lacewing Larvae', *Environmental Sciences Europe* 24: 1–5

Intergovernmental Science-Policy Platform on Biodiversity and Ecosystem Services (2019) 'Summary for Policymakers of the Global Assessment Report on Biodiversity and Ecosystem Services of the Intergovernmental Science-Policy Platform on Biodiversity and Ecosystem Services', Bonn: IPBES

Jasanoff, S. and Wynne, B. (1998) 'Science and Decision-making', in S. Rayner and E. Malone (eds) *Human Choice and Climate Change. Vol 1 The Societal Framework*, Washington DC: Batelle Press: 1–87

Levidow, L. (2017) 'Substituting a Fictional "Science" for Public Accountability: Legitimacy Problems of the EU's Regulatory Framework for GM Products', in L.E. San-Epifanio (ed) *Towards a New Regulatory Framework for GM Crops in the European Union: Scientific, Ethical, Social and Legal Issues and the Challenges Ahead,* Wageningen: Wageningen Academic Publishers

—— (2009) 'Making Europe Unsafe for Agbiotech', in P. Atkinson, P. Glasner and M. Lock (eds) *The Handbook of Genetics and Society: Mapping the New Genomic Era*, Genetics and Society, London: Routledge

—— (2003) 'Precautionary Risk Assessment of Bt Maize: What Uncertainty?', *Journal Invertebrate Pathology* 83: 113–117

—— (2001) 'Precautionary Uncertainty: Regulating GM Crops in Europe', *Social Studies of Science* 31.6: 842

Levidow, L., Carr, S. and Wield, D. (2005) 'European Regulation of Agri-Biotechnology: Precautionary Links between Science, Expertise and Policy', *Science and Public Policy* 32.4: 261–276

Lofstedt, R. (2011) 'Risk Versus Hazard–How to Regulate in the 21st Century', *European Journal of Risk Regulation* 2: 149–168

Mayer, S. and Stirling, A. (2004) 'GM Crops: Good or Bad? Those Who Choose the Questions Determine the Answers', *EMBO Reports* 5.11: 1021–1024

Meyer, G., Folker, A.P., Jørgensen, R.B., Krauss, M.K.V., Sandøe, P. and Tveit, G. (2005) 'The Factualization of Uncertainty: Risk, Politics, and Genetically Modified Crops – A Case of Rape', *Agriculture and Human Values* 22: 235–242

Millstone, E. (2009) 'Science, Risk and Governance: Radical Rhetorics and the Realities of Reform in Food Safety Governance', *Research Policy* 38: 624–636

Millstone, E. and van Zwanenberg, P. (2002) 'The Evolution of Food Safety Policy-Making Institutions in the UK, EU and Codex Alimentarius', *Social Policy and Administration* 36.6: 593–609

National Research Council (1983) *Risk Assessment in the Federal Government: Managing the Process*, Washington, DC: National Academy Press

Office of Science and Technology (2005) *Scientific Analysis in Policy Making*, London: Office of Science and Technology

Panke, D. (2012) 'Being Small in a Big Union: Punching Above their Weights? How Small States Prevailed in the Vodka and the Pesticides Cases', *Cambridge Review of International Affairs* 25.3: 329–344

Pfotenhauer, S.M., Jones, C.F., Saha, K. and Jasanoff, S. (2012) 'Learning from Fukushima', *Issues on Science and Technology* 28.3: 79–84

Santillo, D., Stringer, R., Johnston, P. and Tickner, J. (1998) 'The Precautionary Principle: Protecting against Failures of Scientific Method and Risk Assessment', *Marine Pollution Bulletin* 36.12, 939–950

Stirling, A. (2010) 'From Enlightenment to Enablement: Opening up Choices for Innovation', in A. López-Claros (ed) *The Innovation for Development Report*, London: Palgrave Macmillan

—— (2008a) 'Opening Up and Closing Down: Power, Participation and Pluralism in the Social Appraisal of Technology', *Science Technology and Human Values* 33.2: 262–294

—— (2008b) 'Science, Precaution, and the Politics of Technological Risk: Converging Implications in Evolutionary and Social Scientific Perspectives', *Annals of The New York Academy Of Sciences* 1128: 95–110

van Zwanenberg, P. and Millstone, E. (2005) *BSE: Risk, Science and Governance*, Oxford: Oxford University Press

Wickson, F. and Wynne, B. (2012) 'Ethics of Science for Policy in the Environmental Governance of Biotechnology: MON810 Maize in Europe', *Ethics, Policy and Environment* 15.3: 321–340

Wynne, B. (2014) 'Further Disorientation in the Hall of Mirrors', *Public Understanding of Science* 23.1: 60–70

—— (2006) 'GMO Risk Assessment under Conditions of Biological (and Social) Complexity', in Bundesministerium für Gesundheit und Frauen (BMGF), *The Role of Precaution in GMO Policy* Berlin/Bonn: BMGF: 30–46

—— (1992) 'Uncertainty and Environmental Learning: Reconceiving Science and Policy in the Preventive Paradigm', *Global Environmental Change* 2: 111–137

—— (1983) 'Redefining the Issues of Risk and Public Acceptance: The Social Viability of Technology', *Futures* 15: 13–32

—— (1982) *Rationality and Ritual: The Windscale Inquiry and Nuclear Decisions in Britain*, Chalfont St. Giles: British Society for the History of Science

—— (1975) 'The Rhetoric of Consensus Politics: A Critical Review of Technology Assessment', *Research Policy* 4.2: 108–158

5

CONTROL, MANAGE OR COPE?

A politics for risks, uncertainties and unknown-unknowns

Emery Roe

Introduction

My discussion of a politics of uncertainty is best begun with a lesson in humility. I had the good fortune to be on an interdisciplinary team of researchers investigating the resilience of large-scale socio-technical systems: namely, the chance that levees and dikes would breach in the California Delta. I was the team's policy analyst, and other team members were from backgrounds in engineering, geographic information systems, crisis management and the social sciences. While this was an important US National Science Foundation project, we had been on big research projects and interdisciplinary teams before.

Now, the lesson learned: it was only after a year of regular meetings that the team leader and I realised we were operating under very different operating definitions of resilience. His was the time to recovery after a levee breach, mine was the ability of the levee to absorb shocks before breaching. This was a sobering experience, given the decades of experience of those involved and the explicit project focus on resilience. It is also a good example of the impact of ambiguity as outlined in the Stirling typology of incertitudes, discussed in the introduction to this book.

So, too, definitions of, and assumptions about, risk and uncertainty cannot be taken for granted in high-stakes settings across multiple disciplines. No matter how often we distinguish between, on the one hand, measurable risks (where estimates of the probability and consequences of failure exist) and, on the other hand, non-measurable uncertainties (where estimates of the probability or consequence of failure are missing, if not unobtainable), there are those who insist that risk and uncertainty are not separable. Arguably the most famous example is ISO 31000 'Risk management – Principles and guidelines', which states up front: 'risk [is defined as] the effect of uncertainty on objectives'. Of course, the International Standard goes into more detail about the probabilities and consequences of failure, but the point of departure in uncertainty is unmistakable. So, too, for ordinary language and its deliberate ambiguity when it comes to the terms uncertainty, risk, unpredictability, chance and likelihood, among others.

This chapter demonstrates that another set of distinctions is as crucial as that between risk, uncertainty and the unknown-unknowns of unstudied/unstudiable conditions: it is equally necessary for a politics of uncertainty to distinguish between controlling, managing and coping with those risks, uncertainties and unstudied conditions. Here, too, however, ordinary language – and its lexicographers – take 'control', 'manage' and 'cope' as overlapping, if not synonymous on occasion. I should not then be as surprised – as I usually am – that when I say 'manage' to an audience from other disciplines, they think I'm talking about control. Believe me, there is nothing further away from my mind at that point than illusions of control!

I come from a profession – policy analysis – that has long given up organising notions of Weberian hierarchies, and command and control, in favour of – the names speak for themselves – muddling through, garbage-can processes, adhocracy, coping agencies, goal displacement with means-as-ends, bricolage and, my favourite, managing messes (for more on these notions, see Roe 2013). Of course, control can and does exist, but for policy analysts such as myself any starting assumption that complex systems, let alone contemporary politics and major policies, can macro-control each important micro-operation is misleading, where not outright dangerous.

The argument in what follows is that just as it is dangerous to close down democratic deliberations to risk only, so too is it dangerous to close down that deliberation to the pros and cons of control. A politics of uncertainty recognises that a world where risks must always be controlled falls far short of meeting the transformative challenges involved in better managing uncertainties and coping better with unstudied/unstudiable conditions where control is not possible. Indeed, transformation may be all about managing – or coping better – with so-called existential risks that cannot be controlled.

Preliminaries

This chapter's argument is grounded in research findings on real-time personnel operating large socio-technical systems – think: critical infrastructures for water, energy, telecommunications and transportation (for details see Roe and Schulman 2016; 2008). In ways described later in the chapter, personnel must manage real-time operations *precisely because* they do not have control of the entire system as a system at any one time, and at the same time because coping passively with system-wide shocks that are outside of their direct control is also not an option. Instead, they must actively manage risks they cannot control, as well as actively manage key uncertainties so as to avoid unstudied conditions. Moreover, when they find themselves in unstudied conditions, they cope not just reactively but by planning the next step ahead. Worse behaviour for a politics of uncertainty can be imagined!

What do these professionals mean by control, management and coping? In formal terms, control is when the system's input variance, process variance and output variance are rendered low and stable. Think of the nuclear reactor power plant: guns, guards and gates are used to ensure outside inputs are controlled; processes within the nuclear station are highly regulated by government to ensure few or no mistakes are made (operations and procedures that have not been analysed beforehand are not permissible); and the output of the plant – its electricity – is kept constant, with as low variance as possible (nuclear power is often considered the 'baseload' for a system, on top of which are added other types of electricity generation).

The problem now and in the foreseeable future is that the number of critical infrastructures having low input variance/low process variance/low output variance are fewer and fewer because of increasing political, economic and social unpredictabilities affecting their service provision. Indeed, the very same political, economic and social turmoil has undermined older control-centred notions of the Frankfurt School's 'totally administered society', Harold Lasswell's 'garrison state' and Erving Goffman's 'total institutions' – where key social entities were determined by elites (a theme that is also central to academic discussions of totalitarian politics and societies).

It is the case today that an increasing number of electricity generation sources – and very important ones – face high input variability. Deregulation (involving liberalisation and privatisation) of the integrated utilities has brought with it volatile electricity markets and prices; and, in addition, environmental factors like the climate have become more unpredictable. Consequently, operational processes inside other power plants have had to become more varied (this being the so-called law of requisite variety (Weick 1995; Ashby 1952)), with more options and strategies to process and produce what still must be a low-variance output: namely, electricity at a regulated frequency and voltage. Coping in these systems embraces cases where process variance can no longer be managed to match input variance and/or where output variance is no longer low and stable. Earthquakes, catastrophic fires and tsunamis have had just this effect with default of professional behaviour and operations to coping behaviour.

These initial strategies and types of 'unpredictabilities', as infrastructure operators would call them, are summarised in Table 5.1. To be clear, they are based on the observations of and descriptions provided by infrastructure operators in our research.

Why do these infrastructure distinctions matter for a politics of uncertainty?

The infrastructures we study, like water, energy and transportation, are mandated to operate in a highly reliable fashion – that is, to provide the critical service in question safely and continuously even during (or especially during) turbulent times. To do so requires the variety of operational approaches just described. In like fashion

TABLE 5.1 Forms of unpredictability: definitions and outcomes

Type of unpredictability	Definition	Type of operational approach	Outcome
Risk	Probability and consequences of failure are known and estimated	Control	Low and stable output variance through keeping low input variance and low process variance
Uncertainty*	Either probability or consequences of failure are unknown or not estimated	Manage	High input variance matched by high process variance to ensure low and stable output variance
Unknown-unknowns	Neither probability nor consequences of failure are known for estimating	Cope	High and unstable output variance and/ or inadequate process variance to match input variance

* This definition, consonant with how infrastructure operators see uncertainty, is less expansive than 'uncertainty' in the Stirling framework (Stirling 2010). Note also that the operator term 'unknown-unknowns' does not capture the subjective and intersubjective features conveyed by 'ignorance'.

are politics described as being about – and are expected to be about – underwriting and stabilising respective services, and this too requires varieties of power.

Further, once you realise that operations in critical infrastructures and in politics are undertaken in the face of a host of shared uncertainties and shocks, five inter-knitted features of infrastructures and politics take on prominence:

- **First, infrastructures and politics often have the same operational/ administrative areas.** States and cities, for example, have their own transmission grids and water supplies, including respective political and regulatory oversight. In fact, it is difficult to imagine how modern politics could be undertaken without foundational infrastructures for telecommunications, energy and such like in place.
- **Second, both infrastructures and politics centre on high stakes**. Managing uncertainty is a matter of life and death if critical infrastructure services fail; the often-related high stakes of politics are visible and central across governmental and administrative scales relying on the infrastructures.
- **Third, managing uncertainty in real-time for infrastructures is an ever-present challenge, as it is in politics.** If you cannot manage non-measurable uncertainties now when it matters, why would we believe your promises to control or cope with them better later on?
- **Fourth, non-measurable uncertainties, and not just measurable risks, are to be managed in infrastructures and in politics.** Politicians and

reliability professionals (including their staffs) manage real-time uncertainties in ways that do not stand or fall on undertaking formal risk assessment or standard methodologies. Also, it is notable that the 'public interests' of large, critical infrastructures – ensuring system-wide safety and reliability across political settings – necessitate sensitivities to different types of uncertainty, and their respective management.

• **Fifth, the inevitably major role for real-time uncertainty management remains under-appreciated when it comes to the craft of politics, as well as the craft of infrastructure operations.** Some discipline-based or science-based experts and academics tend to dismiss the professionalism, domains of practice and processes for managing large socio-technical systems and politics.

You can think of real-time managers of infrastructures operating in the same way as those in policy-making and politics who have learned that managing a mess in policy and management (stopping a good mess from going bad or preventing a bad one from getting worse) may be far better than trying to clean that mess up once and for all. Why? Because attempts at achieving a 'once and for all solution' can and often do make major policy messes more difficult to manage (Roe 2013). In the field of critical infrastructures, you see this recognition that management is not control but must be more than coping reactively in the shift from the terminology of 'control rooms' and 'control operators' to, for example, 'operations centres' and the more accurate job titles of 'dispatchers' and 'schedulers'. In order to avoid any confusion with 'controllers', my research colleague, Paul Schulman, and I have termed such infrastructure operators and their real-time support staff 'reliability professionals'.

More detailed argument

Since 'control' and 'manage' are perceived differently, senior staff in some infrastructures we have researched make a big point about how risk controls (read: compliance) are not the whole of risk management. As one high-level risk manager for a large energy utility put it:

> The approach we've taken is that compliance is the first step in risk management. Compliance requirements that are in place are our first obligation in risk management. It's the minimum that we built the rest of our enterprise risk management on. You can do more than just compliance. So compliance and risk management aren't two separate things, where we do one and then the other. You do both at the same time.
>
> For example, we do risk management with respect to compliance: We determine how comfortable we are with respect to our controls for compliance. What problems are there in our compliance programmes? Where do we stand in respect to industry standards or even better on this? (From transcript of an interview held on 30 March 2015, with the senior manager of a risk enterprise unit of a major northern California utility).

TABLE 5.2 Primary approaches to operating for three types of unpredictabilities

		Objective of operational approach		
		Risks	*Uncertainties*	*Unknown-unknowns*
Primary operational approach	*Control* *Manage* *Cope*			

This difference between control and management of risks is graphically displayed in Table 5.2:

Since no existing compliance measure or preset risk control can be expected to be 100 per cent effective, the cell 'Control/Risks' in Table 5.2 is lightly shaded and must be complemented by 'Manage/Risks', the darker shaded cell, for risks that cannot be controlled in real-time or must not be assumed to be controllable right now, when it matters. For example, it is because tomorrow's heat wave is uncontrollable that electric and natural gas grids have to manage the added load requirements for, and associated risks relating to, assets and personnel.

Such management strategies for measurable risks, we found in our research, include having a range of subject matter experts and outside certification programmes and reviews for process safety management and risk management protocols – again, as a way of increasing process options and strategies to match an increasing input variance. The crux, though, is that even in managing risks, the reliability professionals do not rely solely on a single distribution of numbers. Numerical averages and ranges wobble, and this has to be compensated for by experienced and skilled reliability professionals.

It is not only risks that have to be managed because it is dangerous to assume they can be controlled: key non-measurable uncertainties must also be managed. Infrastructure operators typically distinguish uncertainties in terms of missing estimates for the probability or consequence of failure. Since the estimate of risk is defined as the product of the estimates of the probability and consequence of failure, uncertainties are cases where operators have (rough) estimates of probabilities and consequences of failure, but not for both at the same time. The same follows when the logic of risk is cast in terms of threats, exposures and vulnerabilities. Real-time infrastructure operators may have better knowledge of the probability of failure than they do of the consequences of failure; alternatively, they may have better knowledge of consequences than of probability.

Over and over again in our research, and to complicate our initial definition of 'uncertainty' (Table 5.1), real-time operators told us they were able to manage uncertainties about which they may know something more about their consequences than they do about their likelihoods, or *vice versa*. Where utilities know more about probabilities of failure than the expected consequences of failure, we found one management strategy to be planning for or preparing around worst-case scenarios and extra safeguards. Where more is known about the consequences of failure than the likelihood of failure, one management strategy (also for increasing process variance) is the expanded use of simulation studies and of investments in uncertainty reduction with respect to the probability of failure. For example, 'deep dives' into specific cases are undertaken by experienced personnel – and not just subject matter specialists. The cell 'Manage/Uncertainties' has a darker shade in Table 5.2, to reflect this primary approach.

In case it needs saying, for a world where events are sometimes uncontrollable, and in other cases unmanageable (i.e., process options and strategies cannot be increased to reflect increased input variance), there are instances where neither the probability nor consequences of failure are known or studiable under the demands of real-time urgency. (Or, if you prefer, those concerned are at a loss to determine just what are the threats, exposures and vulnerabilities.) Here is where coping behaviour of infrastructure operators in the face of the unknown-unknown is notable – but it is coping with a difference.

When real-time infrastructure operations suffer a shock that pushes those operations into unstudied conditions, the professionals are not only expected to be resilient as regards absorbing the shock, they are at the same time expected to be planning the next step or operation ahead. They do not want to bounce back to the same position that left them vulnerable: they want to bounce forward to better real-time operating conditions. This coping is *coping-ahead* in the face of real-time unknown-unknowns (darker shade in Table 5.2), since it involves planning above-and-beyond reactions in real-time. One such coping-ahead strategy that is directed to planning the next steps for real-time operations is the routine use of variously named 'white hat' teams that are internal to the infrastructure. These teams seek to find ways to undermine real-time system operations so as to anticipate more effectively – predict *and* prepare for – defects that are exploitable by system attack, intentional or otherwise. Planning ahead for addressing defects becomes a template – imperfect as it must be for what are unknown-unknowns – when responding later on to what are encountered in real-time as functionally similar defects.

An emancipatory politics of uncertainty?

This chapter now shifts its register from the descriptive to the normative. The operational strategies and unpredictabilities that society's critical infrastructures seek to handle better are also necessary for the successful enactment of policy. To do otherwise, I suggest, is to open politics to more catastrophe.

Return to Table 5.2 and its highlighted cells. I ask you to see the highlighted cells as principal stepping-stones along a pathway for addressing unpredictabilities in complex, high-stakes systems and processes. (Note the accent on 'principal' leaves aside any complications arising when the empty cells in Table 5.2 are not empty.) I submit that to take a politics of uncertainty seriously centres on demonstrating – constantly – behaviour that recognises the need to better cope-ahead with unknown-unknowns, that recognises the need to manage some uncertainties and risks better than they are now being managed and that recognises control of all this is not possible, where attempts to exert such control create grave political hazards instead.

This politics of uncertainty is, as such, a full-time job for those who treat the politics seriously. How then is it emancipatory? William Kentridge, painter and artist, provides an insight. To the interview question, 'You've been called the patron saint of ambiguity. How do you feel about that?', he responded:

> How do I feel? Ambiguous: I like it and I don't like it. I wish some things could be much clearer that one holds onto without any doubts. *I'm wary of certainty, but I'm very weary of uncertainty, also* (quoted in Buck 2016 [my italics]).

I adapt his insight – wariness of certainties (namely, the pretence to certainty that full control of major politics and policies is achievable) and weariness of having continually to manage and cope-ahead – as the starting point for a politics of uncertainty. This starting point forces us then to ask: why put up with wariness and weariness? What keeps 'us' going? What do we get from these multiple unpredictabilities and having to address them in multiple ways?

For me, the wariness and weariness are associated with emancipation: emancipation from thinking there is no alternative, and emancipation from thinking complex policy problems are wicked and as such intractable. The world cannot be controlled to be only one way; it is far too complex for that, with many components, each component having multiple functions (I am a husband, father, blogger...), and the many interconnections between and among components, functions and the wider environments in which these are embedded enable all manner of interpretations, explanations and descriptions. No single reading can cover, let alone exhaust, that complexity.

The upshot of this inexhaustibility is that complex problems can be cast in multiple ways; or to come at it from another direction, any complex problem that has no description other than 'there's no alternative', 'it's intractable' or 'it's a wicked problem' is an exaggeration that has closed down discussion and analysis long before any insights into alternative possibilities have been obtained. More, those alternative descriptions lie in knowing better than striving for complete control and instead undertaking managing and coping-ahead. Knowing that this is so and acting on the knowledge is, for me, the hard work of emancipating new possibilities. Some would call this recasting of emancipatory possibilities transformative.

Note how different this politics of uncertainty is from the politics of the techno-managerial elites deploying concepts like 'uncertainty' for instrumental advantage, or the politics of international corporations who see uncertainty as blind-eye volatility for capitalist growth, or a conservative politics permanently sceptical of anything like implementing remedies. In the next section, I explore an example of how recasting and transformation can work.

Recasting global climate change locally

Let us assume the situation is one of 'too little/too late' with respect to ameliorating global climate change in global ways. I do this not because I insist it to be true; rather, let us assume this is the worst-case scenario and see if we can, nevertheless, recast it in ways that make it more tractable to positive intervention. If we can recast a worst case by appealing to the distinctions in the pathway of control, management and coping-ahead just discussed, then other scenarios are opened to recasting as well in the face of the very real global climate change now underway.

There are many ways in which the Table 5.2 pathway can be used to recast the too-little/too-late worst-case scenario without denying any of its urgency or validity. Time and space allow for just one illustration. Let us take as our point of departure a recent major review of the published research on the impacts of climate change (Mora *et al.* 2018). Here is what the review article concludes in its main text:

> Our assessment of the literature yielded a small number of positive and neutral responses of human systems to climate hazard exposure (reviewed in Supplementary Note 2). We surmise that the reduced number of positive or neutral impacts may be real, but may also reflect a research bias towards the study of detrimental impacts (discussed under Caveats in the Methods). This small set of positive and neutral impacts, however, cannot counter-balance any of the many detrimental impacts that were uncovered in our literature search, particularly when many of these impacts are related to the loss of human lives, basic supplies such as food and water, and undesired states for human welfare such as access to jobs, revenue and security.

Let us go now to the article's Caveats subsection for details:

> Although our survey of the literature yielded some case examples of adaptations, positive and differential impacts (Supplementary Note 2), these are unlikely to reflect the full scope of the adaptations, opportunities and trade-offs associated with climate hazards. The large array of cases that we uncovered with a systematic literature search on only climatic impacts suggests that a better understanding of those issues (adaptations, positive and differential impacts) will require their own comprehensive analyses.

If the reader's curiosity is piqued, they will turn to Supplementary Note 2, where the following passage is found. (Because this passage is long, the temptation will be to skim it. However, the following recasting depends on the reader giving close attention to the examples.)

> Although the majority of reported impacts were deleterious to humanity, some climate hazards led to beneficial impacts and in other cases no observable responses. Reduction in malaria transmission in Senegal and Niger was

attributed to loss of mosquito breeding habitats brought about by drought and habitat loss. Drought and storms occasionally increased nutrient content in surviving crops, whereas drought in neighboring countries increased availability of game animals in Namibia. Drought and natural land cover change were in some cases reported to improve water quality due to decreased nutrient runoff into streams. Warming reduced seasonal affective disorders, and mortality during winters, although the latter is controversial and unlikely to outnumber increases in heat-related mortality. Flood exposure increased social trust, and the likelihood of people to vote. Changes in ocean chemistry altered the distribution of marine organisms increasing availability in certain fisheries. Warmer temperatures have increased tourism flow toward colder destinations in the UK and the Alps. The Alaskan whale watching industry benefited from changes in ocean chemistry leading to changes in whale migration patterns, allowing for longer viewing seasons. Since the 1970s, there has been significant sea ice reduction in the Arctic providing increasingly navigable waters and shortening the shipping distances between ports. There were also cases where changes in climate hazards did not result in observable responses. For instance, societal impacts of floods and storms have not been found to contribute to the onset of civil conflict as changes in other hazards have. [For ease of reading, text footnotes to each finding have been deleted.]

A close reading of all the passages quoted uncovers a narrative discrepancy in Mora *et al.* – and we know from policy analysis that such textual discrepancies can be the window through which we can re-see a problem differently (Roe 1994). In my re-reading: how did the 'large array of cases that we uncovered' referenced in the Caveat and itemised in detail in Supplementary Note 2 become in the main text '[t]he small set of positive and neutral impacts' that 'cannot counter-balance *any* of the many detrimental impacts that were uncovered in our literature search' (my italics)?

So put, the question brings into focus the local in ways occluded by the term global. The first time you read through the list in Supplementary Note 2, what is itemised might look more like classic coping strategies (e.g., drought-induced hunger leaving people no choice but to do something). But now consider the list when seen through the lens of the more granular differentiation of operational strategies in Table 5.2. Many of the listed examples begin to look like opportunities for coping-ahead and managing at the local level at which the responses were observed.

I do not know if the latter is true and I would be the first to agree with the authors that more research is needed on the topic of *local* positive or neutral responses to *global* climate change. But therein lies the recasting. An uncontrollable climate change globally exhibits a 'large array' of *local* coping and managing options currently under-researched or acknowledged, which admittedly would constitute a 'small set' of positive or neutral responses *globally*. In this recasting, what is 'too little, too late' at the global level remains open with respect to how late and how little this is across a large array of local sites. What better demonstration of a politics of uncertainty?

Note, finally, that the urgency and validity of the worst-case scenario remain, with local particularity persisting in new forms catalysed by global climate change. Am I implying then that global climate change turns out to be a 'good thing'? No. Am I saying that the Mora *et al.* article is representative of climate change meta-analyses? No. Am I saying that all recasting is transformative at the local level? No. What I am saying is that the truth of the matter can be pushed further precisely because global climate change is complex, locally. Recasting is possible because of, not in spite of, the complexity. Further, a large array of local cases could form a distribution across which practices may be emerging for local transformations and emancipations (the plural is deliberate).

Conclusion

If the above is roughly on-point, the worst enemy of a politics of uncertainty is that assumption – shared by the right and the left – that 'management is control and control is power'.

Management is not control, and control is not the only power. Indeed, the power of power lies in acting on the fact that illusions of control have to be replaced by better notions of managing and coping-ahead in a world of multiple shocks, surprises and contingencies. Reverting to formal terms one last time, the desideratum of a politics of uncertainty is more about increasing process variance in terms of options and strategies than it is about 'controlling for' input and output variance. (In this way, think of sustainable development as increasing human opportunities to respond to unpredictable change without killing ourselves and others in the process.)

Nor do we do have to invent a politics of uncertainty. In a planet of seven billion-plus people, with over 190 nations, it must be assumed practices already exist that evince such sensitivities to different types of unpredictabilities or incertitudes, along with different strategies with which to address them more effectively. What can the rest of us learn from these practices and across other scales than global?

Some readers may find the preceding to fall well short of social transformation and human emancipation. That may be true as far as it goes, but it does not go far enough. Only when we differentiate terms like transformation and emancipation across scales of analysis and action is the matter necessarily pushed further. And those wider truths? Just as an emancipatory politics of uncertainty recognises that uncertainty and unknown-unknowns cannot be closed down to measurable risk, so too do those politics require better differentiation among controlling, managing and coping with those risks, uncertainties and the unknown-unknown of unstudied – in real-time, often unstudiable – conditions.

Acknowledgements

The author thanks Ian Scoones and Andy Stirling for their comments on the draft version, and the copyeditors at My Blue Pencil for their considerable attention to the text. I have also benefited from discussions with Petter Almklov, Arjen Boin and Paul Schulman prior to and during our panel on critical infrastructures and reliability at the ESRC STEPS Centre Symposium, 'The Politics of Uncertainty: Practical Challenges for Transformative Action', held on 3–5 July 2019 at the Institute of Development Studies, in Falmer, UK. Detailed examination and citations for the research findings in this chapter are found in Roe and Schulman (2016; 2008) and Roe (2013). An earlier discussion of Tables 5.1 and 5.2 appears in Roe (2020).

References

Ashby, R. (1952) *Design for a Brain*, London: Chapman and Hall

Buck, L. (2016) 'Willian Kentridge: An Animated Life', *The Art Newspaper*, 31 August, www. theartnewspaper.com/feature/william-kentridge-an-animated-life (22 January 2020)

Mora, C., Spirandelli, D., Franklin, E., Lynham, J., Kantar, M., Miles, W., Smith, C., Freel, K., Moy, J., Louis, L., Barba, E., Bettinger, K., Frazier, A., Colburn IX, J., Hanaaki, N., Hawkins, E., Hirabavashi, Y., Knorr, W., Little, C., Emanual, K., Sheffield, J., Patz, J. and Hunter, C. (2018) 'Broad Threat to Humanity from Cumulative Climate Hazards Intensified by Greenhouse Gas Emissions', *Nature Climate Change* 8: 1062–1071

Roe, E. (2020) *A New Policy Narrative for Pastoralism? Pastoralists as Reliability Professionals and Pastoralist Systems as Infrastructure*, STEPS Working Paper 113, Brighton: STEPS Centre, https://steps-centre.org/publication/a-new-policy-narrative-for-pastoralism/ (22 January 2020)

—— (2013) *Making the Most of Mess: Reliability and Policy in Today's Management Challenges*, Durham NC: Duke University Press

—— (1994) *Narrative Policy Analysis – Theory and Practice*, Durham NC: Duke University Press

Roe, E. and Schulman, P.R. (2016) *Reliability and Risk: The Challenge of Managing Interconnected Infrastructures*, Stanford CA: Stanford University Press

—— (2008) *High Reliability Management: Operating on the Edge*. Stanford CA: Stanford University Press

Stirling, A. (2010) 'Keep It Complex!', *Nature* Comment, 23/30 December, 468: 1029–1031

Weick, K. (1995) *Sensemaking in Organizations*, Thousand Oaks CA: Sage

6

EXPANDING CITIES

Living, planning and governing uncertainty

*Sobia Ahmad Kaker, James Evans, Federico Cugurullo,
Matthew Cook and Saska Petrova*

Uncertain cities

The twenty-first century is the urban century. Cities are heralded as the places that will address climate change, reinvent economic growth and create new forms of political and social inclusion. While the city has historically resolved key planning problematics through innovative social, political and technical arrangements, cities are increasingly challenged by the scale and intensity of contemporary planning conundrums. Contemporary cities are chronically underfunded and over burdened, home to deeply divided communities and decrepit infrastructure, and struggling with chaotic unplanned growth and chronic pollution. These divergent narratives of hope and despair spring from a deep uncertainty surrounding the future of humanity as an urbanised species. What will the megacities of the future look like and how will they cope with unprecedented scale and complexity? What new ways of governing, planning and living in cities will emerge to make us happier and healthier? Whose responsibility it is to even address these questions?

These debates brought the authors of this chapter together to question how uncertainty is orienting governments, planners, policy-makers, experts and urban residents to approach urban challenges. The outcome of our collaboration is a consideration of how different forms of uncertainty are experienced, determined and managed in cities, by whom and based on what types of knowledge and techniques of governance. We were interested in excavating the ways in which uncertainty stimulates experimental forms of urban development and governance, and what the political implications of this are.

The contributors to this chapter engage with the concept of uncertainty through the vantage point of their own engagements with cities and urbanism. They approach the problematic of uncertainty from different perspectives. For example, Sobia Kaker and James Evans review how uncertainty is lived, experienced and managed through ordinary urban infrastructures and technologies. They engage with the 'street level' – a form of uncertainty that Sobia Kaker argues is 'ordinary'. Federico Cugurullo and Matthew Cook both focus on the techno-managerial aspects of urban governance. In particular, they engage with technological advancements and smart cities, and how these present uncertain futures (Federico Cugurullo), or how they may offer adaptive, inclusive and innovative solutions to age-old planning conundrums (Matthew Cook). Saska Petrova, on the other hand, crosses scales. She explores how the coming together of energy precarity – a lived condition of individualised suffering – is tied to the intersecting failures of urban planning and governance in light of climate change-related uncertainties.

The authors also recognise the temporal planes of uncertainty. James Evans focuses on the present of uncertainty as an existing condition, while Sobia Kaker speaks of uncertainty as an unfolding process that exists along a timeline. In her example from Karachi, Sobia Kaker discusses how uncertainty is almost made knowable by a forecasting of the future through an experience of the past. Similarly, Federico Cugurullo discusses the adoption of innovative yet uncertain transport technologies in the past to forecast how they may be adopted in the future.

And finally, in their engagement with these issues, each author brings to the fore questions around the politics and ethics of living, planning and managing urban uncertainty. Saska Petrova discusses how under neoliberal frameworks of governing energy deprivation and related uncertainties, the issue of responsibilisation and individualisation perpetuates precarity. Meanwhile, Sobia Kaker points out how the celebratory valorisation of people's anticipatory and speculative practices in response to ordinary uncertainty shifts attention away from the dismal performance of political authorities to ensure citizens' safety and care. Similarly, Federico Cugurullo highlights the political questions of who exerts influence in shaping the emergent city, and how far these voices are democratic, while Matthew Cook presents a more optimistic picture of technological adaptation as a participatory exercise.

The authors each use empirically rich case studies from their ongoing research on expanding cities to present five perspectives on urban uncertainties. In the first section Sobia Kaker presents her case study of ongoing uncertainty in Karachi in Pakistan. In doing so she distinguishes the lived and experienced forms of uncertainty in cities from the techno-scientific/managerial problematic of uncertainty. She terms this everyday form of uncertainty 'ordinary uncertainty'. By showcasing the ways in which everyday information exchange helps urban residents to understand events, speculate how they would unfold and act in the present keeping the unfolding future in mind, she illustrates how governing ordinary uncertainty is an everyday practice for the urban majority. However, she warns that this social practice of collaboratively navigating an uncertain future should not be celebrated as a triumphant moment of urban capabilities of adapting to chronic crisis, nor should it be romanticised as an ideal practice for ensuring urban resilience. She argues that it is important to be mindful of the political nature of information exchange within an environment of precarity and uncertainty, and to develop alternatives that are more grounded in feminist ethics of care.

In the second section James Evans analytically engages with the operation of informal motorcycle taxis in Kampala (*boda boda*s). He showcases how unplanned and self-built transport infrastructures offer a resilient mode of transportation in chaotic, uncertain cities. He explains how *boda bodas* are sustainable, resilient and adaptable modes of transportation which respond to the lived uncertainty that is characteristic of ever-expanding African cities. They are more 'sustainable' than cars, while being highly adaptable in terms of design and as modes of transport, and have the potential to reach places that are otherwise disconnected from the urban fabric due to badly constructed/non-existent road networks. He argues that, while *boda bodas* and similar informal modes of transport are being legislated against by municipalities that are keen to conform to an image of modernity and rational planning, the fact is that formal alternatives are simply not as responsive to the changing needs of people, or to the unplanned and uncertain urban landscape.

In the third section Federico Cugurullo discusses the technology of self-driving cars, and the layers of uncertainty that the adaptation of this new technology brings for urban governors. Not only is there uncertainty regarding the technology itself (whether it is reliable, effective and safe), but also in relation to the uncertain future of the cities within which such technologies will be used. How successful will they be and how well will they be integrated within the existing urban fabric? How can we plan for the uncertain future of these technologies in the present? He explains how, in the past, anxieties surrounding the adoption of new transport technologies were pushed aside by powerful actors who disregarded public concerns to implement their visions of the futuristic city. Presenting the example of self-driving/driverless cars, he argues that a key driver of these technologies is their promotion by companies that are invested in smart urbanism, and that these companies are already automating the management of urban transport infrastructure.

In the fourth section, Matthew Cook presents the case of smart city developments in Milton Keynes in the UK. He explains how a network of IT companies, local business leaders, the Milton Keynes Council, the Open University, Future Wolverton (a community benefit organisation) and other government agencies and bodies came together to develop a local vision of 'smart' for Milton Keynes. He positions the arrival of 'smart' in Milton Keynes in relation to growing worldwide trends in urban planning. Increasingly, big data is used by urban managers to provide agile planning responses to governance conundrums in unruly cities. He rejects critiques of smart city visions as being techno-centric and totalising, and argues that the development of smart city initiatives in Milton Keynes is consistent with the city's experimental and innovative planning history, and is a result of careful negotiation.

In the final section, Saska Petrova discusses energy deprivation and inequalities in the urban context. She foregrounds issues of ethics and politics as central to her discussion. She argues that it is important to use a framework of precarity to understand uncertainty tied to energy provision, especially for vulnerable populations living on the urban margins. She argues that precarity defines the normalisation of contemporary energy uncertainty, especially as the issue of energy deprivation is increasingly understood to be a domestic and private issue, one that responsibilises the individual for their condition. Instead, she argues that urban environmental and ecological conditions, political deadlocks, material inequalities and failures in planning practices come together to marginalise vulnerable populations, whose experience of energy deprivation is magnified by climate change-related uncertainties. She places the responsibility for managing and governing these uncertainties squarely on the shoulders of intersecting political authorities that are implicated in its production.

Ordinary uncertainty and everyday knowledge: perspectives from Karachi

Karachi, the Pakistani port city, is a megacity of over 18 million residents. Everyday life in the city is prone to frequent disruption as a result of infrastructural breakdown, riots and protests, violent ethno-political/sectarian conflict, and insecurity events tied to criminal or terrorist activities. These events regularly interrupt the rhythm of people's everyday lives, disturb the trajectory of their movements across the city, and are generative of an environment of what can be referred to as 'ordinary uncertainty'.

'Ordinary uncertainty' is connected to the techno-scientific understanding of uncertainty as an unknowable future and, in relation to this, a domain of governmental knowledge production, anticipatory action and politics (Anderson, 2010; Callon *et al.* 2009; Adams *et al.* 2009). But it is also markedly different from such conceptions of uncertainty. Instead of understanding it as an exceptional condition that is articulated, managed and solved by policy-makers, governors and/or formal institutions, ordinary uncertainty shifts the perspective of uncertainty to an ordinarily prevailing condition that is at the heart of urban life, as outlined in recent debates in urban studies (Zeiderman *et al.* 2015; Simone 2013). To understand uncertainty as 'ordinary' we must recognise that the experiential domain of uncertainty is very much that of everyday urban life, and that the work of speculation, prediction and governance is an everyday practice for the urban majority.

In Karachi, for example, urban residents navigate uncertainty by applying their knowledge of a shifting future, learned from futures past. For example, news of low-intensity conflict between rival ethno-political parties localised in one part of Karachi may cause taxi drivers (particularly ethnically identifiable ones) to hesitate regarding taking on customers visiting other parts of the city. Karachiites who have experienced similar conflicts in the past know that the contours of security and insecurity are quick to shift in a city where ethno-political violence occurs in an orchestrated form of 'ordered-disorder' (Gayer 2014). Taxi drivers who refuse to take on customers may have experienced harassment first-hand, or may have heard enough stories of ethnically motivated killings of rickshaw and taxi drivers who 'trespass' into ethno-political strongholds to know which routes and places to avoid at what times of day. They are willing to lose some income and a few customers, especially since they are able to predict accurately that things will return to normal within a couple of weeks.

Engagement with such forms of ordinary uncertainty in Karachi resonates with scholarship on crisis and uncertainty (McFarlane and Silver 2017; Newhouse 2017; Cooper and Pratten 2014; Vigh 2009), and reveals that the exchange of information is crucial to its navigation. City residents, police, government officials, private security actors, news reporters and analysts, and risk assessment officials all follow information relating to ongoing insecurity events. They exchange related updates either during casual personal interactions with each other, or with the help of digital and material technologies, such as social media apps, radios and televisions. The circulating information allows participating residents to 'read' disruptive situations, keeping in mind how similar events played out in the past. In doing so, Karachiites can speculate on the trajectory of particular events and manage the spatio-temporal uncertainties associated with them. This form of experiential risk assessment helps urban residents consider whether they should go out into the city, what modes of transport they should take, which places/routes should be avoided, how long to avoid them and at what times of day.

Although such practices of governing uncertainty mostly work in Karachi, we need to be cautious in our celebration of flexibility, adaptive capabilities, everyday forms of hedging, and successful cooperation (Newhouse 2017; Zeiderman *et al.* 2015; Simone 2013) as successful or ideal forms of management. It is important not to displace the responsibility for care in managing uncertainty to already stretched communities. Broader research by Kaker 2017 has carefully analysed relations and processes of information exchange in Karachi, and reveals the limits and politics of information exchange. By tracing the circulation of information around a particular insecurity event in Karachi, the research found that security-related information, which urban residents follow attentively, is often perpetuated with purpose. In its exchange, the information passes through official and unofficial channels, and may be exaggerated, flawed, biased or simply untrue. The socio-technical infrastructures of information exchange are unequally structured, and oftentimes information becomes a political resource that actors use to achieve personal/group advantages. In this context, the social relations of creating certainty themselves become a source of uncertainty.

Uncertainty and urban transport

Urban life is increasingly uncertain, and cities often look most chaotic at street level. Traffic congestion causes harm to billions and jeopardises the planet's sustainability. This is problematic as mobility is a key driver of economic and social development, determining access to jobs, goods and services (UN-Habitat 2010). In Africa alone, 350 million more people will live in cities by 2030 (Pieterse and Parnell 2014), but the region will receive less than 5 per cent of the global investment in transport infrastructure (UN-Habitat 2013). In response, unregulated modes of transport with flexible fares, schedules and routes – like rickshaws, tuk-tuks, minibuses and motorbikes – characterise cities across Asia, Africa and South America (Cervero and Golub 2007). But, while the majority of city dwellers in the global South rely on informal modes of transport for their mobility, these modes of transport are being legislated against by municipalities, as they fail to fit frameworks of planning and investment. At root, informality – whether it is a rickshaw or a self-built house – fails to fit the image of a 'modern' city that is synonymous with both automobility and the ability to plan. As with slum clearance, banning informal modes of transport causes damage to lives and livelihoods, and the formal alternatives are less responsive to the needs of rapidly changing populations and urban landscapes.

Motorcycle taxis epitomise this tension. While unfamiliar in the West, they are used by billions of people across the global South for personal and business transport. For example, in 2010 there were upwards of 200,000 motorcycle taxis serving the Ugandan capital of Kampala, home to some 1.5 million people. Offering affordable transport to the poor, motorcycle taxis are more efficient in terms of fuel, space and maintenance than cars. The bikes themselves are adapted to the landscape, with extra seat padding cushioning against potholes and bumpy mud roads, and high ground clearance keeping passengers and cargo clear of rough surfaces. Motorcycle taxis provide access to peripheral informal settlements, especially during the rainy season, when poorer roads and paths often flood (Goodfellow 2015). Flexible and cheap, they contribute to the connectivity and resilience of the city, being used to run errands and to deliver both goods and information, in addition to providing personal transport. Motorcycle taxis play a major role servicing hard to reach areas, enabling disadvantaged groups to access work and healthcare that is too distant to walk (Porter 2014).

In this way, informal transport is both adapted and highly adaptable to the uncertain conditions that characterise life in informal and fast-growing urban areas. Manifesting what Abdoumaliq Simone terms the distinctive mobility of the African city, where movement is essential to daily survival, *boda bodas* support the 'thickening fields of social relations' (Simone and Abouhani 2005: 1) that city dwellers depend on. Because of this, motorcycle taxis reduce uncertainty for inhabitants, making otherwise impermeable urban landscapes permeable. They reflect the actually existing city – a highly uncertain and unplanned florescence of self-built (infra) structures and informal economic activities. Mobility is an emergent capacity that flows from the combination of motorbikes, drivers, support industries, topography and infrastructure. Understanding how to work with inherent uncertainty in ways that support, rather than undermine, livelihoods of both users and providers applies not just to transport and mobility, but to all aspects of urban informality. Transport is often where these tensions surface as – unlike slums, which are often out of sight – informal transportation permeates and defines the experience of an entire city.

The challenge of 'managing' uncertainty pertains to almost all urban planning. Cities are systems that generate uncertainty – like nuclear power plants or industrialised food production systems, but with two differences. First, urban systems are organic in that they are at least partly designed from the bottom up, rather than by formal structures of control. Second, uncertainty is a permanent lived experience of inhabitants. Rather than an unintended consequence that is experienced acutely, but intermittently, uncertainty is a chronic condition in cities – distributed, pervasive and known. In this sense, the continuing inability of planners and policy-makers to engage meaningfully with uncertainty is particularly unfortunate. Population growth, chronic underfunding and lack of space make it unfeasible for cities to build their way out of trouble – they must work with what already exists.

Self-driving cars and uncertain urban designs

There is a lot of uncertainty surrounding the technology of self-driving. On 18 March 2018 a woman was crossing a road in Tempe, Arizona. A self-driving Uber car moving along the same road did not perceive her. The autonomous car ran over the woman, killing her. Since then, scepticism regarding self-driving cars has been voiced by many in the global media, and such scepticism has been confirmed in sociological studies looking at the attitudes that people have towards self-driving technologies (Cugurullo *et al.* 2020; Stilgoe 2018). Vulnerable road users in particular, such as pedestrians and cyclists, are afraid of this emerging form of urban transport, and these concerns will arguably not disappear until car manufactures like Tesla can demonstrate that a car controlled by artificial intelligence is as safe as one driven by a human being (Penmetsa *et al.* 2019; Taeihagh and Lim 2019).

This layer of uncertainty concerning the extent to which autonomous cars will be integrated within the transport portfolio of cities adds to the uncertainty of urban design. Historically, changes in urban transport have led to changes in the design of cities. In the modernist city of the 1920s, for instance, the popularisation of the car triggered the development of highways and arterial roads that revolutionised the built environment (Sheller and Urry 2000). In the near future, the urban changes that the diffusion of autonomous cars might trigger are uncertain. The future is still opaque, but there are two possible scenarios that are currently being discussed. On the one hand, there is a utopian scenario in which self-driving cars are employed via sharing services. Studies indicate that, especially in large metropolitan areas, people are open to the idea of sharing an autonomous car, instead of owing one (Haboucha *et al.* 2017; Firnkorn and Müller 2015; Fagnant and Kockelman 2014). This attitude could decrease car ownership, improve traffic and, overall, reduce the amount of space that is reserved for cars (Duarte and Ratti 2018). Many parking spaces and roads would become superfluous, and could morph, for example, into bike lanes, pedestrian streets or urban gardens: in essence, places for people, rather than spaces for cars.

On the other hand, the popularisation of autonomous cars could shape a dystopian urban future. Autonomous transport promises productive onboard activities: a promise that might lead to more and longer commutes (Hawkins and Nurul Habib 2019). Take the Volvo 360c model, for instance: an autonomous car that can become a bed, a bar or a living room, depending on the needs of the owner. Such self-driving technologies could improve the experience of travelling in a car, to the point of increasing the demand for cars and for the urban space that they need in the city.

Overarching these uncertain urban designs there is arguably a bigger uncertainty: one that covers like a thick mist the politics of the city, where innovation in autonomous urban transport takes place. If we go back in time to look at urban history we can clearly see that, in the past, dangerous forms of urban transport were integrated into the built environment, regardless of the attitudes that people had towards them. In the Baroque city, for example, as Lewis Mumford (1961: 368, 370) remarks, the stagecoach 'killed more people annually than the railroad that followed it', and 'in France, parliament begged the king to prohibit vehicles from the streets'. In strongly undemocratic contexts, this dissent was not taken into account, and politically powerful actors imposed their urban visions.

What will happen in the future when autonomous cars are operational is an open question, but the present has already given us two important hints. First, with the automation of the management of urban infrastructure and services as one of its key foci, smart urbanism is the matrix through which autonomous urban transport unfolds (Batty 2018). Second, we know that current practices of smart urbanism are often top-down and driven by neoliberal rationales of economic growth (Cugurullo 2018; Karvonen *et al.* 2018; although see below). Therefore, while being important, people's feelings towards emerging autonomous technologies might, in the end, play only a marginal role in determining future urban designs (Acheampong and Cugurullo 2019). Whoever rules the city is likely to dictate its shape, and questions of technological innovation and urban design thus become questions of urban governance under conditions of uncertainty.

Uncertainty and the governance of smart city developments

Cities are viewed by many as having considerable agency to resolve key issues (such as climate change), stimulate new forms of economic development and foster innovative political and social arrangements (Rohracher and Späth 2017; EC 2012). However, at the same time, cities are suffering from the effects of over a decade of austerity, and are experiencing increasing income and social inequalities, poorly maintained infrastructure and significant pollution problems (North *et al.* 2017). Thus, while somewhat optimistic urban futures are often posited, their realisation may also be framed as uncertain. In many instances, ways to address these framings of urban futures involve knowledge of the city by collecting so-called 'big data' to inform city management responses. Indeed, sensors, big data hubs and apps have been built in many cities to form urban digital platforms under the auspices of the 'smart city' (Kitchin *et al.* 2019; Caprotti and Cowley 2019; Cowley and Caprotti 2019). Such development visions are spreading and, indeed, continue to spread across a field of actors, including IT companies and policy-makers, consultants and government institutions associated with cities (Bouzarovski and Haarstad 2019; Haarstad and Wathne 2018).

Smart city visions have inflected developments in many cities, including Milton Keynes (MK) in the United Kingdom. MK was developed in the late 1960s as part of a wave of new town developments to relieve post-war development pressures, mainly for housing. Situated some 60 miles north of London, it is the fastest growing UK city, with a population of 245,750, set to expand to 308,500 by 2026 (Destination MK 2019; MKI 2017). MK's development has been inflected by multiple global circulations. For example, the grid road system upon which it is based was exported from Los Angeles by Mervin Webber, 'applied' and 'adapted' in MK (Walker 1982). It also pioneered self-build housing and low-carbon housing developments (PRP Architects 2010). As such, MK is open to new ideas and 'smart' is the latest in a long line of socio-technical developments to inflect developments in the city (Valdez *et al.* 2018).

Smart 'arrived' in MK via a network of actors – not a city to city network, but a network of private and public bodies, including consultants, government agencies, land developers, business leaders and leaders of community organisations. Smart inflected MK developments via governance practices situated in the formal and informal institutional landscapes associated with MK. For example, in the city council; in public fora open to the public, but largely attended by a semi-regular group of elite actors, such as the events organised by the Fred Roche Foundation; in the meetings of community groups, such as the Future Wolverton association or on the doorsteps of the households surveyed by volunteer community engagement organisations, such as Community Action MK.

In such institutional spaces, actors such as MK Council and the Open University played a major role in making and curating relations to form the basis of smart city initiatives. Different versions of MK and different versions of 'smart' were co-constructed and responses to the uncertainty associated with such developments emerged. *Post hoc*, a step-wise engagement with 'smart' can be discerned. Initially, policy-makers met IT consultants to learn about their smart city offerings. Subsequently, the MK:Smart project was developed. Funded by the UK government, and led by the Open University and MK Council, this project focused on the development of an urban platform built around a data hub and various 'apps' to augment infrastructure, such as transport, energy and water infrastructure. Finally, informed by the outcomes of the MK:Smart project, 'smart' is now focused in MK on aspects of the city where it closely aligns with governance and policy rationalities, such as transport planning (Cook *et al.* 2018).

Here, such governance practices comprise a 'learning' journey: moving from the generic claims of smart visions to identifying specific outcomes and potentialities of 'smart' in MK. From the outset, MK policy-makers acknowledged the uncertainties associated with smart city claims; there was never an intention to make MK a 'smart city', but rather to explore the potentialities of 'smart' for MK, and to encourage this to influence developments. Within MK, this approach is entirely consistent with the historically contingent set of 'flexible' governance practices sedimented in the city since its inception. More generally, although smart city visions have been widely critiqued for their techno-centrism and seemingly totalising force (Luque-Ayala and Marvin 2015; Greenfield 2013), actually existing smart city developments are often somewhat tentative and exhibit an experimental modality that valorises pragmatic learning over coordinated actions to realise specific goals, such as environmental sustainability (Caprotti and Cowley 2019; Cugurullo 2018; Caprotti and Cowley 2017).

Seen in this way, smart city initiatives are emblematic of growing trends in urban governance that have emerged in response to an increased awareness of the world as complex, uncertain and non-linear. Indeed, despite the rhetorical claims of various planning epochs, planning practice has perhaps never been a modern technocratic institution, but one mainly founded on negotiation, identifying and realising 'windows of opportunity', and, crucially here, embracing uncertainty.

Urban(ising) energy precarity: uncertainty and scales of action

Energy and fuel poverty have traditionally been explored as domestic issues, expressed by the inability to secure adequate levels of energy services in the indoor environment of the home (Bouzarovski and Petrova 2015). As such, they have been principally discussed in terms of vulnerabilities and uncertainties centring on the residential sector. However, energy deprivation principally occurs in an urban context.

With their specific material and environmental circumstances (green areas, air pollution, the effect of heat islands) cities are directly implicated in how energy deprivation is produced, experienced and addressed. What is more, cities are political entities where multiple practices and relations of power, authority and governance are intertwined across a multiplicity of regulatory arenas. All of this points to the need for an integrated perspective to understand the nexus between energy inequality and the urban.

The 'energy precarity' framework provides a stepping-stone for understanding how energy deprivation is articulated and conditioned beyond the home. It develops conceptual tools to examine the everyday experiences associated with uncertain energy infrastructures in urban geographies. Energy precarity also draws attention to the multiple ways in which domestic energy deprivation is politically induced as a lack of 'rights to the city'. This approach has been employed as a means of uncovering the spaces where energy deprivation is produced, experienced and contested. It has highlighted the inherently relational nature of energy demand, through which energy deprivation metaphorically and physically overflows the limits of the home, creating multiple modalities of injustice and deprivation (Petrova 2018).

There are strong links between energy precarity and uncertainty. In a broader sense, precarity, precariousness and precarisation have been used as signifiers of uncertainties, risks and vulnerabilities (Thieme 2017). Precarity has come to define the normalisation of uncertainty and anxiety under a neoliberal capitalist regime that promotes individuality and self-responsibility. Energy deprivation has also been approached in this very manner – as a domestic and private issue. In dominant framings, energy and fuel poverty are burdened with stigma and social exclusion (Hards 2013; Day and Hitchings 2011), rather than being seen as the consequence of inadequate and exclusive urban planning and governance practices that produce unequal spatialities. People who live in energy deprivation tend to be presented in a trivialised and stylised manner: an elderly lady covered in a blanket in front of a radiator or electric heater; a miserable-looking child in a dark, damp room. The wider story of who these people are is often missing, even if their domestic vulnerability remains personified and exposed to the public. The urban settings that they inhabit remain erased and ignored. This is despite the fact that most vulnerable people tend to inhabit marginalised urban areas, with poor-quality housing and a lack of environmental amenities (such as poor access to green areas), in addition to experiencing elevated levels of air pollution as well as limited or expensive public transport connections.

Climate change-related uncertainties are likely to lead to further pressures on energy deprivation, due to the increased prevalence of summertime cooling challenges stemming from the overheating of homes and cities. This is precisely why solutions to the multiple political and spatial uncertainties that underpin energy precarity cannot be found solely in the domain of socio-technical and spatial fixes. Instead, they require more radical thinking in terms of how cities construct and govern their energy systems, taking into account the rising tide of decentralised and citizen-led efforts to govern energy flows.

Conclusion

The five perspectives on urban uncertainties presented above are drawn from the authors' extended research on urban challenges in expanding cities. Taken together, they broaden our understanding and conceptualisation of uncertainty. Through their rich, empirical examples on how present and future uncertainties link to the past, the authors showcase that uncertainty exits along a temporal continuum. In addition to this, by focusing on the range of actors collaborating to plan for and govern uncertainty (informal, formal, government, communities, corporations) over extended periods of time, the authors present a picture of uncertainty as an ongoing process – one that is lived, experienced, planned, negotiated and governed by a multiplicity of actors, operating across variegated space and time. Through their discussion of ordinary uncertainties tied to insecurity in Karachi, informal negotiations of urban circulation in Kampala, technology adaptation in the futuristic city, smart city developments in Milton Keynes and climate change-related precarity and energy deprivation, the authors assemble an understanding of uncertainty as an ongoing temporal, experiential and political process.

Yet the authors' focus on expanding cities also opens up a debate on the politics of uncertainty, and, more importantly, on the ethics of governing uncertainty. As cities become more informal, demands on services more acute and environmental conditions more extreme, it becomes evident that neoliberal governance settings often fail urban majorities. Kaker, Evans and Petrova warn that uncertainty and precarity are often co-constructed, and reproduce urban inequalities. However, as long as these concerns are recognised and taken seriously, and urban residents, governors and corporations collaborate to foster a progressive socio-political milieu, then perhaps it could be possible to find flexible, innovative and equitable solutions to governing uncertainty.

References

Adams, V., Murphy, M. and Clarke, A.E. (2009) 'Anticipation: Technoscience, Life, Affect, Temporality', *Subjectivity* 28.1: 246–265

Anderson, B. (2010) 'Preemption, Precaution, Preparedness: Anticipatory Action and Future Geographies', *Progress in Human Geography* 34.6: 777–798

Batty, M. (2018) 'Artificial Intelligence and Smart Cities', *Environment and Planning E: Urban Analytics and City Science* 45.1: 3–6

Bouzarovski, S. and Haarstad, H. (2019) 'Rescaling Low-Carbon Transformations: Towards a Relational Ontology', *Transactions of the Institute of British Geographers* 44.2: 256–269

Bouzarovski, S. and Petrova, S. (2015) 'A Global Perspective on Domestic Energy Deprivation: Overcoming the Energy Poverty–Fuel Poverty Binary', *Energy Research & Social Science* 10: 31–40

Callon, M., Lascoumes, P. and Barthe, Y. (2009) *Acting in an Uncertain World: An Essay on Technical Democracy (Inside Technology)*, Cambridge, Massachusetts and London, England: MIT Press

Caprotti, F. and Cowley, R. (2019) 'Varieties of Smart Urbanism in the UK: Discursive Logics, the State and Local Urban Context', *Transactions of the Institute of British Geographers* 44.3: 587–601

—— (2017) 'Interrogating Urban Experiments', *Urban Geography* 38.9: 1441–1450

Cervero, R. and Golub, A. (2007) 'Informal Transport: A Global Perspective', *Transport* Policy 14.6: 445–457.

Cook, M., Horne, R., Potter, S. and Valdez, A.M. (2018) 'Exploring the Epistemic Politics of Urban Niche Experiments', in J.S. Jensen, P. Späth and M. Cashmore (eds) *The Politics of Urban Sustainability Transitions: Knowledge, Power and Governance*, London: Routledge

Cooper, E. and Pratten, D. (eds) (2014) *Ethnographies of Uncertainty in Africa*, Berlin: Springer

Cowley, R. and Caprotti, F. (2019) 'Smart City as Anti-planning in the UK', *Environment and Planning D: Society and Space* 37.3: 428–448

Cugurullo, F. (2018) 'Exposing Smart Cities and Eco-Cities: Frankenstein Urbanism and the Sustainability Challenges of the Experimental City', *Environment and Planning A: Economy and Space* 50.1: 73–92

Cugurullo, F., Acheampong, R.A., Gueriau, M. and Dusparic, I. (2020) 'The Transition to Autonomous Cars, the Redesign of Cities and the Future of Urban Sustainability', https://doi.org/10.1080/02723638.2020.1746096

Day, R. and Hitchings, R. (2011) '"Only Old Ladies Would Do That": Age Stigma and Older People's Strategies for Dealing with Winter Cold', *Health & Place* 17: 885–894.

Destination MK (2019) '101 Facts About MK', www.destinationmiltonkeynes.co.uk/About-us/101-Facts-about-MK

Duarte, F. and Ratti, C. (2018) 'The Impact of Autonomous Vehicles on Cities: A Review', *Journal of Urban Technology* 25.4: 1–16

European Commission (2012) 'European Initiative on Smart Cities', https://setis.ec.europa.eu/set-plan-implementation/technology-roadmaps/european-initiative-smart-cities

Fagnant, D.J. and Kockelman, K.M. (2014) 'The Travel and Environmental Implications of Shared Autonomous Vehicles, Using Agent-Based Model Scenarios', *Transportation Research Part C: Emerging Technologies* 40: 1–13

Firnkorn, J. and Müller, M. (2015) 'Free-Floating Electric Carsharing-Fleets in Smart Cities: The Dawning of a Post-Private Car Era in Urban Environments?' *Environmental Science & Policy* 45: 30–40

Gayer, L. (2014) *Karachi: Ordered Disorder and the Struggle for the City*, Oxford: Oxford University Press

Goodfellow, T. (2015) 'Taming the "Rogue" Sector: Studying State Effectiveness in Africa Through Informal Transport Politics', *Comparative Politics* 472: 127–147

Greenfield, A. (2013) *Against the Smart City: A Pamphlet. This is Part I of 'The City is Here to Use'*, New York City: Do projects

Haarstad, H. and Wathne, M.W. (2018) 'Smart Cities as Strategic Actors: Insights from EU Lighthouse Projects in Stavanger, Stockholm, and Nottingham', in A. Karvonen, F. Cugurullo and F. Caprotti (eds) *Inside Smart Cities: Place, Politics and Urban Innovation*, London: Routledge

Haboucha, C.J., Ishaq, R. and Shiftan, Y. (2017) 'User Preferences Regarding Autonomous Vehicles', *Transportation Research Part C: Emerging Technologies* 78: 37–49

Hards, S.K. (2013) 'Status, Stigma and Energy Practices in the Home', *Local Environment* 18: 438–454

Hawkins, J. and Nurul Habib, K. (2019) 'Integrated Models of Land Use and Transportation for the Autonomous Vehicle Revolution', *Transport Reviews* 39.1: 66–83

Kaker, S.A. (2017) Karachi: Circulating Uncertainties, in: A. Zeiderman, S.A. Kaker, J. Silver, A. Wood and K. Ramakrishnan (eds) *Urban Uncertainty: Governing Cities Through Turbulent Times*, London: LSE Cities: 23–26

Karvonen, A., Cugurullo, F. and Caprotti, F. (eds) (2018) *Inside Smart Cities: Place, Politics and Urban Innovation*, London: Routledge

Kitchin, R., Coletta, C., Evans, L., Heaphy, L. and MacDonncha, D. (2019) 'Smart Cities, Algorithmic Technocracy and New Urban Technocrats', in M. Raco and F. Savini (eds) *Planning and Knowledge: How New Forms of Technocracy Are Shaping Contemporary Cities*, Bristol: Policy Press: 199

Luque-Ayala, A. and Marvin, S. (2015) 'Developing a Critical Understanding of Smart Urbanism?' *Urban Studies* 52.12: 2105–2116

McFarlane, C. and Silver, J. (2017) 'Navigating the City: Dialectics of Everyday Urbanism', *Transactions of the Institute of British Geographers* 42.3: 458–471

MKI (2017) 'Population Bulletin 2017', www.miltonkeynesccg.nhs.uk/modules/downloads/download.php?file_name=1965

Mumford, L. (1961) *The City in History: Its Origins, its Transformations, and its Prospects*, New York: Harcourt, Brace & World

Newhouse, L.S. (2017) 'Uncertain Futures and Everyday Hedging in a Humanitarian City', *Transactions of the Institute of British Geographers* 42.4: 503–515

North, P., Nurse, A. and Barker, T. (2017) 'The Neoliberalisation of Climate? Progressing Climate Policy Under Austerity Urbanism', *Environment and Planning A: Economy and Space* 49.8: 1797–1815

Penmetsa, P., Adanu, K.A., Wood, D., Wang, T. and Jones, S.L. (2019) 'Perceptions and Expectations of Autonomous Vehicles–A Snapshot of Vulnerable Road User Opinion', *Technological Forecasting and Social Change* 143: 9–13

Petrova, S. (2018) 'Encountering Energy Precarity: Geographies of Fuel Poverty Among Young Adults in the UK', *Transactions of the Institute of British Geographers* 43: 17–30.

Pieterse, D. and Parnell, S. (2014) *Africa's Urban Revolution*, London: Zed Books

Porter, G. (2014) 'Transport Services and their Impact on Poverty and Growth in Rural Sub-Saharan Africa: A Review of Recent Research and Future Research Needs', *Transport Reviews* 34.1: 25–45

PRP Architects (2010) *Milton Keynes – A Sustainable Future: A Low Carbon Prospectus*, Milton Keynes: Milton Keynes Council

Rohracher, H. and Späth, P. (2017) 'Cities as Arenas of Low-Carbon Transitions: Friction Zones in The Negotiation of Low-Carbon Futures', in *Urban Sustainability Transitions*, London: Routledge: 287–299

Simone, A. (2013) 'Cities of Uncertainty: Jakarta, the Urban Majority, and Inventive Political Technologies', *Theory, Culture & Society* 30.7–8: 243–263

Simone, A.M. and Abouhani, A. (eds) (2005) *Urban Africa: Changing Contours of Survival in The City*, London: Zed Books

Sheller, M. and Urry, J. (2000) 'The City and the Car', *International Journal of Urban and Regional Research* 24.4: 737–757

Stilgoe, J. (2018) 'Machine Learning, Social Learning and the Governance of Self-Driving Cars', *Social Studies Of Science* 48.1: 25–56

Taeihagh, A. and Lim, H. (2019) 'Governing Autonomous Vehicles: Emerging Responses For Safety, Liability, Privacy, Cybersecurity, And Industry Risks', *Transport Reviews* 39.1:103–128

Thieme, T.A. (2017) 'The Hustle Economy: Informality, Uncertainty and the Geographies of Getting By', *Progress in Human Geography* 42.4: 529–548

UN-Habitat (2013) 'Planning and Design for Sustainable Urban Mobility: Global Report on Human Settlements, Nairobi', Nairobi: UN Habitat

—— (2010) 'Sustainable Mobility in African Cities', Nairobi: UN Habitat

Valdez, A.M., Cook, M. and Potter, S. (2018) 'Roadmaps to Utopia: Tales of the Smart City', *Urban Studies* 55.15: 3385–3403

Vigh, H. (2009) 'Motion Squared: A Second Look at the Concept of Social Navigation', *Anthropological Theory* 9.4: 419–438

Walker, D. (1982) *The Architecture and Planning of Milton Keyes*, London: The Architectural Press Ltd

Zeiderman, A., Kaker, S.A., Silver, J. and Wood, A. (2015) 'Uncertainty and Urban Life', *Public Culture* 27.2(76): 281–304

7

UNCERTAINTY IN MODELLING CLIMATE CHANGE

The possibilities of co-production through knowledge pluralism[1]

Lyla Mehta and Shilpi Srivastava

Introduction

Uncertainty is at the core of the climate change problem. Uncertainty is defined by the Intergovernmental Panel on Climate Change (IPCC) as 'a state of incomplete knowledge that can result from a lack of information or from disagreement about what is known or even knowable' (Barros *et al.* 2012: 128). Considered to be a 'super-wicked problem' by scientists and policy-makers (Curry and Webster 2011; van der Sluijs 2005), climate change policy-making is often dominated by efforts to minimise and control uncertainty, and 'attempts to quantify it in one way or another' (Hallegatte *et al.* 2012: 10). This approach has been increasingly critiqued for not providing a useful basis for meaningful policy responses (Vogel and Olivier 2019; Shackley and Wynne 1996), and at the same time it does not reflect the lived realities of local people, who are often at the frontline of climatic uncertainty but far removed from the decision-making processes. In the *Fifth Assessment Report*, the IPCC (2014) acknowledges that there are uncertainties that we will never know and that the best response is to understand and cope with them. In this light, alternative perspectives have emerged over recent years that focus on embracing uncertainty through 'robust' decision-making (Lemos *et al.* 2016) or engaging with and integrating local or indigenous understandings through citizen science (D'Souza and Kale 2018; Panda 2016).

Why is this important? Decisions are made today that will affect future vulnerabilities – and, in turn, impacts – from extreme environmental change, including climate change. There is a growing recognition that the global, national and subnational responses to uncertainty have been inadequate (Stirling *et al.* 2007; Wynne 1992). The largely Northern-focused literature of science and technology studies has been critical in elucidating the narrow ways in which uncertainty is often conceptualised by modellers, scientists and planners (Mehta *et al.* 2019; Wynne 1992).

Despite the increasing recognition of growing complexity, dynamism and uncertainties, decision-making is still predominantly driven by techno-managerial solutions that may either falter in the face of local social dynamics and uncertainties or end up harming certain groups, usually the poor (Leach *et al.* 2010; Mehta *et al.* 1999). These top-down processes fail to take into account more embodied experiences of uncertainty, which culminate from the broader political-economic and historical experiences of exploitation, discrimination and dispossession. They tend to privilege 'modernist' environmental practices and disparage other forms of knowledge as primitive, irrational or vernacular (Arora 2019; Ranganathan and Bratman 2019).

In this chapter, we focus on how uncertainties are characterised in scientific models, explore their inherent limitations and argue that responding to climate-related uncertainties requires a combination of different knowledges and methodological approaches. We first begin by conceptualising uncertainty in climate change. This is followed by a discussion of the limitations that arise out of modelling, and the practices of working with uncertainty, focusing on how uncertainty is negotiated, maintained and represented in forecasting models. Using the case of two projects in South Asia, we explore the opportunities and challenges of knowledge co-production between the scientific, policy and lay communities. Our core proposition is that investigating and unpacking the gaps in diverse conceptions of uncertainty can facilitate processes that embrace rather than eliminate uncertainty. This is because, as Melissa Leach *et al.* (2010) and Andy Stirling *et al.* (2007) argue, subjective judgements, multiple knowledges and diverse interpretations around uncertainty are inevitable and must be central to responses to uncertain situations, in turn shaped by historical and socio-cultural processes (Lyons *et al.* 2019).

Conceptualising uncertainty in climate change

Climate shocks and stresses, such as cyclones, floods, droughts, changing rainfall patterns and extreme temperatures are some examples of uncertainties that planners and local people in the global South regularly confront. Climate-related uncertainty refers to the inability to predict the scale, intensity and impact of climate change on human and natural environments (Curry and Webster 2011). Uncertainties in climate change projections remain particularly high and, combined with economic and political drivers of change, they make local-level effects difficult to predict (Barros *et al.* 2012).

Thus, there is now a growing acknowledgement that climate science is better at dealing with uncertainties arising due to macro trends, such as temperature extremes and sea level rise, than understanding the effects at the local level, due to downscaling challenges (Bhave *et al.* 2016). These local-level effects include the impacts of land use change, water management trends and socio-political and economic processes that can increase uncertainties for local people (Swart *et al.* 2009). These are what Robert Wilby and Suraje Dessai refer to as 'the envelope of uncertainty' (Wilby and Dessai 2010: 181), which intersects with social, political, economic, cultural and scientific domains.

Warren Walker *et al.* define uncertainty as 'any deviation from the unachievable ideal of completely deterministic knowledge of the relevant system' (Walker *et al.* 2003:5). Three types of uncertainties are relevant for our discussion. First, aleatoric uncertainty, referring to natural fluctuations, a high degree of variability and disequilibrium dynamics having unknown effects (cf. Achutarao 2016). Second, knowledge or epistemic uncertainties, which refers to indeterminate knowledge about changes and their impacts (Barros *et al.* 2012). Third, uncertainties linked to larger political economy conditions, including unanticipated outcomes due to socio-political interventions, and how they are experienced by diverse groups (Mehta *et al.* 1999; Wynne 1992). All these uncertainties are experienced, framed and interpreted differently by different actors and are linked to relations of power that justify different institutional practices and responses (Rein and Schön 1993). While acknowledging aleatoric uncertainty, our focus in this chapter is on epistemic uncertainty and the interaction with wider institutional and socio-political processes.

Given the 'deep uncertainty' (Hallegatte *et al.* 2012: 4) presented by climate change, new approaches are needed as it is difficult to 'eliminate' uncertainty all together. This has given rise to a growing 'family of approaches' focused on providing robust outcomes in the face of a range of possible changes, ranging from large computer-based models to qualitative assessments. Approaches include a focus on 'no regrets', reversibility and flexibility in the face of uncertainty, building in safety margins, and reducing decision-making time horizons (Hallegatte *et al.* 2012), alongside approaches that emphasise the importance of more bottom-up methods of climate assessment and adaptation (Conway *et al.* 2019). Common to these approaches is that they acknowledge and embrace uncertainty, rather than trying to avoid or minimise it. However, despite these good intentions, there is still a tendency to manage uncertainty through top-down, techno-managerial practices and framings in contemporary climate discourse and practice: for example, through the current notions of the 'climate emergency' and a 'war on climate change'. As argued by Mike Hulme (2020) and Sinichiro Asayama *et al.* (2019), portraying climate change as 'black and white' obscures both deep uncertainties in science as well as the local-level impacts, concealing the inherently political nature of the term. In the worst case, the 'emergency' could be used as a justification for techno-managerialism on a massive scale, such as solar geo-engineering or authoritarian forms of regulation.

We recognise that knowledge about climate is co-produced alongside the social orders in which it is shaped and driven (cf. Jasanoff 2009). Hence, our notion of co-production does not principally relate to bringing different groups of people together to create new knowledge (cf. Ostrom 1996): rather, it is more about teasing out forms of knowledge that are often overlooked or undervalued by more traditional forms of knowledge-making. This includes embodied, emotional and tacit ways of knowing and representing the world. This requires a pluralist sensitivity to and appreciation for a persistent diversity of understandings (Stirling *et al.* 2018). We contend that transformative change – that is non-linear, involves deep-seated structural change and challenges the *status quo* of existing development structures (O'Brien 2012; Pelling 2011) – is only possible if such plural pathways of knowledge-making are facilitated and encouraged.

Can we know better? Modelling for climate change

Climate change involves such complex systems that one of the few, but fundamentally pervasive, ways to deal with it is through computer models. Models are simplified representations of complex systems, and as such are never the 'real' thing – a fact that is often ignored. Computer models of climate change are often riddled with uncertainty and may not fully represent the complexity of climate processes. While model structure uncertainty refers to uncertainty about the form of the model itself, technical uncertainty arises from the implementation of these models. Other challenges include attempts to synthesise disparate sources and sets of data, and the impossibility of using experimentation to test hypotheses (Swart *et al.* 2009). Therefore, several choices need to be made while constructing a climate model and deciding how these processes are represented. These choices also concern the parameters chosen and the values attributed to these parameters. Other sources of uncertainty in climate projections and modelling include internal variability and natural fluctuations, model uncertainty (i.e., that different models simulate different responses in the climate), and scenario uncertainty (e.g., demographic change, emissions pathways) (Hawkins and Sutton 2009).

Social scientists studying the 'social life of models' tell us that climate modelling takes place according to diverse reasoning and across different scales (Hastrup 2013). In this process, nature is conceptualised and futures are reimagined. At the centre of the scientific practice is the creation of boundaries and distinct binaries (Douglas 1986) between the subjective and the objective, between the abstract climate and the particularities of weather (Heymann 2019; Hulme 2017). The abstract and supposedly 'objective' is represented by the hard science of modelling, which can ignore or externalise the subjective dimensions of uncertainties or neglect their political dimensions (cf. Jasanoff 2009). Such scientific approaches are just one of the many ways people anticipate and prepare for the future, and they need to be viewed together with the day-to-day strategies used by people who live with the uncertainties of climate (Hastrup 2013). However, a certain politics of knowledge results in particular domains (especially so-called hard science) gaining authority over others. Yet, all forms of knowledge (including so-called expert knowledge) are culturally and socially embedded and moulded by particular social, power and gender relations. Models are also embedded in narratives and storylines about a future based on certain assumptions (cf. Hajer, 1995), but, through a range of political practices and boundary-ordering devices, they gain authority over other forms of knowledge (Heymann 2019; Shackley and Wynne 1996).

Historically, local communities have developed practices and strategies to plan for and live with ecological uncertainty and variability (Hastrup 2013). These practices include seasonal mobility, crop diversification or risk-averse behaviours to cope with resource fluctuations. However, climatic change presents a radical rupture with what communities have been attuned to in the past. Thus, following Lyla Mehta *et al.* (2019), we distinguish between uncertainty from 'above' and uncertainty from 'below', recognising that there are overlaps and nestings between these two relational categories. We also recognise that bridging these two domains requires actors and knowledge systems that can translate across the domains, hence the notion of the 'middle', representing actors and space(s) of negotiation of knowledges and practices.

Uncertainty from 'above' is represented by climate scientists, policy elites and decision-makers. The standard approach for conceptualising uncertainty is to quantify it in terms of probabilities (e.g. Sigel *et al.* 2010), reducing it to risk through statistical models that accommodate sophisticated data with multiple variables across a range of spatial and temporal scales (Edwards 2001). Of course, many modellers acknowledge the limits to models and their predictions due to limited understandings of the climate system (Curry and Webster 2011), although there will be hierarchies and multiple rationalities within these systems (Curry and Webster 2011).

Uncertainty from 'below' concerns the framings of lay people, as differentiated by gender, class and caste. It is experiential, non-official knowledge – not necessarily played out verbally or articulated formally but instead a more 'practical' or 'tacit' form of knowledge (cf. Bourdieu 1977). While our concern is largely with marginalised groups and perspectives, lay knowledge can also be linked to a very heterogeneous group consisting of both rich and poor, more powerful and powerless people. A wide literature from anthropological, sociological and political ecology traditions has demonstrated how local people live with and adapt to uncertainty (e.g. Scoones 2019; Hastrup 2013). Many indigenous knowledge systems evolve through adaptive learning based on developing a complex knowledge base of the environment and lessons from past mistakes – a version of 'post-normal' science (cf. Funtowicz and Ravetz 1993). Thus, such knowledges not only complement more macro perspectives but perhaps also reveal aspects that can be missed by more macro and global perspectives.

We, of course, acknowledge that climate change and uncertainty from 'above' and 'below' have different relative strengths and epistemological entry points, and have potential for complementarity. Both are culturally and socially embedded in local institutions, practices and power relations. Both, however, tend to approach temporal and spatial concerns differently, as we discuss further below. Neither scientists nor local people are homogenous and we do not intend to privilege one form of knowledge over the other. There are clear power differentials between the two, and power relations shape these categories and their relations with each other. That said, there is potential space for collaboration and bridging, where knowledges are negotiated across actors. As Hulme (2020) points out, such differences can be worked out iteratively, through negotiation within power structures and institutional processes.

We now turn to how stakeholder dialogues and roundtables that seek to break down political power and disciplinary divides can provide diverse actors with opportunities to engage with and learn from diverse perspectives (Bhatt *et al.* 2018). Such emerging dialogues stress the importance of bringing to the fore hidden and alternative perspectives and solutions, while highlighting the need to address the power imbalances that prevent the application of alternative ways of valuation and epistemic diversity, which are so urgently required to address growing climate-related uncertainties. We highlight two such experiments below, and the challenges and opportunities that they present for the co-production of knowledge.

Starting a dialogue with different perspectives: experiments in bridging through roundtables on climate change uncertainty

Climate change is like an elephant in the story, and while people see different things (e.g. ear, tail, trunk), we need to look at it as one whole animal (Roundtable participant, Gandhinagar 2018). This quote from an NGO participant in a roundtable discussion nicely summarises the many ways in which climate and its associated uncertainties are characterised by actors from the above, middle and below. Although epistemic divides can lead to confrontational politics, they can also open up possibilities and opportunities for learning from diverse perspectives (Bhatt *et al.* 2018). We convened four roundtables in different settings in India and Europe.[2] The objective was to bring together perspectives and experiences of government officials, academics, scientists, practitioners and activists on climatic uncertainty in order to examine how discourses on uncertainty from 'below' and 'above' are contested, accommodated or hybridised in these politically charged spaces.

The Oslo roundtable was organised as a dialogue between natural scientists and social scientists, while the other three roundtables, which were organised in India, were rooted in their site-specific contexts (the dryland dynamics of Kutch in Gujarat; the rapidly urbanising context of the metropolis Mumbai and the deltaic islands of the Indian Sundarbans). All the roundtables ended up being quite distinct in both orientation and scope. This was due to the different locations (e.g., whether at a university, a government institute or a neutral seminar venue) and the role played by the local partners and co-hosts. For example, in Oslo, we largely had researchers from different disciplinary backgrounds and just two policy-makers. In Mumbai, the audience at the Indian Institute of Technology–Bombay largely comprised natural and social scientists, with some NGOs and local fisher activists. In both of these settings the discussions were preoccupied with academic discourses on uncertainty. By contrast, the Gujarat meeting, perhaps due to its location in the state capital (Gandhinagar), was dominated by government officials and policy-makers from different departments, who welcomed the opportunity to engage with each other's work, alongside many researchers and NGOs. Similarly, in Kolkata, the meeting had a good mix of different scientists, researchers and NGOs, as well as government officials. In all cases, but in different ways, power differentials were evident.

The roundtables played a key role in highlighting different understandings of uncertainty, while simultaneously opening up opportunities for sharing and learning. For some participants, the roundtable was a new experience and they appreciated the opportunity to engage with and learn from diverse perspectives. For others, the roundtable rehearsed well-known diverse views and brought to the fore the challenge of reconciling these plural perspectives (Mehta 2018).

Several key messages emerged. First, the importance and relevance of social science perspectives as regard challenging the dominant positivist framings of climate science. For example, sea level rise and flooding in Mumbai gets more complex once you start to unpack the social and political dimensions of these challenges, such as the grabbing of land on the coastline – including fragile mangrove ecosystems – by property developers and a total disregard of the natural creeks and rivers that offer natural drainage for the city. Second, issues related to scale and modelling. For local people, who are focused on uncertainty from 'below', there is more engagement with local weather variability (or everyday change) (cf. Hulme 2017), and they draw on multiple rationalities and intersecting explanations. Climate scientists, by contrast, are concerned with long-term climate change and short-term forecasting, but usually construct understandings statistically and not experientially. This is also exemplified in the quote below from a natural scientist at the Oslo roundtable:

> There is a complete mismatch between what people think uncertainty means and what scientists think uncertainty means, so if we could talk about certainty instead it would help a lot. The climate models are made to look at effects of emissions or scenarios, and those changes or these differences only come into play after about 30 years, so every uncertainty before that is not really dealt with. Such models should be used only for things that are relevant at that kind of time scale – for instance, should we build a dam in this site or that. Going to the local level, where people are uncertain about some things, the models do not help. There is a fundamental misconception that climate models can do anything in the here and now, locally (Oslo roundtable, August 2017).

Third, policy-makers prefer to rely on scientific expertise to understand climate change, rather than the subjective understandings of local people, which they often dismiss as anecdotal evidence – as occurred in the Gandhinagar roundtable. We also observed that policy-makers argue for the use of 'certain' 'evidence', because uncertainty, they believe, creates policy paralysis. This was explained by a senior bureaucrat in Gujarat:

> Policy-makers usually like to be certain about the course of action and they can work with likely scenarios but not with something that is highly uncertain. We need to justify our decisions. Uncertainty creates policy chaos, and the decision cannot be taken if the range of uncertainty is too high (Paraphrased, Gujarat roundtable, January 2018).

While the climate scientists and meteorologists admitted to the limits of working with uncertainty, we observed resistance on the part of the bureaucrats, who preferred to 'control' and 'minimise' and, if possible, 'eliminate' uncertainty as much as possible.

Fourth, several field-level bureaucrats also argued that discussions of climate change usually suffer from an elite bias because most of the deliberation and scientific investigations are conducted in English, ignoring understandings of climate uncertainty in the local vernacular. For many policy-makers, we found that the local level was a black box and uncertainty was messy and not clearly articulated.

As mentioned earlier, the roundtables were not designed to resolve or harmonise these differences: rather, they served as a platform to bring these differences to the fore and to demonstrate how discursive, social and institutional power shapes the understanding and framing of climate uncertainty. They did indeed help bring to the surface many different possibilities and issues. We started with the idea of 'bridging', but this seemed too restrictive, suggesting a link between similar groups. Instead, we began to think in terms of crossroads or junctions, which suggest meeting points and confluence between different actors and perspectives. Here too the importance of bringing to the fore diverse ways of valuation and epistemic diversity is key. Whose voices and priorities are privileged over others (as none of these spaces are power-neutral)? For example, is it possible for a camel herder in Kutch to have a seat around the table with policy-makers, and, if it is, how will different expressions of uncertainty interact with the institutional hierarchies and structural inequalities? Convening such spaces may open up the possibility of experiments with Habermasian communicative rationality, participation and deliberation (Dryzek 2002; Honneth and Joas 1991), but the hidden and invisible dimensions of power also need to be addressed as we bring these perspectives into dialogue with each other. This requires methodological innovations, not only to engage in dialogue but also to facilitate synergies in knowledge production.

Moving towards transformative change through co-production

Co-production involves the negotiation of knowledge as well as power; through co-production both new knowledges and social orders are produced (Jasanoff 2004). In roundtables, as in other forms of engaged research, knowledge is produced through relations of power and their intersection with historical, social and economic processes. For example, in another project, TAPESTRY,[3] we focus on how bottom-up transformation takes place in marginal environments that are facing high levels of uncertainty associated with droughts, floods and cyclones, influenced by the uneven impacts of capitalist expansion that is threatening people's well-being and sense of place and identity in India and Bangladesh. Across these sites, alliances between hybrid actors – local communities, NGOs, scientists and some state agencies – are seeking socially just and ecologically sound alternatives, based on local people's plural understandings of what transformation entails. In each of the sites, the team is facilitating an engaged process of situated learning, working with locally based partners who both research and also co-produce transformative action with local communities. For example, fishers in Mumbai are challenging the growth-led paradigms of urban expansion, while also carving out ways to address plastic pollution, which is damaging their fishing habitats. Equally, in the deltaic Sundarbans in India and Bangladesh, climatic threats have undermined many islanders' well-being and collaborative efforts between civil society organisations, local communities and scientists are helping to restore ecology and livelihoods. Meanwhile, in the drought-prone drylands of Kutch in Gujarat, India civil society organisations and villagers are challenging dominant state paradigms regarding drylands and pastoralism, while also improving poor people's quality of life and enhancing biodiversity.

Although such initiatives provide the scope to re-imagine nature–society relations in uncertain, marginal environments, these emergent processes may be resisted by incumbent players, and may not always challenge underlying inequalities associated with class, ethnicity, gender or caste. They also involve a delicate power relationship between civil society organisations and diverse communities, begging the question who is imagining what, and for whom? We must equally ask: how does one ensure that the voices of the most marginalised, who are at the forefront of climatic uncertainty, are able to come to the fore? In response, we need to think of methodologies and consider the ethics around these experiments in co-production, while we re-imagine uncertainty as an opportunity.

Communicating uncertainty: reflections on methods

Creative and participatory methods can potentially open up new and existing conversations that otherwise might be impeded by hierarchical social structures, such as caste traditions or gender inequities. These may include storytelling, mural paintings, photovoice, photostories and a range of methods that seek to address power imbalances and ensure that hidden and subaltern perspectives are central. For example, we used the community-based participatory action research method photovoice to capture the embodied experiences of uncertainty.[4] Although scientists and policy-makers may see uncertainty in the form of coastal erosion or warming temperatures, local people experience uncertainty in more tacit and affective ways. This manifests itself in loss of culture, place and identity due to threats to traditional pastoralist livelihood practices due to a decline in the camel population and changing access to their traditional grazing lands on mangrove islands. Besides capturing these responses, the photovoice methodology also opens up ways of communicating understandings of uncertainty to different stakeholders. This is because visual images can break down language and disciplinary barriers, which often impede climate change communication and knowledge co-production and engagement.

All roundtables began with a powerful photovoice presentation highlighting the precarity of ordinary people in regard to climate change-related uncertainties, illustrating how they make sense of, live with and adapt to them. The visual stories demonstrated how uncertainties at these local scales are further compounded by wider socio-economic changes, such as industrialisation along with the coast or port developments, which often destroy the commons, whether grazing lands, mangroves or fishing habitats. The interlinkages between resources, livelihoods and socio-economic change are often bypassed in siloed mainstream policy processes, through departmental jurisdictions and policy programming. Photovoice thus helped in revealing some of these blind-spots in climate policies and implementation.

For example, as part of our research on climatic uncertainty in pastoral communities in the border district of Kutch in Gujarat, India, we organised a photovoice series to understand the gendered experiences of uncertainty, focusing on the lives of women within these communities. In this context, photovoice played a transgressive role in two key ways. First, within the mainstream scholarship on pastoralism, women's role is under-represented and under-theorised. Hence, the focus on women brought to light powerful images of the 'invisible' care economy that sustains the pastoral system on a day-to-day basis. Second, in contrast to the dominant framings of climatic uncertainty in the form of high temperatures, erratic patterns of rainfall and sea level rise, the photovoice method revealed more embodied, socially and culturally embedded experiences of uncertainty. Some examples include frequent trips to drying wells in the summer, picking fodder leaves, milking buffaloes and washing the calves, and the role of faith and religion in coping with climatic uncertainties. Thus, through photovoice, we were able to tease out tacit and embedded forms of knowledge and experience that are often undervalued and overlooked by traditional forms of research and top-down policy processes.

Our experience with photovoice shows that the use of such methods provides agency to local actors to frame problems in ways that are seen as relevant and appropriate to their knowledge and lived experiences. These embodied understandings can also facilitate dialogue with scientists and policy-makers. For instance, women from the Sundarbans used photovoice to make a representation of their demands to the Sundarbans Development Board in West Bengal (Ghosh *et al.* 2019). Such iterative learning can provide new insights and perspectives in combining diverse knowledge, can challenge and reframe mainstream narratives and can also open up possibilities for dialogue and communication between a range of actors.

Conclusion

In this chapter, we have highlighted the divergent framings of uncertainty in relation to climate science, and how these come to be negotiated, maintained and shaped in forecasting models, through scenarios and projections, as well as in their interactions with science and policy processes. We have also highlighted the epistemic disjuncture in the framing of uncertainty and drew on the heuristic of the 'above', 'middle' and 'below' to demonstrate the divergent frames and understandings that shape these cognitive lenses. Drawing on creative methodological experiments, we argued that there is a potential to harness this diversity to facilitate practices of engagement and co-production between diverse stakeholders. Such emerging dialogues stress the importance of bringing to the fore hidden and alternative perspectives and solutions, while highlighting the need to address the power imbalances that prevent the application of alternatives ways of valuation and epistemic diversity, which are so urgently required for transformative change.

Roundtables present a potentially fruitful way of bringing divergent perspectives into dialogue with each other. However, as we have shown, these spaces are politically charged and disagreements about the use of the term uncertainty abound. Although the interactions with climate scientists in some of these spaces have been fruitful – encouraging them to open up to the experiences of others – the majority of the scientists involved had reservations. Especially in India, the sentiment persisted that 'we can teach people, but have nothing to learn from them'. The roundtables were not envisaged as spaces of harmonisation and reconciliation, but were meant to allow us to bring the diversity of perspectives to the fore, as well as to observe the workings of power and how these are negotiated and shape understandings of uncertainty.

The use of visual methods such as photovoice and photostories can effectively capture lived and tacit experiences of uncertainty. Besides providing agency to local people, who have often been categorised as 'subjects' of research, such approaches provide a voice to vulnerable and marginalised communities, making them active participants in research and the creation of knowledge. Such co-produced research can potentially empower people to shape the conditions of their lives, creating spaces to produce and disseminate knowledge and actively shape development and research processes. However, sustained engagement is required in building relations of trust and reciprocity, as well as addressing power relations – and also in the research process.

Hence, co-production of climate knowledge will require altering the modernist and homogenising frame of knowledge production and dissemination that has long colonised practices through target-oriented top-down framings. This means embracing more decentralised and plural ways of knowing, with the aim of co-producing both new knowledges and social orders. In this chapter, we have also outlined the challenges involved in such processes when tackling existing power relations and existing social and gender inequities. This makes it important to develop methodologies and practices that open up new forms of dialogues among a diversity of actors and knowledges. These must both challenge existing social orders and embrace the multiple modalities of future-making and the plural practices of anticipation and living with uncertainty.

Notes

1 This chapter draws on Mehta *et al.* (2019). We are grateful to Ian Scoones and Andy Stirling for their helpful comments and to Ruby Utting for her help with the references and formatting of this chapter.
2 These roundtables were convened as part of the *Climate Change, Uncertainty and Transformation* project, funded by the Norwegian Research Council, www.nmbu.no/en/faculty/landsam/department/noragric/research/our_projects/projects/node/21234.

3 TAPESTRY is short for Transformation as Praxis: Exploring Socially Just and Transdisciplinary Pathways to Sustainability in Marginal Environments. TAPESTRY is financially supported by the Belmont Forum and NORFACE Joint Research Programme on Transformations to Sustainability, which is co-funded by Economic and Social Research Council, Research Council of Norway, Japan Science Technology Agency, International Science Council and the European Commission through Horizon 2020. https://steps-centre.org/project/tapestry/.

4 https://steps-centre.org/project-related/photovoiceuncertainty/.

References

Achutarao, K. (2016) 'Uncertainty from Above: Can it be Reduced?', paper presented at workshop on Climate Change and Uncertainty from Above and Below, New Delhi, January 2016, www.slideshare.net/Stepscentre/krishna-achutarao-uncertainty-from-above-can-it-be-reduced

Arora, S. (2019) 'Admitting Uncertainty, Transforming Engagement: Towards Caring Practices for Sustainability Beyond Climate Change', *Regional Environmental Change* 19.6: 1571–1584

Asayama, S., Bellamy, R., Geden, O., Hulme, M. and Pearce, W. (2019) 'Why Setting a Climate Deadline is Dangerous', *Nature Climate Change* 9: 570–574

Barros, V., Dahe, Q., Field, C. and Stocker, T. *et al.* (eds) (2012) *Managing the Risks of Extreme Events and Disasters to Advance Climate Change Adaptation,* A Special Report of Working Groups I and II of the Intergovernmental Panel on Climate Change (IPCC), New York: Cambridge University Press

Bhatt, M.R., Mehta, L., Bose, S., Adam, H.N., Srivastava, S., Ghosh, U., Movik, S., Narayanan, N.C., Naess, LO., Parthasarathy, D., Wilson, C. and Pathak, V. (2018) *Bridging the Gaps in Understandings of Uncertainty and Climate Change: Round Table Reports*, Experience Learning Series 76, Ahmedabad: All India Disaster Mitigation Institute

Bhave, A., Conway, D., Dessai, S. and Stainforth, D. (2016) 'Barriers and Opportunities for Robust Decision Making Approaches to Support Climate Change Adaptation in the Developing World', *Climate Risk Management* 14.1: 1-10

Bourdieu, P. (1977) *Outline of a Theory of Practice*, Cambridge: Cambridge University Press

Conway, D., Nicholls, R.J., Brown, S., Tebboth, M.G., Adger, W.N., Ahmad, B., Biemans, H., Crick, F., Lutz, A.F., De Campos, R.S., Said, M., Singh, C., Zaroug, M.A.H., Ludi, E., New M. and Wester, P. (2019) 'The Need for Bottom-up Assessments of Climate Risks and Adaptation in Climate-Sensitive Regions', *Nature Climate Change* 9: 503–511

Curry, J. and Webster, P. (2011) 'Climate Science and the Uncertainty Monster', *Bulletin for the American Meteorological Society* 92.12: 1667–1682

D'Souza, M. and Kale, E. (2018) *Using Transformative Scenario Planning to Think Critically About the Future of Water in Rural Jalna, India*, Second TSP Report, www.uct.ac.za/sites/default/files/image_tool/images/138/South_Asia/WOTR/WOTR%20Overall%20TSP%20Report%20-%20Aug%202018_For%20Online%20FINAL.pdf

Douglas (1986) *How Institutions Think*, New York: Syracuse University Press

Dryzek, J.S. (2002) *Deliberative Democracy and Beyond: Liberals, Critics, Contestations*, Oxford: Oxford University Press

Edwards, P. (2001) 'Representing the Global Atmosphere: Computer Models, Data and Knowledge about Climate Change', in P. Edwards and C. Miller (eds) *Changing the Atmosphere: Expert Knowledge and Environmental Governance*, Cambridge MA: MIT Press

Funtowicz, S. and Ravetz, J. (1993) 'Science for the Post Normal Age', *Futures* 25.7: 739–755

Ghosh, U., Bose, S. and Sen, B. (2019) 'Photo Voice as a Participatory Approach to Influence Climate Related Health Policy in the Sundarbans', *The Lancet Planetary Health* 3: S22, doi.org/10.1016/S2542-5196(19)30165-2

Hajer, M.A. (1995) *The Politics of Environmental Discourse: Ecological Modernization and Policy Process*, Oxford: Clarendon Press

Hallegatte, S., Shah, A., Lempert, R., Brown, C. and Gill, S. (2012) *Investment Decision Making Under Deep Uncertainty: Application to Climate Change*, World Bank Policy Research Working Paper 6193, Washington DC: The World Bank

Hastrup, K. (2013) 'Anticipating Nature: The Productive Uncertainty of Climate Models', in K. Hastrup and M. Skrydstrup (eds) *The Social Life of Climate Change Models: Anticipating Nature*, London: Routledge

Hawkins, E and Sutton, R. (2009) 'The Potential to Narrow Uncertainty in Regional Climate Predictions', *Bulletin of the American Meteorological Society* 100: 12

Heymann, M. (2019) The Climate Change Dilemma: Big Science, the Globalizing of Climate and the Loss of the Human Scale, *Regional Environmental Change* 19.6: 1549–1560

Honneth, A. and Joas, H. (eds) (1991) *Communicative Action: Essays on Jürgen Habermas's The Theory of Communicative Action*, Cambridge, MA: MIT Press

Hulme, M. (2020) 'Is it too Late (to Stop Dangerous Climate Change)? An Editorial', *WIREs Climate Change* 11, https://doi.org/10.1002/wcc.619

—— (2017) *Weathered: Cultures of Climate*, London: Sage

Intergovernmental Panel on Climate Change (2014) *Climate Change 2014: A Synthesis Report*, Switzerland: Intergovernmental Panel on Climate Change, www.ipcc.ch/report/ar5/syr/ (19 January 2017)

Jasanoff, S. (2009) *The Fifth Branch: Science Advisers as Policymakers*, Cambridge MA: Harvard University Press

—— (2004) 'The Idiom of Co-Production. States of Knowledge: The Co-Production of Science and Social Order', in S. Jasanoff (ed) *States of Knowledge: The Co-Production of Science and the Social Order*, London: Routledge

Leach, M., Scoones, I. and Stirling, A. (2010) *Dynamic Sustainabilities: Technology, Environment, Social Justice*, London: Earthscan

Lemos, M.C., Lo, Y.-J., Nelson, D.R., Eakin, H. and Bedran-Martins, A.M. (2016) 'Linking Development to Climate Adaptation: Leveraging Generic and Specific Capacities to Reduce Vulnerability to Drought in NE Brazil', *Global Environmental Change* 39: 170–179

Lyons, I., Hill, R., Deshong, S., Mooney, G. and Turpin, G. (2019) 'Putting Uncertainty Under the Cultural Lens of Traditional Owners from the Great Barrier Reef Catchments', *Regional Environmental Change* 19.6: 1597–1610

Mehta, L. (2018) 'Overview', in M.R. Bhatt, *et al.* (ed) *Bridging Gaps in Uncertainty and Climate Change*, Experience Learning Series 76, Ahmedabad: All India Disaster Mitigation Institute

Mehta, L., Leach, M., Newell, P., Scoones, I., Sivaramakrishnan, K. and Way, SA. (1999) *Exploring Understandings of Institutions and Uncertainty: New Directions in Natural Resource Management*, Institute of Development Studies Discussion Paper 372, Brighton: Institute of Development Studies

Mehta, L., Srivastava, S., Adam, H.N., Bose, S., Alankar, Ghosh, U. and Kumar, V.V. (2019). 'Climate Change and Uncertainty from "Above" and "Below": Perspectives from India', *Regional Environmental Change* 19.6: 1533–1547

O´Brien, K. (2012) 'Global Environmental Change II. From Adaptation to Deliberate Transformation', *Progress in Human Geography* 36.5: 667–676

Ostrom, E. (1996) 'Crossing the Great Divide: Coproduction, Synergy, and Development', *World Development* 24.6: 1073–1087

Panda, A. (2016) 'Exploring Climate Change Perceptions, Rainfall Trends and Perceived Barriers to Adaptation in a Drought Affected Region in India', *Natural Hazards* 84.2: 777–796

Pelling, M. (2011) *Adaptation to Climate Change: From Resilience to Transformation*, Oxon: Routledge

Ranganathan, M. and Bratman, E. (2019) 'From Urban Resilience to Abolitionist Climate Justice in Washington, DC', *Antipode,* https://doi.org/10.1111/anti.12555

Rein, M. and Schön, D. (1993) 'Reframing Policy Discourse', in F.J. Fischer and J. Forester (eds) *The Argumentative Turn in Policy Analysis and Planning*, London: Duke University Press

Scoones, I. (2019) *What is Uncertainty and Why Does it Matter?*, STEPS Working Paper 105, Brighton: STEPS Centre

Shackley, S. and Wynne, B. (1996) 'Representing Uncertainty in Global Climate Change Science and Policy: Boundary-Ordering Devices and Authority', *Science, Technology, & Human Values* 21.3: 275–302

Sigel, K., Klauer, B. and Pahl-Wostl, C. (2010) 'Conceptualising Uncertainty in Environmental Decision-Making: The Example of the EU Water Framework Directive', *Ecological Economics* 69.3: 502–510

Stirling, A., Leach, M., Mehta, L., Scoones, I., Smith, A., Stagl, S. and Thompson, J. (2007) *Empowering Designs: Towards More Progressive Appraisal of Sustainability*, STEPS Working Paper 3, Brighton: STEPS Centre

Stirling, A., Marshall, F. and Ely, A. (2018) 'How is Transformative Knowledge "Co-Produced?"', *Integration and Implementation Insights,* https://i2insights.org/2018/04/03/co-producing-transformative-knowledge/ (accessed 17 January 2020)

Swart, R., Bernstein, L., Ha-Duong, M. and Petersen, A. (2009) 'Agreeing to Disagree: Uncertainty Management in Assessing Climate Change, Impacts and Responses by the IPCC', *Climate Change* 92: 1–29

Van Der Sluijs, J. (2005) 'Uncertainty as a Monster in the Science–Policy Interface: Four Coping Strategies', *Water Science Technology* 52.6: 87–92

Vogel, C. and Olivier, D. (2019) 'Re-imagining the Potential of Effective Drought Responses in South Africa' *Regional Environmental Change* 19.6: 1597–1610

Walker, W.E., Harremoës, P., Rotmans, J., van der Sluijs, J., van Asselt, M.B., Janssen, P. and Krayer von Krauss, M.P. (2003) 'Defining Uncertainty: A Conceptual Basis for Uncertainty Management in Model-Based Decision Support', *Integrated Assessment* 4.1: 5–17

Wilby, R.L. and Dessai, S. (2010) 'Robust Adaptation to Climate Change', *Weather* 65.7: 180–185

Wynne, B. (1992) 'Uncertainty and Environmental Learning: Reconceiving Science and Policy in the Preventive Paradigm', *Global Environmental Change* 2.2: 111–127

8

DISEASE OUTBREAKS

Navigating uncertainties in preparedness and response

Hayley MacGregor, Santiago Ripoll and Melissa Leach

Introduction

Concern about deadly infectious diseases with local outbreak or pandemic potential has grown significantly, in a world characterised by increasing global mobility and significant social, economic and ecological transformations. In recent years such fears have crystallised in the restructuring of institutional architectures within agencies with a global health remit, alongside initiatives to predict, prepare and respond to epidemics. Underlying the fears of global actors is the reality of limited knowledge about many aspects of outbreaks, coupled with predictions of potentially devastating consequences – both rapidly unfolding and fatal. A better delineation of the contours of uncertainty in global planning and practice is vital, we argue, to understanding the assumptions made about appropriate measures, the allocation of responsibility and the justifications of actions.

The 2013–2015 Ebola outbreak in West Africa was a key episode in galvanising global attention towards disease-preparedness activities, geared towards pre-emptive control in the event of outbreaks. Practices focused on prediction and control concentrate on turning uncertainties into 'risk', through surveillance, modelling, early warning and scenario planning (e.g. WHO 2017). Alongside the scientific uncertainties that are the focus of these efforts, a further source of uncertainty has increasingly come into view for scientific and policy communities: the behaviour of affected populations and the social and political dynamics and geographies of disease 'hotspots'. This has catalysed an increased recognition of social science perspectives and the value of disseminating knowledge about the contexts in which disease outbreaks occur – socio-economic, political and ecological (Leach 2019; GLOPID-R 2019). Thus, a growing recognition of 'context' in the epidemics science-policy space has been a significant development. We argue here that new discourses and practices have emerged around this realisation. These can be detected in initiatives such as those to standardise risk communication and community engagement, to develop social science protocols to inform outbreak response, or to obtain synthesis briefings from social scientists for frontline workers – in an attempt to make the unpredictable and lesser known spaces of 'social context' more discretely intelligible and legible.

As social scientists working on epidemics we too have beaten the drum about the fact that 'context matters and must be known'. We have actively contributed to this discourse in the hope that it could serve as a bridge to the inclusion of perspectives beyond the biomedical, and in an attempt to avoid potential harm from interventions that might be naive as regards on-the-ground realities. We have led and participated in initiatives to brief epidemic responders on context, such as the Ebola Response Anthropology Platform (www.ebola-anthropology.net) and Social Science in Humanitarian Action Platform (SSHAP) (www.socialscienceinaction. org). And yet we also cannot help but reflect critically on how agencies have employed this knowledge, and how such initiatives can also be viewed as part of a broader suite of technologies to transform uncertainties – in this instance social, political and structural realities – into calculable risks, tamed and streamlined for communication to publics. In the official discourse of preparedness and response, local people have been variously objectified as a source of uncertainty, including now as (behavioural and social) 'context'.

In this chapter, we seek to open up a richer dialogue about the different understandings and experiences of outbreaks and of uncertainty that prevail among global science-policy communities, and the 'communities' that are envisaged as the focus of global-level efforts, informed by, but also self-critically engaged with, these recent efforts to make 'context' and local responses knowable. We address and illustrate the potential contestation between the official response efforts of public health agencies, and alternative ways of knowing and responding to outbreaks, grounded in practice and mobilisation that might be more salient and trusted at local level. We suggest that, while there has been growing attention to these gulfs and how to bridge them in *response* efforts, there has been less attention to *preparedness* efforts and their understanding at local level, and how these might relate to everyday experiences of and responses to uncertainty. But our main concern here is to go further, to reflect on the limits in comprehending the ontological dimensions of uncertainty, particularly as experienced in places where outbreaks are happening, by people whose lives are precarious, with misfortunes and 'emergencies' – health-related and otherwise – that are as likely to be of the 'slow' (Anderson *et al.* 2019) as the acute kind. For people living in these settings, we suggest, it is not 'context' that is salient but the ongoing flow – or text – of social and ecological life, in which a host of everyday uncertainties are constantly faced, with variable outcomes.

Attention to the dynamics of different levels, forms and realities of uncertainty raises questions about whose versions of uncertainty dominate in imaginaries of future outbreaks, and corresponding global response and preparedness strategies. Moreover, it is essential to consider whose knowledge and experiences count in preparing and responding, as well as whether uncertainties related to disease outbreaks are always resolvable. Are alternative processes possible for formulating international planning frameworks, ones that are more open to considering different forms of knowledge and more attentive to views 'from below' that might reveal alternative priorities and ways of being-in-the-world? Or is a more radical departure necessary, where a new process for organising international responses does not rely foremost on roadmaps developed remotely from national and local-level realities?

The framings and dynamics of uncertainty at the global level

Conventional epidemic response institutional architecture is based on the 'outbreak narrative' that highlights particular aspects of an epidemic and is blind to others (Dry and Leach 2010). The outbreak narrative is a 'formulaic plot that begins with the identification of an emerging infection, discussion of global networks through which diseases travel, and a chronicle of the epidemiologic work that results in disease containment' (Wald 2008: 2). This 'outbreak narrative' focuses on particular disease dynamics – 'sudden emergence, speedy, far-reaching, [and often] global spread' – and on particular types of response – 'universalised, generic emergency-oriented control, at source, aimed at eradication' (Leach *et al.* 2010: 372). This narrative tends to prioritise the 'global citizen' at risk of contagion, disproportionately referring to citizens of the global North. This global bio-security paradigm is characterised by a move from public health technologies of prevention to preparedness, deploying particular military and security techniques for the 'construction of potential futures' in the realm of disease threat (Lakoff 2008: 401). Preparedness involves a complex and rapidly developing set of concepts, architectures and practices aimed at creating a 'vigilant alertness for the onset of surprise' and an 'anticipatory imagination' among policy-makers (Lakoff 2017: 20).

At the global level, at least three different forms of uncertainty can be delineated with respect to 'expert' scientific knowledge and outbreak responses. Firstly, in a situation where an actual outbreak of a known disease has occurred, there are uncertainties that arise in terms of how the disease will unfold, which populations will be most affected, how people might behave in response and what the overall effects will be. Secondly, considering a particular disease with epidemic potential, there are uncertainties regarding where the next outbreak will occur and how this might develop, such as whether efficient human-to-human transmission might occur. Thirdly, there is the situation of extreme unknowns: which Disease X might emerge in the near future, how organisms might be mutating and how preparedness can be maximised.

All three forms of uncertainty, as states of limited knowledge, are acknowledged by scientists. Discussions about 'closing the gaps' in scientific understandings frequently form the focus and grist of numerous expert meetings, such as those convened on the WHO priority diseases (WHO 2019a). The paradigm of evidence-based response is held as the gold standard approach for guiding action, and as such there are calls for urgent research to address outstanding questions, with the assumption that risk mitigation can be replaced by risk elimination as evidence becomes more complete. In pursuit of prediction in order to manage and reduce risk, preparedness and response architectures prioritise technologies of control, with practices concentrated on turning uncertainties into risk, such as surveillance and modelling of disease, and scenario planning. These involve the intensified collection and use of public health and epidemiological data, supported by clinical and laboratory information, as well as novel (e.g. digital) means to collect and share it.[1] The common framework is to move from 'reactive' to 'predictive and proactive' approaches to pathogens. R&D is also prioritised, with the assumption that vaccines, immune therapies and novel drugs are the 'game-changers' in the control of risk, and should be fast-tracked through human trials and into production.

These control-driven approaches are understandable, given the urgency associated with outbreak response. The stakes are often high and public health and response professionals are under intense scrutiny and pressure to intervene definitively and with assurance. While scientists might readily acknowledge the knowledge gaps among themselves, and discuss the tensions of balancing scientific uncertainties and difficulties with prediction against the need to act, this openness is not readily expressed beyond their professional community. A lack of certainty creates particular discomfort among public health professionals in discussions of 'risk reduction' messages directed at the general public and the media.

Scientists might acknowledge that the dynamism of complex interacting biological and ecological systems make it likely that limits to forms of scientific knowing in regard to 'priority diseases' will persist, on the shifting sands of new and emerging uncertainties. In designing responses and engaging with publics, health professionals also increasingly recognise that social worlds cannot be ignored – from individual beliefs about disease and health-seeking behaviours to diverse cultural logics and conditions of life and livelihood that affect relevant social relations and responses (Bedford *et al.* 2019). But, as we now show, this attention is often framed in terms of 'behaviour' and 'context' – and as further sources of uncertainty that in turn need to be tamed and controlled.

The uncertainty of behaviour and context

The 2013–2015 West African Ebola outbreak helped focus a spotlight on the uncertainties associated with social factors, as well as the dangers of action that is 'context-blind', even in a situation of great urgency and high mortality and a virus capable of epidemic spread. Social scientists working with local populations in efforts such as the Ebola Response Anthropology Platform highlighted the social processes and concerns shaping viral transmission patterns; care and burial practices; local innovations and institutions in addressing the outbreak; and the relationships and learning among community members and health workers, and the histories and political economies shaping these (e.g. Wilkinson *et al.* 2017; Richards 2016). Communicated to response agencies through accessible briefings in near-real-time, and then the subject of global reports and reflections (e.g. GLOPID-R 2019), these efforts have contributed to greater appreciation of local social dimensions of epidemic response. This has been termed 'behaviour' of affected populations by response agencies, although there is increasing recognition that this domain of 'context' includes cultural logics, social responses, political factors and media reports, and that the formal outbreak response itself can shape rumours and local reactions that in turn will shape the evolution of the outbreak. Many scientists now reflect more openly on contextual factors and local responses as a major form of uncertainty in attempting modelling and other forms of prediction.

For global agencies, this growing appreciation of 'behaviour' and 'context' presents a new set of uncertainties that must now be grappled with in responding to, but also preparing for, outbreaks. To date, the dominant approach to dealing with this unruly contextual space has focused attention on 'risk communication' and 'community engagement' (e.g. WHO 2018: 14). Agencies and initiatives such as the WHO's new Health Emergencies programme are rapidly commissioning social science tools, methods, protocols and procedures to support these emphases, as well as to make social contexts legible and manageable.[2] While contributing to such efforts through initiatives such as SSHAP,[3] we have also been at pains to point out the narrow and over-simplistic ways that 'communities', 'communication' and 'social context' are addressed (Leach 2019).

Central to our argument, however, is also the way that such approaches once again 'close down' on uncertainties – attempting to reduce them to predictable and manageable risk (Leach et al. 2010). In this regard, there is a push to get a more complex understanding of context onto the radar of response agencies and modellers, including an understanding of the dynamic, non-linear interactions between different social, political and ecological processes that shape disease emergence and outbreaks. Two examples of recent outbreak responses – Nipah in Bangladesh and Ebola in the DRC – show advances in appreciating local social realities, yet also the persistence and limits of reductive approaches to the uncertainties of behaviour and context.

Outbreaks linked to Nipah virus in Bangladesh have brought to the fore the disjunctures that can exist between scientific and local understandings of disease events. Interdisciplinary research assisted in uncovering human–bat contact as central for 'spillover' to people who drank raw palm sap contaminated by bat secretions (Luby et al. 2006). Yet, since collection of palm sap was a key livelihood strategy, and consumption of the sap was also a widespread social practice, interventions to address the risk of transmission had to consider that local people would not simply stop harvesting sap as a consequence of the sharing of new scientific facts. Innovative adaptations of methods of sap collection to reduce risks took this into account and low-cost interventions were advocated (ibid.). Furthermore, careful social science research revealed that people held distinct beliefs regarding illness causation – such as that the bodily symptoms had been sent by Allah – which did not concur entirely with a germ theory (Parveen et al. 2016; Blum et al. 2009). People were sceptical of the links that professionals were making to palm sap, as their observed experience over time did not accord with the idea that consumption caused fatal illness. They were thus not initially inclined to change their behaviour.

Local beliefs needed to be taken into account in 'risk communication' and the development of public health messages (*ibid.* 2016). For scientists leading an outbreak response under time pressure and media scrutiny, unexpected local responses that do not appear to accept scientific findings or respond in expected ways to risk reduction measures are cause for disquiet as they appear to counteract strategies based on medical facts. Again, much has been done in such cases to work with local people to shift 'behavioural' risk factors, such as with respect to the care of relatives with Nipah infection in ways that respect prevalent expectations and moral economies of care, while still being attentive to public health concerns about risk of transmission (Islam *et al.* 2013; Blum *et al.* 2009). Vaccine and immunoglobulin developments might be sought as a way to bypass or neutralise the vagaries of human behaviour, but it is likely that the dynamics of this disease, and the responses to it, will remain unpredictable.

The Ebola outbreak in North Kivu and Ituri in the DRC (ongoing since August 2018) has focused attention on the context of conflict as an extreme form of social and contextual uncertainty, and one even less likely to be amenable to strategies of control. In the second largest Ebola outbreak after the West African pandemic, a vaccine that was fast-tracked for trial and development has been available and has, by most accounts, reduced the impact of the outbreak. But despite these conventional approaches to controlling disease, the political realities have necessarily shaped the humanitarian response. This response has incorporated the importance of 'understanding context', along with many of the lessons learned from the West African pandemic. For example, social science analysis has been effectively generated remotely by networks like SSHAP, and on the ground by institutions such as CASS (*Cellule Analyse Science Sociale* – the Social Sciences Analysis Cell).[4] Another advance has been collaboration between field agencies and SSHAP in the analysis of community feedback data: this community feedback is gathered, analysed and communicated to response teams. This is important because the response generates social uncertainties as much as the disease itself, and shapes the perceptions and actions of affected populations.

Yet the DRC Ebola response has also opened up a myriad of uncertainties that cannot be contained by community engagement. Military action has curtailed humanitarian access in particular locations and times, and concerted attacks on Ebola treatment centres by armed groups have reduced the effectiveness of the response. In SSHAP discussions this has raised the importance of peacebuilding and political economy expertise in social science analyses.

Even more importantly, the uncertainty of chronic conflict has permeated people's everyday lives. Under continuous threat of physical violence, people seek to prioritise the immediate need for physical security over Ebola-related activities. An example of this was the 'Ebola strike' that occurred in October 2018, when many community members halted Ebola activities in protest at the lack of security. An historical political marginalisation vis-à-vis a central government that is also unable to protect people generates distrust of health services and enables plausible explanations of Ebola as a government plot. Conventional methods of case management – listing contacts – become fraught with difficulty, as fear and mistrust towards the response make the act of giving that information highly risky. As the main method of the Ebola vaccine on trial was ring vaccination, the incompleteness of these lists of contacts had an important impact on the efficacy of vaccination. For much of the response, the number of Ebola deaths at home (rather than in treatment centres) of people who were not on the case management contact list was high, reaching up to a third of cases (WHO 2019b). In addition, Congolese citizens wonder why Ebola is prioritised over other health priorities in an already limited health system. In turn, this mistrust is exacerbated by the disruptive Ebola economy, and the unequal access to finance and resources that have accompanied the response among fragmented local political authorities. Thus, the roll-out of the response has inevitably generated a new set of deep uncertainties between local socio-political dynamics and response activities.

While these examples represent stories of success in the institutionalised appreciation of social issues, and measures to deal with the uncertainties of behaviour and context, the attempts are limited in various respects. In both cases, the initiatives remained part of a managerial framework that aimed to reduce uncertainty to risk, and was unable to do so. Furthermore, social science inputs have to date been 'layered' on top of the response architecture, rather than contributing to transforming the philosophy or the constitution of the response itself.

Alternative experiences of uncertainty: the view 'from below' and the text of life

For agencies, the unpredictable influence of social and political realities on outbreak responses has thus come to be packaged as 'context'. Yet what are the experiences of those actually living this 'context', for whom it is, in effect, not context but the text of life? This experiential reality is not uncertainty that needs to be reduced and rendered into risk, but is manifested as an ongoing flow of situations, to be lived with and negotiated. Nor are these uncertainties fully amenable to elimination through knowledge, since they are part of the lived, embodied fabric of social, ecological and political life – what one might term 'ontological uncertainties'.

In the growing, but still marginal, advocacy to include local people's own perspectives in outbreak preparedness and response, there has been little attention to people's lived experiences or embodiment of uncertainty. Yet exploring people's experiences and responses to uncertainty in the form of everyday threats to health and life could provide an alternative view on how preparedness and response might be understood and mobilised 'from below'. Such enquiry would explore what could be learned from those who live with multiple uncertainties in areas affected by infectious disease outbreaks. It would ask how people draw on formal and informal institutions, forms of public authority, social relations and practices as they anticipate and respond to health and other threats on a daily basis – not as some hangover of 'traditional' past beliefs, but in social responses to new forms of adversity that come about amid social, ecological and political transformations. It could reveal and support ways for people to harness their own resources and practices, in new hopes and possibilities for socially-sensitive epidemic preparedness and response. In these ways, appreciation of lived, ontological uncertainties could become part of an alternative epidemic 'preparedness from below'.

While this is still an open field of enquiry,[5] its salience is suggested by ethnographic examples from diverse settings, which also point to some of its key dimensions. Such work highlights how ontological uncertainties are woven into people's everyday lives and existential realities, becoming particularly relevant in circumstances of precarity – whether related to subsistence, violence or disease. Thus in post-invasion Iraq, Al-Mohammad and Peluso explore people's lives in uncertain, violent spaces as the 'rough ground of the everyday' (2012: 42). The horizon of lives of people in conflict are not determined solely by 'contextual' categories, such as kinship, tribalism, religion or sectarianism, but rather as 'living-in-action – that is, as phenomenologically, experientially, and sensibly grounded' (2012: 44).

Uncertainties in precarious everyday lives carry particular temporalities. Thus Paul Richards' work shows that Hausa farmers do not deal with the uncertainties of subsistence farming by looking forward and planning, and then rolling out those plans. While a technique like intercropping may seem like premeditated design, it is by virtue of the performance of sowing and the difficulties that arise in the emergent moment that the choice of seeds and their spatial location is chosen (Richards 1993: 67). In illness a similar emergent temporality unfolds in the pursuit of care: the emergent symptoms, the social meaning attached to them (that often go beyond the biomedical) and the available and desirable avenues of care are a form of navigation, rather than it being a case of those who are ill following an established route of a health-seeking pathway, as James Fairhead *et al.* (2008) have shown for infant health in Guinea. Improvisation in the present can also draw on past repertoires: thus, Mende villagers' implementation of locally managed quarantines in the 2013–2015 Ebola outbreak re-mobilised principles and authority relations (such as placing youth as guards on bush paths) that had been used in the 1991–2002 civil war, as well as in twentieth-century outbreaks of smallpox and measles.[6]

In dealing with uncertainties of violence and disease, people may strive for further autonomy and control, aiming to 'create and find some continuity in their lives, in the face of hostile circumstances and their own vulnerability' (Jenkins *et al.* 2005: 11). Yet such desire for control does not necessarily translate into a desire for certainty, or the medicalisation of illness. For example, Marita Eastmond highlighted a preference of refugees in Sweden to frame their ailments as a product of traumatic lives outside the medical concepts imposed by bureaucratic systems, as a way to emphasise their normality and ability to work (Eastmond 2005). Further, people may seek to resist the certainty of an unwanted outcome, such as a medical diagnosis with a poor prognosis. Thus Nyole people in Uganda often prefer to open up possibilities for healing by seeking counsel from alternative health providers, and if these fail, through divination in rituals, which in turn can open up particular social explanations (Whyte 1997). In precarious circumstances it might be more comfortable to live with ongoing uncertainties than with the certainty of a bad outcome.

In other extreme circumstances, the uncertainties of a world where there is 'too much death and too much loss' can generate a resignation in which violence, or the loss of life, is accepted and awarded a particular meaning (Scheper-Hughes 2008: 29). Nancy Scheper-Hughes (1993) speaks of the difficult decisions that poor mothers in north-eastern Brazil had to make when resources were so scarce that their attention to the survival of some infants would mean letting the weakest die. Scheper-Hughes depicts this as an act of resilience, as people struggle to affect the elements they can control in a particular moment while living in precarious environments – in other words, caring for those children who show a 'knack for life' (1993: 446), while letting go of those who do not.

Such examples highlight that experiences of disease and other forms of 'misfortune' in everyday life cannot be understood solely at an individual level – or as a matter for unified 'communities' – but are embedded in social relations. Thus 'care, and also neglect and violence, ravel and unravel the entanglings of lives with other lives' (Al-Mohammad and Peluso 2012: 45). For Nyole people in Uganda, the explanation of misfortune, including illness, goes beyond the body and the self and also lies in uncertainties about the intentions and actions of others – living, dead or supernatural (Whyte 1997).

In light of this, activities that are linked to narrow or immediate material concerns (such as farming or health-seeking), can only be understood as part of a wider 'performance' of social life, with all its uncertainties (Richards 1993). Richard Jenkins *et al.* suggest further that as a result of our human capacity to imagine futures and possible worlds and our desire to control particular outcomes, new uncertainties emerge:

> A blessing and a curse of human cognition is our talent for the complex imagination of options, alternatives, possibilities and 'what ifs'. Confronted by the routine uncertainties of the environment and the actions of other humans, individual and collective decision-making in the attempt to establish some predictable control over matters-at-hand necessarily involves imagining options, alternatives and so on. The result is at least as likely to be further uncertainty as anything else (Jenkins *et al.* 2005: 28).

Towards alternative approaches to disease outbreaks amid uncertainties

Such explorations of everyday uncertainties and how people negotiate them amid precarious lives start to open up different, and richer, understandings of uncertainty as it relates to disease outbreaks. These understandings involve moves from context to text; from epistemology to ontology; from individual/community perspectives to social relational ones; and from narrow temporalities (the immediate outbreak, the future plan) to multiple ones, as past, present and imagined future dynamics inform each other. Perhaps above all, they suggest that uncertainties are not always amenable to being reduced to risk, and managed and controlled – and that, furthermore, attempts at control may simply spawn further uncertainties.

The reality of a multitude of forms of uncertainty, temporalities and experiences does not mean that we should dismiss the urgency of outbreak response, or suggest that efforts to research pathogens, engage with models and predict and indeed prepare for epidemics are not important. Understanding everyday uncertainties and their implications for epidemic preparedness and response must emerge from continuous engagement, as responses to such lived uncertainties can be revealing of local efforts that are of relevance for outbreak preparedness – for instance, as forms of local mobilisation were in response to Ebola in West Africa (Parker *et al.* 2019). While we recognise the limitations of foregrounding 'coping strategies' in settings where the 'staff, stuff, space and systems' for combating infectious outbreaks are sparse on the ground (Farmer 2014: 39), it is nevertheless important to ask whether different, and more inclusive, processes are possible. Thus, several provisional conclusions can be drawn at this point.

Conclusion

As we have argued, the dominant narratives and approaches of global public health and humanitarian agencies have privileged formal science and epidemiological knowledge over local models of disease and response, and have emphasised 'blueprint' and 'roadmap' approaches to preparing for and managing outbreaks. While recent efforts have seen greater attention to multiple types of uncertainty, the emphasis is on reducing these to manageable risk through better scientific knowledge, scenarios and surveillance.

Increasingly, the uncertainties associated with complex social, ecological and political processes, both 'potential' (affecting future outbreaks) and 'actual' (as they unfold in the dynamics of current outbreaks) are seen as important (Samimian-Darash 2013). Yet the dominant response has been either to reduce these uncertainties to a narrow set of risk communication and community engagement issues, and/or to treat them as a 'social context' to be rendered legible and manageable through narrow forms of 'social science intelligence'.

Thus the watershed event of the West African Ebola pandemic led to a reconfiguration of epidemic responses, with 'contextual' knowledge now likely to be incorporated into future interventions. However, there is a strong tendency to include social knowledge around socio-cultural dynamics and political economy within existing managerial technologies, reconfiguring social uncertainties as calculable risks. Social knowledge is then mapped onto the conventional epidemic risk management approach of 'predict, prepare and control'. In parallel to the prediction technologies of epidemic modelling and reading 'virus chatter', vulnerable populations can be identified according to their socio-cultural and demographic characteristics, and recruited for 'participatory surveillance'. In planning responses, social knowledge can be used to identify the role different social groups may play in enabling or resisting interventions, as well as to design strategies to recruit support. Lastly, in terms of control, vaccination, treatment and drug-testing are rolled out in parallel to social science-informed community engagement activities that aim to enhance uptake and community acceptance. People and the social uncertainties they live with and enact are thus 'tamed' and controlled through activities informed by social sciences, such as public health communication, community engagement, behavioural change interventions or even allegedly participatory approaches, such as decentralised 'surveillance' and community feedback.

Despite the fact that many of these activities have succeeded in enhancing both the impact of epidemic response and its accountability, we have equally argued that this approach is often based on illusory assumptions about the full knowability of 'the social'. Our case studies show that there is a degree of radical and irreducible uncertainty that pervades all social life, but that this can become particularly salient in situations of precarity – and perhaps most heightened where an epidemic is unfolding within a violent conflict. Beyond the limits of social science in depicting social realities, there are limits as regards acknowledging the range and depth of uncertainties and their ontological dimensions. For people living in precarious environments, context is less relevant than how uncertainty is phenomenologically experienced as they navigate the flow, or text, of life through 'structured improvisation' (Scheper-Hughes 2008: 47). Striving for control in the face of uncertainty brings with it the need to imagine other worlds and possibilities, in which we are closely entangled with others. This in turn will almost inevitably generate further uncertainties.

In terms of epidemic response, this can create conflict between the risk-mitigating strategies of the response and the unruly uncertainties and vernacular responses that emerge 'from below'. What are the implications of this for a different kind of preparedness and response? Is there a way of promoting preparedness and response 'from below'? The meanings, practices and place of this, and how to promote it, are a work-in-progress, but some key features can be identified. This alternative approach would not be instigated by external agencies on the basis of maximising the use of social science information about the context. It requires a more respectful and empowering approach, in which people – especially in precarious contexts – shape the core of this response in a more autonomous way. The role of external agencies would be to support and build on these practices, enabling local ideas, innovations, institutions, resources and responsibilities to flourish. Such an approach also requires a more nimble, responsive, adaptive mode, eschewing fixed plans in favour of flexibility, and ongoing iterative adaptation and learning. Further, epidemic preparedness and response 'from below' would need to acknowledge difference and contestation in how diseases and outbreaks are understood and experienced, and the different kinds of politics that emerge, deliberating and co-constructing strategies accordingly. Finally, an approach is needed that responds not just to the immediate needs of a time-bound outbreak, but that also embeds this in people's broader and longer-term needs, including with respect to 'slow emergencies' (Anderson *et al.* 2019). This means an approach that is not just (or necessarily) disease-specific, but that is also engaged with other priorities around security, livelihoods and the ability to live a meaningful and dignified personal and social life. Embracing such approaches will require a step change among global agencies and science-policy communities, but the current and future challenges of preparing and responding well and humanely to disease outbreaks amid uncertainties demands nothing less.

Notes

1 For example, the Global Virome project and the Global Viral Forecasting aim to listen to the 'chatter' of viruses and other microbes and contain them 'at source'. Programmes like the USAID-funded PREDICT (www.usaid.gov/news-information/fact-sheets/emerging-pandemic-threats-program) and the Eco-Health Alliance (www.ecohealthalliance.org/program/emerging-disease-hotspots) have looked at disease emergence to identify genetics, geographies and species to remain alert to.
2 www.who.int/features/qa/health-emergencies-programme/en/.
3 www.socialscienceinaction.org/.
4 CASS is ground-breaking as it does not sit under the Risk Communication-Community Engagement pillar of response, but under the Strategic Commission of the DRC Ministry of Health, so feeding into all pillars of response.
5 The idea of 'preparedness from below' is being explored through the Wellcome Trust-supported project 'Pandemic preparedness: local and global concepts and practices in tackling disease threats in Africa', co-led by Leach and MacGregor (www.ids.ac.uk/programme-and-centre/pandemic-preparedness/).
6 Personal communication, village chief in Sierra Leone.

References

Al-Mohammad, H. and Peluso, D. (2012) 'Ethics and the "Rough Ground" of the Everyday: The Overlappings of Life in Post-Invasion Iraq', *Hau* 2

Anderson, B., Grove, K., Rickards, L. and Kearnes, M. (2019) 'Slow Emergencies: Temporality and the Racialized Biopolitics of Emergency Governance', *Progress in Human Geography*, https://doi.org/10.1177/0309132519849263

Bedford, J., Farrar, J., Ihekweazu, C. *et al.* (2019) 'A New Twenty-First Century Science for Epidemic Response', *Nature* 575: 130–136

Blum, L., Khan, R., Nahar, N. *et al.* (2009) 'In-Depth Assessment of an Outbreak of Nipah Encephalitis with Person-to-Person Transmission in Bangladesh: Implications for Prevention and Control Strategies', *The American Journal of Tropical Medicine and Hygiene* 80: 96–102

Dry, S. and Leach, M. (2010) 'Epidemic Narratives', in S. Dry and M. Leach (eds) *Epidemics. Science, Governance and Social Justice*, London: Earthscan

Eastmond, M. (2005) 'The Disorders of Displacement: Bosnian Refugees and the Reconstitution of Normality', in R. Jenkins, H. Jessen and S. Vibeke (eds) *Managing Uncertainty: Ethnographic Studies of Illness, Risk and the Struggle for Control*, Copenhagen: Museum of Tusculanum Press

Fairhead, J., Leach, M., Millimouno, D. and Diallo, A. (2008) 'New Therapeutic Landscapes in Africa: Parental Engagement with Infant Health Care in the Republic of Guinea', *Social Science and Medicine* 66.10: 2157–2167

Farmer, P. (2014) 'Diary', *London Review of Books* 36.20: 38–39

Global Research Collaboration for Infectious Disease Preparedness (2019) *Towards People Centred Epidemic Preparedness and Response*, www.glopid-r.org/wp-content/uploads/2019/07/towards-people-centered-epidemic-preparedness-and-response-report.pdf (13 February 2020)

Islam, M.S., Luby, S., Gurley, E. (2013) 'Developing Culturally Appropriate Interventions for Preventing Person-to-Person Transmission of Nipah Virus in Bangladesh: Cultural Epidemiology in Action', in C. Banwell *et al.* (eds) *When Culture Impacts Health*, London: Academic Press/Elsevier

Jenkins, R., Jessen, H. and Vibeke, S. (2005) *Managing Uncertainty: Ethnographic Studies of Illness, Risk and the Struggle for Control*, Copenhagen: Museum of Tusculanum Press

Lakoff, A. (2017) *Unprepared: Global Health in a Time of Emergency*, Oakland, CA: University of California Press

—— (2008) 'The Generic Biothreat, Or, How We Became Unprepared', *Cultural Anthropology* 23: 399–428

Leach, M. (2019) 'Epidemics and Anthropologists. Guest Editorial', *Anthropology Today* 35.6: 1–2

Leach, M., Scoones, I. and Stirling, A. (2010) 'Governing Epidemics in an Age of Complexity: Narratives, Politics and Pathways to Sustainability', *Global Environmental Change* 20.3: 369–377

Luby, S., Rahman, M., Hossain, M. *et al.* (2006) 'Foodborne Transmission of Nipah Virus, Bangladesh', *Emerging Infectious Disease* 12.12: 1888–1894

Parker, M., Hanson, T., Vandi, A. *et al.* (2019) Ebola and Public Authority: Saving Loved Ones in Sierra Leone', *Medical Anthropology* 38.5: 440–454

Parveen, A., Islam, M.S., Begum, M., *et al.* (2016) 'It's Not Only What You Say, It's Also How You Say It: Communicating Nipah Virus Prevention Messages During an Outbreak in Bangladesh', *BMC Public Health* 16: 726

Richards, P. (2016) *Ebola: How a People's Science Helped End an Epidemic*, London: Zed Books

—— (1993) 'Cultivation: Knowledge or Performance?', in M. Hobart (ed) *An Anthropological Critique of Development: The Growth of Ignorance*, London: Routledge: 61–78

Samimian-Darash, L. (2013) 'Governing Future Potential Biothreats: Toward an Anthropology of Uncertainty', *Current Anthropology* 54.1: 1–22

Scheper-Hughes, N. (2008) 'A Talent for Life: Reflections on Human Vulnerability and Resilience', *Ethnos* 73.1: 25–56

—— (1993) *Death Without Weeping: The Violence of Everyday Life in Brazil*, Berkeley: University of California Press

Wald, P. (2008) *Contagious: Cultures, Carriers, and the Outbreak Narrative*, Durham: Duke University Press

Whyte, S.R. (1997) *Questioning Misfortune: The Pragmatics of Uncertainty in Eastern Uganda*, Cambridge: Cambridge University Press

Wilkinson, A., Parker, M., Martineau, F., Leach, M. (2017) 'Engaging "Communities": Anthropological Insights from the West African Ebola Epidemic', *Philosophical Transactions of the Royal Society B* 372: 20160305, DOI: 10.1098/rstb.2016.0305

World Health Organization (WHO) (2019a) 'Prioritizing Diseases for Research and Development in Emergency Contexts', www.who.int/activities/prioritizing-diseases-for-research-and-development-in-emergency-contexts (accessed 13 February 2020)

—— (2019b) *Ebola Virus Disease – Democratic Republic of the Congo*, Disease Outbreak News: Update, www.who.int/csr/don/14-november-2019-ebola-drc/en/

—— (2018) *WHO's Work in Emergencies: Prepare, Prevent, Detect and Respond*, Health Emergencies Programme, Annual Report, Geneva: World Health Organization, www.who.int/emergencies/who-work-in-emergencies/en/ (accessed 13 February 2020)

—— (2017) *A Strategic Framework for Emergency Preparedness*, Geneva: World Health Organization

9

DISASTERS, HUMANITARIANISM AND EMERGENCIES

A politics of uncertainty

Mark Pelling, Detlef Müller-Mahn and John McCloskey

Introduction

A central tenet of disaster risk management is reducing uncertainties to manageable risks, such that, where possible, probabilities of outcomes are known or at least predictable. Thus, the starting points for research and policy are to reduce uncertainty through improved knowledge of hazard processes to enable better event forecasting, but also to understand better how information on risk is communicated and accessed, and the social and political processes that constrain what individuals and organisations can do with such information – since early warning needs early and inclusive action. This approach has delivered considerable gains in regions exposed to weather extremes, including coastal lands and rainfall-dependent agricultural communities.

One of the greatest global achievements for this style of risk-based science has been the reduction in the number of people killed and harmed by flood events since records began in the 1980s (UNISDR 2019). Global loss data are available from the 1980s to present, allowing long-term trend analysis over this period. This shows declining mortality even when the number of flood events has increased. Losses to property and people affected have increased over this period, indicating the further challenge of reducing risk that goes beyond effective evacuation. This success is as a direct outcome of reduced uncertainty across all aspects of flood warning and response drawing together inputs from natural and social sciences. This gain is especially impressive when seen alongside the increased number of reported flood events from all causes, and the increasing number of people made homeless and suffering property damage. Flood risk is increasing as more people and property are exposed to flood hazard, with climate change acting as a hazard multiplier, but reduced uncertainty in knowledge about the likelihood of outcomes and how to act on early warning has enabled more people to make decisions to avoid personal harm.

The success of this type of approach to reduce flood risk is important because it highlights the multiple factors required for success. Yet uncertainties are present in all areas of knowledge production and decision-making in the knowledge chain that underpins such early warnings. One of the key lessons from the success referred to is that reducing uncertainty in ways that can allow individuals to make decisions and avoid harm is best achieved through interdisciplinary knowledge production coupled with cross-sectoral policy action. The length of the knowledge production chain is captured well by the World Meteorological Organisation HiWeather project (http://hiweather.net) (Figure 9.1). This identifies six specific stages of technical expertise as components of a knowledge chain. At each step, different combinations of science are needed to address specific technical challenges, and so to better articulate knowledge and identify knowledge gaps to describe the significance of remaining known uncertainties. Each of these stages helps describe known uncertainty brought about by incomplete data, modelling and theoretical assumptions and biases in understanding and communication. Because knowledge to reduce risk is produced across multiple stages, additional uncertainty is introduced through the transfer or exchange of data, understanding and information from one site of expertise to another. Such exchanges often require data transformation, for example where model output and input work at different spatial scales or where additional variables have to be interpolated to allow analysis. Although uncertainties may of course not be reduced through such a knowledge chain, the hoped-for result is not a compounding of but a reduction in uncertainty in understanding for the end-user: the citizen at risk contemplating evacuation. It is worth noting the origin of Figure 9.1, which reflects the ambition of weather forecasters to make their work as relevant as possible to end-users. The result in this figure is a representation of a knowledge chain that is linear and emphasises formal scientific knowledge. This allows a clear delimitation of opportunities to improve the quality of early warnings – through each stage and bridges between them. It also prompts the question 'How would other actors view knowledge production?' from a more bottom-up viewpoint. For example, it might be that these stages are compressed into compound acts of assessment, often including informal or local knowledge based on experience. It is likely, from this perspective, that the final decision stage might be more central.

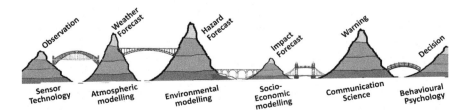

FIGURE 9.1 The knowledge chain for flood early warning
Source: Crown copyright (Golding *et al.* 2019)

The historical progression in disaster studies from a hazard to a people-centred approach, and more recently to an integrative and multidisciplinary framing where a range of epistemic logics has been recognised (including local knowledge), has increased awareness of uncertainties and the ambiguities buried deep in multiple knowledge production and communication efforts. More than this, the extension of disaster studies into interdisciplinary analysis (where physical and social science approaches are blended or synthesised) – for example in risk analysis that combines hazard likelihood with the susceptibility, coping and adaptation of people and their asset systems – has brought to the surface the political nature of knowledge. Science does not have a unique claim on legitimacy for knowledge production, even where its methods are more transparent and defendable. Local knowledge based on personal experience and indigenous knowledge rooted in cultural identity are increasingly recognised as being part of the conversation out of which knowledge becomes relevant to specific decision-makers' needs. Here the robustness and transparency of the scientific method is also key in bringing accountability to decision-making and confidence to action. The scientific method, with its roots in replicability and falsification of analysis, brings clarity to linear questions of cause and effect – as exemplified in Figure 9.1. Recent innovations in disaster science have pushed at the boundaries of complexity theory, where cause and effect are less clearly connected – with multiple intervening and dynamic variables. This makes scientific work less transparent to non-experts. A central dilemma facing disaster studies is how expert analysis interacts with other knowledge traditions in developing more integrated understandings.

Where different knowledge traditions are clear about embedded uncertainties and open to a reinterpretation of positions, together with evidence-based science, there is scope for a nuanced confrontation of uncertainty. Where science or other knowledge traditions reject each other's assumptions, value positions and findings, uncertainty is likely to be ignored and improved outcomes are more difficult to anticipate.

Uncertainty has become more visible as research has expanded its knowledge base through interdisciplinary and multidisciplinary work and the increasing inclusion of local/traditional knowledge. There is much debate on how to best do this, from weather forecasting in a daily news bulletin to flagging future climate scenarios integrated with specific economic futures. The latter places less emphasis on describing uncertainty as a qualifier on analysis and rather works in a constant state of contestation where few complex concepts like poverty, vulnerability, resilience or development have a concrete meaning or material expression.

The remainder of this chapter explores these two traditions from particular viewpoints, reflected in the authorship of this chapter. The next section, emerging from a social science perspective, examines the social construction of uncertainty and certitude within studies of social vulnerability and resilience in Africa, while the following section, taking a more physical science perspective, takes us from weather and climate science to an exploration of risk and uncertainty and the implications for earthquake science and modelling. Both sections reflect on a common set of themes outlined in Box 9.1, to which we return again in conclusion to tease out similarities and differences between these two traditions of disaster risk research.

BOX 9.1 FOUR AREAS OF QUESTIONING TO EXPLORE THE POSITION OF UNCERTAINTY IN DIFFERENT KNOWLEDGE PRODUCTION CONTEXTS

Knowledge: Where does uncertainty or ambiguity sit? Is it inherent within the methodologies deployed, inherited from external inputs or consequential through the use others make of knowledge and data that have been produced?

Communication: How, if at all, is uncertainty communicated? Is this a major or minor aspect? Is the balance right or are disciplinary norms and expectations for the communication of uncertainty in need of revision?

Response: If we accept that uncertainties are always present in science and decision-making then are there progressive or productive uses to which uncertainty can be put? What kinds of actors or discourses tend to dominate when the level of uncertainty is high? Can such actors be enabled to open space for more inclusive processes of knowledge production and progressive outcomes for knowledge application in decision-making?

Ethics: What are the ethical implications for researchers in managing uncertainty and its communication? Is the existing ethical approach right for the complexities we face in integrating physical and social science with local or indigenous knowledge?

A social science perspective: uncertainty as a challenge for disaster risk management in Africa

Uncertainty presents a serious challenge for disaster risk management because it impedes pre-emption. As a consequence, precaution becomes imperative but difficult to achieve. Disaster prevention and management require the reduction of uncertainty – or, more precisely, the translation of forms of uncertainty and ignorance into calculable probabilities (i.e. risk). But what if this is not possible? What if disaster risk management cannot avoid knowledge gaps and unpredictable events? Embracing uncertainty first and foremost requires an understanding of its causes and consequences. Situations characterised by uncertainty may originate from lack of knowledge and experience, unprecedented events or new and unpredictable conditions. Climate change is a major driver of newly emerging uncertainties, especially in poor countries. This section of the chapter focuses on the social construction of uncertainty in the context of climate change and natural disasters in Africa. The African continent is often portrayed as the continent that is most seriously affected by climate change due to its exposure to extreme events, high vulnerability and limited coping capacities (IPCC AR-5 2014). This raises a number of questions: How is uncertainty socially constructed and communicated? In which way are real and constructed uncertainties related? And how does this matter for disaster risk management? These themes are explored in the four sub-sections below, linking to the questions posed in Box 9.1.

Uncertainty, just like risk, can be viewed from a realist and from a constructivist perspective. The realist perspective claims to build upon scientifically produced 'facts'. It acknowledges that some aspects of the future are simply not predictable, such as events related to tipping points, complex human–environment relations and unforeseeable system changes. The constructivist perspective, on the other hand, embraces people´s perceptions, imaginations and feelings of unknown futures (Cooper and Pratten 2015). It refers to the ways in which individuals or societies live with uncertainty, how they get along with insufficient knowledge and how they navigate their future without a clear vision of what to expect. From a constructivist view, the shapes and contents of both knowledge and uncertainty are partly constituted not just by 'the facts' (as highlighted in the realist view), but by social orders acting on the processes of knowledge production. In other words: to a realist, knowledge (and uncertainty) are effectively shaped solely by the conditions of the focal objects; to a constructivist they are also shaped by the conditions of the subjects of knowledge.

The distinction between realist and constructivist concepts is important because human behaviour does not so much respond to the world as it is, but rather as it is perceived. In practice, however, 'real' and 'socially constructed' uncertainties are difficult to differentiate, as can be seen in the context of climate change.

Climate-related uncertainties in Africa can be traced back to diverse origins (IPCC AR-5 2014; Niang *et al.* 2014). First, the future effects of climate change on the continent are expected to be highly heterogeneous in space. As a consequence, place-specific predictions are often quite inaccurate. While most of the continent is likely to receive less rainfall, eastern Africa will probably receive more – but highly erratic – rains. Second, model-based forecasts of future climate change in Africa are less refined than in other parts of the world due to a relatively weak data base and short time of observation. Third, environmental change is caused not by climate alone but by complex human–environment interactions that cannot be predicted. Fourth, societal transformations play an essential role in future disaster risks and coping capacities in Africa, but they are not predictable. And, finally, cross-scalar influences and power relations are decisive for local agency and the struggle for control.

A recent IPCC special report mentions the impact of climate change on growing disparities and social disintegration in Africa (IPCC 2019). It leaves no doubt that there has been an increased frequency of droughts in African drylands over the past few decades, which, together with population pressure, exacerbates land degradation. This is affecting the productivity of land use systems in large parts of the continent, leading to a deterioration of food security and local livelihoods. The report, in turn, draws attention to regional heterogeneity, cascading risks, telecoupling[1] and socially differentiated effects on women, the elderly and the poor (IPCC 2019: 17).

To give an example, the Afar pastoralists in Ethiopia have a long experience of living with multiple risks, including highly variable rainfall, recurring droughts and famines, sudden outbursts of violent clashes and disruptions of trade connections and markets due to changing international relations between Ethiopia, Eritrea, Djibouti and Somalia (Müller-Mahn *et al.* 2010). The overlapping livelihood challenges are today further enhanced by newly emerging uncertainties. Rainfall anomalies are occurring more frequently. The expansion of irrigated farms and new infrastructure reduces access to pasture lands, while the uncontrollable invasion of alien species undermines rangeland quality. Under these conditions, the Afar feel that they are surrounded by enemies. They experience uncertainty not only in terms of unpredictability, but – worse than that – as a situation in which they are losing control over what is happening, and the capacity to cope.

The social construction of uncertainty is based on communication among actors about shared future visions. In situations where the outcome of ongoing processes cannot be foreseen, and where future conditions remain concealed, decision-making lacks clear reference points. People are therefore searching for collective orientations. They rely on each other in order to obtain clues for decision-making. Communication over uncertainties may lead to 'fictional expectations' (Beckert 2016): in other words, shared imaginations regarding what is going to happen in the future. These joint expectations are essential for making people act collectively. By sharing visions of the future, people come to an understanding about what may be expected, or feared, and how to prepare for it.

Experts and lay people frame uncertainty differently, which has consequences for how uncertainties are responded to. While experts encounter uncertainty as a limitation of scientific methods, forecasts and planning, others instead view it as a quotidian experience, something they cannot influence – and thus have to take for granted. Against this backdrop, communication among and between experts and lay people becomes important in order to find common understandings and orientations.

To give another example, a case study in Côte d'Ivoire revealed how farming communities respond to climate-related uncertainties that go beyond the 'normal' rainfall variability of previous years (Müller-Mahn *et al.* 2020). Over the past two decades many farmers adopted new crop varieties that are more resilient to dry spells, or they shifted cultivation to areas with better water supplies. But today the increasingly unpredictable onset of the rainy season makes it extremely difficult for farmers to decide when to start cultivation. They cannot fully rely on traditional experience, nor do they trust the weather forecasts. While people are waiting for the beginning of the rainy season, the feeling of uncertainty among community members passes through stages of unrest, hope and despair. People communicate intensively over their assessment of the situation, with the effect that some simply follow the practices they know, while others feel more inclined towards new strategies to secure household incomes outside of agriculture.

How can the uncertainties of drought and famine be responded to in practice? Development cooperation and humanitarian assistance have developed a number of instruments for that purpose, which aim at strengthening local resilience against drought, or improving external assistance to alleviate its consequences. An example of a resilience-building approach is the drought cycle management model. It provides a disaster risk management strategy that uses the periods between droughts to prepare for the next one by better linking activities of development, relief and rehabilitation. The approach is based on an analysis of the underlying causes of vulnerability at household levels and the dynamic pressures that enhance vulnerability further, and an assessment of coping capacities and disaster preparedness (Brüntrup and Tsegai 2017).

An example of improved external assistance is the Famine Early Warning Systems Network that is used for the organisation of famine relief. FEWSNET is an information platform that provides data on current and expected food insecurities at country and regional levels for most parts of the world, including all of Africa (see: https://fews.net/). It was established by the US Agency for International Development in 1985, and it has since helped to manage food crises more effectively by analysing data on rainfalls, yields, markets, prices and regional food stocks. These data are combined with observations on local livelihoods, trade and the political environment. FEWSNET publishes monthly bulletins that classify the observed state of food insecurity, from stress to emergency and famine. Such early warning systems use scenarios that link the observation of present food security assessments with informed assumptions about future events. Based on these assumptions and future scenarios, it is possible to prepare for emerging crises, for example by concentrating food stocks in regions that are expected to be most seriously affected.

However, critical voices point out that the combination of drought cycle management and famine early warning is insufficient to overcome the challenges of uncertainty. Managing the uncertainties of drought and famine in Africa more effectively would require a better integration between short-term humanitarian assistance, long-term development and political activities to support peace and human security. This is often lacking, especially in areas affected by violent conflicts, such as Somalia (Medinilla *et al.* 2019).

In designing responses to climate uncertainty, ethical implications arise concerning the acknowledgement of local knowledge, felt needs and local perspectives. Uncertainty does not only present a challenge for the future, it also represents an opportunity: can uncertainty open up new spaces for alternative developments, innovation and desirable futures?

Uncertainty in Africa, like anywhere else, may concern all aspects of life, with negative as well as positive connotations (Cooper and Pratten 2015). This raises the question whether there is anything special about uncertainty in Africa. The understanding of uncertainty in Africa is embedded in the historical relations between the global North and South. This relationship has stimulated controversial debates about the dynamics of contemporary world society, and about uncertainty as a distinguishing characteristic of societies in the global North and South. Current debates on the concepts of 'risk society' (Beck 1992) and 'imagined futures' (Beckert 2016) are informed by the historical experience of the industrialised North, where technological risks are seen as unavoidable side-effects of modernity. It would, however, be misleading to view the global South simply in juxtaposition to this, as the realm of uncertainty, where future changes in nature and society cannot be properly predicted and managed (Bloemertz *et al.* 2012).

A physical science perspective: the challenges of forecasting earthquakes

On 28 March 2005 the magnitude 8.7 Nias earthquake ruptured the Sunda megathrust fault where the Indo-Australian plate is being forced under the Eurasian plate. The earthquake, at the time the fourth biggest ever instrumentally recorded, produced strong shaking in the islands of the Sumatran forearc and along the densely populated west Sumatran coastline, causing significant damage and more than 1,000 deaths (Hsu *et al.* 2005). While the impact of such a large earthquake was not surprising, and perhaps less severe than might have been expected, this earthquake was unique in that its approximate location and energy release had been forecast in a paper that was published in an international peer-reviewed science journal only 11 days previously (McCloskey *et al.* 2008). On the one hand, this forecast could be viewed as a confirmation of the physical understanding of crustal physics that enabled it, but, on the other, for many – including its authors – it confirmed the fundamental intractability of earthquake prediction: a step change in precision from forecasting where, when and how big future events might be.

Earthquakes communicate by stress transfer. A large earthquake deforms the earth's crust around it, changing the stress field on neighbouring earthquake faults (Stein 1999; King *et al.* 1994), bringing some closer to failure and triggering aftershocks, some of which can be very large. In the decade before the Nias event, physical scientists had developed techniques for calculating this so-called Coulomb stress and identifying particular faults that were made more dangerous by the occurrence of any large earthquake (Hubert-Ferrari *et al.* 2000; Nalbant *et al.* 1998). Statistical assessments of aftershock sequences had repeatedly demonstrated that these calculations had the ability to explain the distributions of triggered events (e.g. Toda *et al.* 2011). Estimation of the Coulomb stress from the great Sumatra-Andaman earthquake, which produced the Indian Ocean tsunami, resolved onto neighbouring active fault segments, combined with considerations of their seismic history, allowed researchers to suggest an increased risk that was confirmed by the Nias event.

Remarkably, the causative stress change was less than 0.1 megaPascal (Nalbant *et al.* 2005), which is less than the stress caused by a handshake. The precise mechanism whereby this geologically imperceptible perturbation broke the grip holding some small part of the opposing sides of the fault together is not properly understood, but the resulting non-linear amplification of the rupture process eventually broke an area of 50,000km^2, displacing the fault by as much as 15 metres and releasing energy equivalent to 1,000 times the bomb dropped by the US on Hiroshima. This avalanche of energy release was probably initiated 20km below the seafloor. The following paragraphs draw on this case, and other earthquake events, to explore the set of questions outlined earlier, from a physical science perspective.

Geophysical scientists frequently distinguish two sources of uncertainty. Aleatory, or statistical, uncertainty results from lack of knowledge of the time-varying state of a system – here, the precise distribution of the stress on, and the strength of, the Nias fault segment, the precise distribution of slip on the Sumatran-Andaman earthquake, and the precise history of tectonic stress accumulation on the plate interface. Epistemic – or systematic – uncertainty, by contrast, emerges from an insufficient understanding of the physical processes that govern the earthquake event. In this case, tectonic convergence of the plates increases their mutual stress for hundreds of years and interactions with neighbouring earthquakes increase it rapidly and locally. Thus, the forecast of the Nias event was successful because the epistemic uncertainty in the problem was relatively small, the seismic and tectonic history were reasonably well understood, and the physical link between cause (the Sumatra-Andaman earthquake) and effect (the Nias earthquake) was well enough described by the equations governing the Coulomb stress calculations.

Perhaps more importantly, the problem was sufficiently well posed to promote the epistemic clarity of the physical process above the aleatory uncertainty in the initial conditions. While uncertainty in the precise initial conditions precluded specification of the exact hypocentral location, and lack of knowledge of the loading history precluded specification of the event origin time, the large area of interaction identified, and the lack of specificity in the forecast, cast the net wide enough that many different futures were consistent with a successful forecast. This does not imply any duplicity. Rather, it reflects a careful consideration of the physical process (through accurate calculation of the Coulomb stress resolved on large areas of appropriate active structures with a known seismic and tectonic history) maximising the chances of an accurate forecast over an unspecified time into the future.

While the location and size of a magnitude 8.7 earthquake being deterministically forecast 11 days before it happened might be considered a success of physical science, this success came at a very high price. Firstly, this case demonstrates that large earthquakes can be triggered by almost infinitesimally small perturbations, and that, despite the underpinning determinism of the process, this – paradoxically – probably precludes deterministic forecasting of particular events. The precision with which the initial conditions are required to be known 20km below the ocean floor makes such prediction of this, or any other, rupture initiation an impossibility. Secondly, the non-linear amplification of the initial rupture required to produce a massive failure is controlled by the detail of the stress on the Nias fault segment and recent observations expose the fractal complexity of earthquake slip, and suggest that slip, even after rupture initiation, is also inherently unpredictable. The earthquake is one possible outcome of a game of tectonic bagatelle and successive events on the same fault are completely different (Lindsay *et al.* 2016; Nic Bhloscaidh *et al.* 2015; Philibosian *et al.* 2014).

This – now rarely disputed – observation provides the final blow to hopes of useful deterministic earthquake forecasting. If it were possible to identify segments of active faults with a high likelihood of rupture in the near future, and if, as in the Nias case, previous history made it possible to estimate the likely magnitude of the impending earthquake, even then we would be unlikely to make useful forecasts. Consider, for example, how tsunamis are generated by megathrust earthquakes. Strain, accumulated over hundreds of years, depresses the near-shore sea floor by metres and large earthquakes rupture the plate interface, allowing this century-scale strain energy to be released in seconds, forcing the seafloor upward over a vast area and producing a 10 billion tonne bulge in the sea surface. The collapse of this bulge generates a tsunami, the impact of which might be expected to be related simply to the earthquake magnitude. However, several studies (McCloskey *et al.* 2008; Geist 2002) have shown that this is not the case. Again, the non-linear amplification, this time of small differences in the relationship between water depth and earthquake slip, result in very different impacts when viewed, for example, from the coastal city of Padang in western Sumatra. Almost identical earthquakes on the same segment of the off-shore fault might produce a 50cm wave for the city or a 5m wave – killing no one or possibly hundreds of thousands (Borrero *et al.* 2006). Similar numerical experiments examining the shaking produced by possible earthquake scenarios for Istanbul show similar divergence, both in wave amplitude measured at particular places and in estimated fatalities.

These observations have important philosophical as well as practical implications for the application of physical science to earthquake risk management. Despite undeniable advances in the understanding of the physical processes underlying large earthquakes, several seismic butterfly effects ensure that the outcome will always be a surprise (cf. Lay 2012). Consider a world in which earthquake physics was completely known and where Laplacian determinism[2] would only require accurate assessment of the initial conditions fully to constrain the future (and the past). Even then, the hope that these initial conditions might be estimated with sufficient accuracy to yield actionable forecasts by the techniques of geology and geophysics are dashed by Lorenzian exponential[3] (or even super-exponential) divergence of dynamical trajectories. The immutable aleatory uncertainty in our observations, no matter how good our epistemic understanding, forbids useful prediction of the outcome. In this world, conservative estimates of impact might wildly underestimate the consequences of particular decisions and unfulfilled forecasts of the worst impacts would leave physical scientists exposed to accusations of crying wolf, fundamentally undermining their collective credibility.

What are the implications of this perspective for physical science in earthquake risk management? Many physical scientists now recoil from traditional pronouncements made with certainty and clarity that effectively made science and engineering the decision-makers in many development environments (cf. Chiarabba *et al.* 2009). For some, this is a cause for celebration but, spurious as this over-confidence might have been, the potential vacuum thus created is unlikely to be filled by better assessments of risk. Allowing this, the challenge becomes a reassessment of what can be learned by scientific risk estimation, and finding a more nuanced, and perhaps a more modest, role for its insights.

In the Global Challenges Research Fund Urban Disaster Risk Hub (www. tomorrowcities.org), attempts are being made to use the enduring convening power of physical science simulation, rather than its certainty. In this approach, simulations of the consequences of particular development choices are used to convene multidisciplinary teams of decision-makers who provide multiple perspectives to illuminate complex development decisions. Rather than usurping decision authority, science now becomes a tool for decision support. Rather than scientists providing definitive forecasts, they relegate the consequences of immutable aleatory uncertainty and promote the epistemic certainty of well-constrained physical principles to a supporting role in a multidisciplinary process. Time will tell if this is a more effective, sustainable role for geophysical science.

Conclusion

Responding to the questions posed in Box 9.1, the accounts of uncertainty presented here, from quite different perspectives and in very different contexts, agree on four fundamental properties of knowledge production in the context of disaster risk management and international development:

Uncertainty is prevalent throughout disaster research. Uncertainty is a product of the complexities of physical and social processes and their interactions. There are some areas that are more predictable than others: flood risk as a consequence of upstream river catchment rainfall and river level rise is highly predictable when all catchment characteristics are known in detail. However, anticipating the probabilities of outcomes becomes difficult where non-linear physical or social processes distance observable phenomena from potential outcomes – in time, space and scale. It is much harder to predict flooding accurately in urban catchments due to the complexity and dynamism of land use, or to predict earthquakes based on observable changes in crustal stress.

As knowledge has grown, so has awareness of the uncertainties that constrain this knowledge. Researchers have been very successful in their mission to resolve knowledge gaps in the understanding and predictability of social and physical systems behaviour. However, the history of disaster studies shows that greater depth of knowledge, while offering specific insights, tends then to reveal further the complexity, context-specificity and ambiguity of revealed knowledge.

Uncertainties are likely to continue into the future and so must be embraced. Research that seeks to push forward the frontiers of knowledge is key to scientific endeavour and its social contribution. It is tempting for researchers to claim to have reduced uncertainty through their work. For research findings to be useful to society it is important also to recognise that uncertainties remain even as knowledge grows. The pressures on academics to publish results that emphasise comprehensiveness and certainty does not allow broader uncertainties embedded in question framing, methodology and interpretation to be fully expressed. This is compounded in aggregate reviews and integrated assessments, where uncertainties may be systematically overlooked. This challenge is especially important for disaster risk studies, which are often interdisciplinary or multidisciplinary. With knowledge crossing domains of expertise it becomes more difficult for researchers to bring expert judgement to questions of uncertainty embedded in research processes and yet not made explicit through publication or other formal reporting.

Managing the presentation of uncertainty is a challenge for scientists working with policy-makers and the public, who look to science to reduce uncertainty. The case of L'Aquila in Italy, where seven public officials were tried for having allegedly given out misleading and incorrect information to the public before the 6 April 2009 earthquake, has highlighted how exposed scientific comment (and scientists) can be when knowledge is taken into politicised and emotive contexts (Alexander 2014). There remains a popular assumption that the role of science is to make the world more understandable, not to reveal its uncertainties. Indeed, the public legitimacy of scientists as 'speakers of truth through evidence' rests on this. As science moves more deeply into researching the behaviour of non-linear systems and processes of production of risks and uncertainties, so the gap between popular (and political) expectations of science, and the actual practice of science, grows.

These four fundamentals of uncertainty within the context of disaster studies reveal an increasing tendency for science to move from providing society with increased certainty and having its legitimacy built on bringing clarity, towards a situation where natural, physical and social science is one arbiter among other arbiters of diverse knowledges that are always partial and contingent. This challenge matches the movement of science from providing linear to providing non-linear conceptualisations of nature and society. The value of natural and physical science in offering a transparent and robust way into the uncertainty of non-linear systems, and a key challenge for the future, is to continue to communicate the value of the contribution of a broader interdisciplinary science. This does not mean that only the formal natural-physical scientific methodology is legitimate – but it does emphasise the importance of a particular type of quantitative rigour in the presentation of underlying conceptual and methodological frameworks, and the ability to communicate these in non-specialist language to allow such contributions to grow into the interdisciplinary spaces demanded of complex and non-linear phenomena.

At the same time, there is a danger that the technical expertise needed to understand such cutting-edge research could push this type of science into elite spaces – with only experts being seen as having the analytical tools to make sense of uncertainty; or that the burden for decision-making under uncertainty is unreasonably placed into the hands of local actors with constrained access to appropriate interpretive tools. Instead, researchers have a responsibility to work with uncertainty in disaster management as a mechanism for the levelling of formal expertise. Realising this opportunity is perhaps the greatest challenge facing contemporary research that aims to make a difference in the world.

Notes

1 Telecoupling refers to interactions between distant social-ecological systems (Hull and Liu 2018).
2 The mathematician Pierre Simon Laplace argued, in 1814, that if we knew the precise location and momentum of every atom in the universe, the entire past and future could be calculated from the laws of classical mechanics. Thus, if we knew the physical law perfectly (no epistemic uncertainty), knowledge of the precise state of the fault would allow the perfect description of all past and future events.
3 Ed Lorenz was the meteorologist who, in his paper of 1963, first described the butterfly effect. Tiny changes in initial conditions are amplified through dynamics to render the future extremely unpredictable.

References

Alexander, D. (2014) 'Communicating Earthquake Risk to the Public: The Trial of the L'Aquila Seven', *Natural Hazards* 72.2: 1159–1173

Beck, U. (1992) *Risk Society. Towards a New Modernity*, London: Sage

Beckert, J. (2016) *Imagined Futures: Fictional Expectations and Capitalist Dynamics*, Cambridge, Massachusetts: Harvard University Press

Bloemertz, L., Doevenspeck, M., Macamo, E. and Müller-Mahn, D. (eds) (2012) *Risk and Africa. Multi-Disciplinary Empirical Approaches.* Berlin, Münster: Lit

Brüntrup, M. and Tsegai, D. (2017) Drought Adaptation and Resilience in Developing Countries, Briefing Paper, No. 23/2017, *Deutsches Institut für Entwicklungspolitik* (DIE), Bonn, http://hdl.handle.net/10419/199811 (accessed 11 February 2020)

Borrero, J.C., Sieh, K., Chlieh, M. and Synolakis, C.E. (2006) 'Tsunami Inundation Modelling for Western Sumatra', *PNAS* 103.52: 19673–19677

Chiarabba, C., Amato, A., Anselmi, M., Baccheschi, P., Bianchi, I., Cattaneo, M., Cecere, G., Chiaraluce, L., Ciaccio, M.G., De Gori, P., De Luca, G., Di Bona, M., Di Stefano, R., Faenza, L., Govoni, A., Improta, L., Lucente, F.P., Marchetti, A., Margheriti, L., Mele, F., Michelini, A., Monachesi, G., Moretti, M., Pastori, M., Piana Agostinetti, N., Piccinini, D., Roselli, P., Seccia, D. and Valoroso, L. (2009) 'The 2009 L'Aquila (Central Italy) MW6.3 earthquake: Main Shock and Aftershocks', *Geophysical Research Letters* 36: L18308

Cooper, E. and Pratten, D. (eds) (2015) *Ethnographies of Uncertainty in Africa*, London: Palgrave Macmillan

Geist, E.L. (2002) 'Complex Earthquake Rupture and Local Tsunamis', *Journal of Geophysics Research* 107.B5: 2086

Golding, B., Ebert, E., Mittermaier, M., Scolobig, A., Panchuk, S., Ross, C. and Johnston, D. (2019) 'A Value Chain Approach to Optimising Early Warning Systems'. Contributing paper to GAR2019. UNDRR, www.preventionweb.net/publications/view/65828

Hsu, Y.J., Simons, M., Avouac, J.P., Galetzka, J., Sieh, K., Chlieh, M., Natawidjaja, D., Prawirodirdjo, L. and Bock, Y. (2005) 'Frictional Afterslip Following the 2005 Nias-Simeulue Earthquake, Sumatra', *Science* 435.7046: 1921–1926

Hubert-Ferrari, A., Barka, A., Jacques, E., Nalbant, S.S., Meyer, B., Armijo, R., Tapponnier, P. and King, G.C. (2000) 'Seismic Hazard in the Marmara Sea Region Following the 17 August 1999 Izmit Earthquake', *Nature* 404.6775: 269–273

Hull, V. and Liu, J. (2018) Telecoupling: A New Frontier for Global Sustainability. *Ecology and Society* 23.4:41

Intergovernmental Panel on Climate Change (2019) 'Climate Change and Land. an IPCC Special Report on Climate Change, Desertification, Land Degradation, Sustainable Land

Management, Food Security, and Greenhouse Gas Fluxes in Terrestrial Ecosystems', www.ipcc.ch/srccl/

—— (2014) 'Summary for Policymakers', in *Climate Change 2014: Impacts, Adaptation and Vulnerability – Contributions of the Working Group II to the Fifth Assessment Report*: 1–32 www.ipcc.ch/report/ar5/wg2/

King, C.P., Stein, R.S. and Lin, J. (1994) 'Static Stress Changes and the Triggering of Earthquakes', *Bulletin of the Seismological Society of America* 84.3: 935–953

Lay, T. (2012) 'Why Giant Earthquakes Keep Catching us Out', *Nature* 483: 149–150

Lindsay, A., McCloskey, J. and Nic Bhloscaidh, M. (2016) 'Using a Genetic Algorithm to Estimate the Details of Earthquake Slip Distributions from Point Surface Displacements', *Journal of Geophysical Research Solid Earth* 121.3: 1796–1820

Luhmann, N. (2002) *Risk. A Sociological Theory*, New York: Routledge

McCloskey J., Antonioli, A., Piatanesi, A., Sieh, K., Steacy, S. and Nalbant, S. (2008) 'Tsunami Threat in the Indian Ocean from a Future Megathrust Earthquake West of Sumatra', *EPSL* 265.1: 61–81

Medinilla, A., Shiferaw, L.T. and Veron, P. (2019) *Think Local. Governance, Humanitarian Aid, Development and Peacebuilding in Somalia*, European Centre for Development Policy Management Discussion Paper No. 246, ECDPM, Brussels

Müller-Mahn, D., Moure, M., Gebreyes, M. (2020, forthcoming): 'Climate Change, the Politics of Anticipation, and Future Riskscapes in Africa', *Cambridge Journal of Regions, Economy, and Society*

Müller-Mahn, D., Rettberg, S. and Alemu, D.D. (2010) 'Pathways and Dead Ends of Pastoral Development Among the Afar and Karrayu in Ethiopia', *European Journal of Development Research* 22.5: 660–677

Nalbant, S.S., Hubert-Ferrari, A. and King, G.C.P. (1998) 'Stress Coupling Between Earthquakes in Northwest Turkey and the North Aegean Sea', *Journal of Geophysics Research* 103.B10: 24469–24486

Nalbant, S., Steacy, S., Sieh, K., Natawadjaja, D. and McCloskey, J. (2005) 'Earthquake Risk on the Sunda Trench', *Nature* 435: 756–757

Niang, I., Ruppel, O.C., Abdrabo, M.A., Essel, A., Lennard, C., Padgham, J. and Urquhart, P. (2014) 'Africa', in V.R. Barros, C.B. Field, D.J. Dokken, M.D. Mastrandrea, K.J. Mach, T.E. Bilir, M. Chatterjee, K.L. Ebi, Y.O. Estrada, R.C. Genova, B. Girma, E.S. Kissel, A.N. Levy, S. MacCracken, P.R. Mastrandrea and L.L. White (eds) *Climate Change 2014: Impacts, Adaptation, and Vulnerability. Part B: Regional Aspects. Contribution of Working Group II to the Fifth Assessment Report of the Intergovernmental Panel on Climate Change*, Cambridge, United Kingdom and New York, NY, USA: Cambridge University Press

Nic Bhloscaidh, M., McCloskey, J., Naylor, M., Murphy and S., Lindsay, A. (2015) 'Reconstruction of the Slip Distributions in Historical Earthquakes on the Sunda Megathrust, W. Sumatra', *Geophysical Journal International* 202.2: 1339–1361

Philibosian, B., Sieh, K., Avouac, J-P., Natawidjaja, D.H., Chiang, H-W., Wu, C-C., Perfettini, H., Shen, C-C., Daryono, M.R. and Suwargadi B.W. (2014) 'Rupture and Variable Coupling Behavior of the Mentawai Segment of the Sunda Megathrust During the Supercycle Culmination of 1797 to 1833', *Journal of Geophysical Research. Solid Earth* 119.9: 7258–7287

Stein, R. (1999) 'The Role of Stress Transfer in Earthquake Occurrence', *Nature* 402: 605–609

Toda, S., Lin, J. and Stein, R.S. (2011) 'Using the 2011 M_w 9.0 off the Pacific Coast of Tohoku Earthquake to Test the Coulomb Stress Triggering Hypothesis and to Calculate Faults Brought Closer to Failure', *Earth Planet Sp* 63: 39

United Nations International Strategy for Disaster Reduction (2019) *Global Assessment Report 2019*, https://gar.unisdr.org/report-2019

10

INTERTWINING THE POLITICS OF UNCERTAINTY, MOBILITY AND IMMOBILITY

Dorte Thorsen

Introduction

The idea of uncertainty lingers beneath mobilities involving the search for work, better fortunes and different lives. This is regardless of whether these mobilities involve short-term circular labour migration or have no temporal limits, or whether they traverse regional or transnational spaces. But the conception of how uncertainty and mobility are linked, and with what outcome, varies.

From one perspective, the combination of uncertainty and risk in the so-called sending countries instigates mobility. People are forced to leave their home areas to counter poverty and deficiencies in opportunity – what is often spoken about as the root causes of mobility. From the perspective of the so-called host countries, the influx of (certain types of) migrants is perceived potentially to unsettle the existing state-of-affairs. Strategies to mitigate this risk attempt to deter migrants by informing potential migrants about the dangers encountered when crossing borders undocumented, and by creating an hostile environment in which migrants are unable to achieve their goals or the costs of trying to do so become too high. A third perspective is that of migrants themselves. Although they are not at all a homogenous group, and their experiences are differentiated by race, ethnicity, class, gender and age, migrants have in common that uncertainty can create barriers and be productive at the same time. At the individual level, uncertainty can be 'a social resource [that] can be used to negotiate insecurity, conduct and create relationships, and act as a source for imagining the future with the hopes and fears that entails' (Cooper and Pratten 2015: 2).

The way that risk and uncertainty are conceptualised in these three perspectives is inherently social and political, and it is important to recognise that institutions of different types are central in producing *and* resisting uncertainty. On the one hand, we have a global political economy of deep structural inequality that permits the angst of publics and policy-makers to set the agenda for how mobilities are understood. This perspective undergirds restrictive regimes of mobility and hardened border controls. And it denies legal mobilities to an increasing proportion of populations in the global South, cutting them off from ways of achieving a better life for themselves and their families (Kleist 2016). On the other hand, we have informal institutions – such as families, marriage, social networks – that do not figure prominently in policy discussions of uncertainty, despite the fact that these informal institutions are just as central in shaping the distribution of risk, uncertainty and opportunity (Thorsen 2017). Being very diverse, and inherently socio-cultural, these institutions contribute to the contours of uncertainty in quite a different manner.

This chapter is the outcome of a roundtable discussion exploring how the politics of preventing (irregular) migration and migrants' subtle practices of contesting the power of states intersect with the fundamental sentiments of contemporary mobilities: hope, anticipation, precarity and disappointment. The contributors[1] to the roundtable discussion study mobilities, immobilities and migration in Africa to illuminate the larger issues of social change, political economy and material cultures. Reflecting long-term and deep engagements with the field, this chapter leans on phenomenological approaches to explore a lived politics of uncertainty in migrants' life-worlds.

The chapter starts by reflecting on how migration policies produce a mobility paradox for many Africans, who project their ideas about the good life onto other places, and how this paradox spills over into the capacity to hope. The following section examines the disconnect between information campaigns to prevent irregular mobilities and the persistent actions among irregular migrants to realise the hoped-for future. Then, with a focus on gender, the chapter discusses the influence of the state and informal institutions on individuals' agency.

Contours of uncertainty and hope in African mobilities

Policies and interventions surrounding mobility have become increasingly centred on management, prevention and crisis control over the past few decades. Although labour markets globally thrive on the circulation of workers, the dominant rhetoric intimates an uncontrolled over-supply of labour, often of the wrong type, which in turn nourishes discursive distinctions between wanted and unwanted migrants (Fassin 2011; Squire 2011). In this language, mobility is associated with risk and uncertainty in countries and regions perceived to be at the receiving end of migratory flows, and this discourse sanctions a technocratic approach that seeks to stem the influx of unwanted migrants.

Although the dominant rhetoric is a product of politics in the global North, it is not foreign in the African context. For decades, foreign nationals have been labelled as irregular migrants, their local mobility has been curbed and expulsions of migrants have been articulated as part of national security concerns during conflict or crisis, or as part of broader efforts to curb migration (Adepoju 2005; Bredeloup and Zongo 2005). Migrants across Africa have experienced a hostile environment – their identity papers and residence cards are inspected at random by state authorities and others, who regularly demand levies whether the papers are incomplete or not (Bredeloup 2012; Landau and Freemantle 2010; Whitehouse 2009). 'Irregularity' and 'illegality' in these cases is a political construction that is used to criminalise and exclude certain groups of migrants (Bredeloup 2012; Inda 2011).

However, the rhetoric that has mushroomed in regional and local discourses on cross-border mobilities in sub-Saharan Africa is not about expulsion. Since 2000, strategic advocacy by Northern states and agreements such as the Cotonou Agreement and the Rabat Process, which focus on the relationships between the EU and Africa, have tied the patrol of European borders into development assistance (Mazzella and Perrin 2019; Aguillon 2018). These compacts impel African countries to formulate national migration strategies and legislate about permissible and non-permissible mobilities of their citizens (Glick Schiller and Salazar 2013). Through controlling its subjects, the state becomes actively implied in the distribution of hope, by facilitating some types of mobilities but not others and, in some countries, by regulating the costs of regular migration.

The tightening of borders has happened at a time when rising inequalities globally and locally have paved the way for new uncertainties and disenchantment with the *status quo*. Yearning for a different type of life relates to aspirations to acquire purchasing power and upward social mobility, but there is also a more existential side to mobility: discovering other places and other life conditions (Awedoba and Hahn 2014; Bredeloup 2014). The shrinking of legal mobility opportunities and the rising popularity of projecting ideas of what constitutes 'the good life' onto Europe, the Middle East or elsewhere amounts to a mobility paradox for many African migrants (Kleist and Thorsen 2016).

And yet, the preference in the global labour market for temporary legal mobilities to plug labour gaps offers opportunities, often to new categories of migrants with the desired skills, gender and age. As national regimes of mobility target several types of mobilities, including that of their own citizens, this shift is premised on states allowing their subjects to accept overseas opportunities. Moreover, since new mobilities generate wide and deep repercussions in regard to the social fabric of migrants' home communities, a shift also requires that the gatekeepers of informal institutions accept that normative boundaries for what hitherto has been seen as appropriate behaviour are pushed (e.g. in Ethiopia – Thorsen *et al.* forthcoming; Fernandez 2020). Additional dimensions are thus added to uncertainty and the mobility paradox, in as much as the outcome of mobility often varies between different categories of migrants.

For many people in Africa, and especially those from resource-poor backgrounds, mobility for work is an important model of realising a different and better life. It is premised on hope. According to Ernst Bloch (1972) hope is an horizon of opportunity and limitation. In other words, hope encompasses the potentiality of a future elsewhere, along with a degree of uncertainty because both the future and the qualities of elsewhere are unknown. For migrants and their families, the potentiality of mobility is within the realm of the imaginable. Hope inspires action, but entails waiting. It requires migrants and their relatives to cope with difficulties and journeys that have high costs, in anticipation of the future. However, hope can be disappointed. The inherent uncertainty means that hope always has a grain of doubt about achieving the hoped-for future, or having the capacity to achieve it (Bachelet 2016; Kleist 2016; Mar 2005).

In the contexts of West Africa and the Horn of Africa, migratory projects are rooted in a shared expectation of mobility being a means of economic security and social mobility after some time of waiting. Hope vested in both regular and irregular mobility is individual and at the same time collective. Adding an extra layer to the idea of hope, I return to the point made above about the role of formal and informal institutions in producing and resisting uncertainty and potential. In Ghassan Hage's conceptualisation, a collective form of hope, societal hope, is produced in societies or (transnational) networks in a specific social and historical context. The core content of what constitutes societal hope is shared, but hope is not distributed equally. Institutions like the state, society or a transnational network provide a mechanism for evaluating who belongs to the distributional network, in which way and to what degree (Hage and Papadopoulos 2004; Hage 2003).

In exploring a politics of uncertainty in migrants' life-worlds, we need to bear in mind that their horizons of societal hope result from an amalgam of sources. While migrants and prospective migrants may feel the lightness of being able to access opportunities or the pressure of obstacles to mobility issued by the state, it is important to explore which state. Migrants are subjected to multiple state authorities: from their homeland, to their current and possibly to their future place of abode. Likewise, they draw on diverse informal distributors of dominant forms of societal hope: the family and social networks of different kinds, stretching transnationally and relaying different experiences. In combination, we begin to see the complex intertwining of several dominant forms of societal hope, which may generate or be a response to uncertainties.

The following sections explore how this intertwining materialises in the mobility paradox, and how it shapes the distribution among migrants and their families of potentialities and uncertainties across race, gender and age.

Politics of uncertainty in the mobility paradox

Contemporary mobilities are increasingly inscribed in restrictive regimes of mobility and much effort is spent on deterring so-called irregular migrants. The dominant idea that has lingered among policy-makers and practitioners for quite some time is that such prospective migrants are ignorant. Thus, information campaigns that highlight the risks, dangers and uncertainties in irregular mobilities are believed to dampen the interest in going. This is a fundamental misunderstanding. It is based on an assumption that many prospective migrants are unaware of the risks incurred along the overland and sea routes travelled. This way of thinking also makes implicit links to a conceptualisation of migrants as individual actors deceived by criminal smugglers.

Evidence from West Africa and the Horn of Africa reveals that many of the migrants taking these irregular paths have migrated several times and they know that the journey can be uncertain and dangerous, even if they cannot foresee or imagine in detail what they might experience. Those who are travelling along a particular route for the first time seek information and advice from other migrants at home, at different points along the way and elsewhere (Darkwah *et al.* 2019; Kleist 2017). Many also prepare for their journeys spiritually and devote considerable sums of money to diviners and sacrifices (Tine and Thorsen 2019). However, as roundtable contributor Hans Peter Hahn stressed, prevention and information campaigns are more effective in controlling how imminent departures are handled than in deterring them. In Senegal, like elsewhere, routes have changed in response to border patrols, but a more significant change is the way that the planning of a journey has been moved out of the public realm and into the private. Secrecy now surrounds departures, in order to avoid detection and to avoid shame if the journey does not work out.

Roundtable contributor Nauja Kleist drew attention to how a video produced by the International Organization for Migration illustrates the disconnect between the way in which practitioners and migrants conceptualise uncertainty and potentiality. The video zooms in on people narrating their experiences as irregular migrants, as this is assumed to provide effective and authentic evidence of the risks incurred on irregular journeys. One individual in the video describes his adventure as playing the lotto. For IOM, the reference to a lotto is meant as a deterrent, in the belief that others will not dare or be willing to play the lotto with their life. However, in the discussion Nauja Kleist argued that for migrants the reference to lotto is read differently. For them, it is an uncertainty *and* a potentiality because it is possible to win. The potentiality, in turn, fuels notions of luck and chance. These differences in the understanding of what uncertainty means are important and they shed light on the ambivalences and arbitrariness in the distribution of hope.

In contrast to the institutions that seek to deter irregular migration through legislation or information campaigns, Sébastien Bachelet's work with young stranded migrants from Cameroon and Côte d'Ivoire in Morocco teases out that for them uncertainty is not an all-consuming state of life, marked by fear or doom, but also a ground for action (Bachelet 2016). Their self-identification as adventurers – an important trope among young male migrants from West and Central Africa, and increasingly also among young female migrants – signifies that, although they are 'looking for their lives' – a common phrase used in West and Central Africa that suggests the search for better opportunities and well-being in mobility – their journeys are not just endeavours for an economic end, but are also about physical and existential mobility. The social hope they share with migrants in similar situations has a significant element of chance – of being in the hands of God. The outcome of their actions, then, is beyond them. They cannot influence how long they have to wait because that falls under the jurisdiction of God, but they can increase the likelihood of being in the right place when their time comes (*ibid.*).

In the Moroccan context, they seek to do exactly that on the border. Time after time, they board inflatable boats to cross the Mediterranean or participate in what they call 'massive attacks' on the border fences of the Spanish enclaves Ceuta and Melilla.[2] Both types of attempted border crossing are high-risk and require what the young men describe as the essential characteristics of an adventurer: courage, and mental and physical strength. Migrants 'attacking' the sea and land borders never know if they will succeed; the only way to find out is to try. They will realise that the right time has come only when they have physically crossed the border and registered with the authorities.

The logic among adventurers of linking the unknowable – the chance – with the active and persistent pursuit of the hoped-for, but unpredictable, future is a way of coping. They navigate complex terrains, locally and transnationally. Regardless of whether they inhabit the forests, coastal cities, Rabat or Casablanca, the social terrain in Morocco is constantly in flux, with border patrols waxing and waning both temporally and spatially. Random controls of papers in the street can, in a space of months, turn into systematic screening of the neighbourhoods where many migrants live, or to military campaigns to evict the forest dwellers. Authorities may leave migrants to work in construction sites or trade in the streets and then, a few months later, carry out mass deportations to the border region of Algeria, or mass relocations to remote areas in the south of the country. Similar fluxes happen within migrants' transnational social networks, stretching across several countries. At one moment they receive assistance from a relative who is already abroad, or occasionally from home, at another moment they are requested to contribute money to solve an emergency. Young adventurers thus contend with a social environment in which uncertainties, burdens and potentialities unfold and change (Thorsen 2017).

Uncertainty and unpredictability in their everyday lives spill into the decisions they make and, as Bachelet noted, every decision, small or large, may be decisive for the outcome of their project – and yet they are acutely aware of the limitations on their agency (Bachelet 2016: 226). Their aspirations to live the good life of their social imaginaries are essential for understanding why they do not give up, as is the fact that these are not simply their individual aspirations, but those embedded in the societal hope of their families and communities. In research with a wider group of sub-Saharan migrants living in Rabat in 2012, I found that societal hope surrounding mobility has become vested in individuals' ability to endure hardship, to find ways of circumventing barriers, to maintain hope despite hardship and to wait. As long as they are seen actively to pursue a better future, their courage and resistance to restrictive regimes of mobility and structural violence in the border zones is applauded by their relatives. However, if they are perceived not to do enough or not to have the mental strength to endure, they are subject to critique (Thorsen 2017).

The self-representation of young migrant men as adventurers, as well as the expectations families have of them, is thus premised on having considerable agency to turn uncertainty into a social resource.

The question of agency and uncertainty

In order to identify where the power to embrace uncertainty comes from, it is useful to return to those ideas that underpin the mobility paradox. The assumption that African migrants engage in irregular migration due to a lack of information implicitly implies that they have made this choice from a position of relative privilege and that different choices could have been made. Drawing on her research in Ethiopia, Lebanon and Kuwait with migrant domestic workers, roundtable contributor Bina Fernandez noted that for the majority of people in Ethiopia, both men and women, the decision to migrate is based on a realistic assessment of their limited prospects. In short, there is no viable alternative to migration. The sources of uncertainty and vulnerability in Ethiopia are differentiated by class, gender and age. The demographic youth bulge puts pressure on land availability and on the possibility of land-based livelihoods in rural Ethiopia in particular. Although primary education and some degree of secondary education has expanded, most youth do not complete secondary education. As a result, there is a large group of young men and women who have enough education to produce aspirations for a better job, but not enough to secure a decent job. Thus, employment opportunities are limited and, for young women, there is almost certainty that they will be unemployed, whereas young men might find work in Ethiopia, albeit often casual in nature and low-paid (Fernandez 2020).

Young men and women are not simply individual rational actors. Their decisions to migrate are firmly embedded in family livelihood strategies and driven by the fundamental inability of families in Ethiopia to reproduce and sustain their life given economic and political instability. At the same time, the global labour market adds new dimensions to the differentiation of uncertainty and vulnerability in Ethiopia. Due to their skills in domestic work, young women have a comparative advantage over young men in the migrant labour market in the Gulf States. Hence, they mostly become regular migrants, whereas young men are more likely to become irregular migrants in a broader range of countries and experience uncertainties akin to those encountered by young West African adventurers. Labour market demands have thus facilitated an upset in the traditional gender hierarchy, in that young women working in the Gulf States earn more than their male counterparts. This has longer-term effects in that young men do not have the resource base that consolidated men's privileged social positions in the past. In families where choices have to be made due to a tight economy, parents may choose to support a daughter's mobility rather than a son's, thereby exacerbating the differential earning power of young men and women. Young female migrants anticipate that their achievements abroad have a positive effect on their statuses at home, and bestow on them a new and less subordinate position in the household (Thorsen *et al.* forthcoming).

The potentiality of mobility for young Ethiopian women does not lie in the move away from vulnerability and inequality in the social terrain at home but in their return. This is not the focus of the Ethiopian state, however. Given the global rhetoric focused on stemming unwanted mobilities and the intersection of mobility regimes, the Ethiopian state has produced a whole range of regulations, which, under the guise of protecting migrants, seek to control the mobilities of its subjects. In reality, however, some of the regulations produce conditions that lead to greater precarity and greater uncertainty. However, the state is operating in a context where it has few enforcement capabilities and many other actors continuously facilitate escape from the state's control. The role of the state is similar in the Gulf States. There, migrants are regulated by the Kafala system, which is a mechanism of control whereby their work permit is attached to the employer. Inherent instabilities in this system give migrants the possibility to escape, to exit from that form of contract and live as irregular migrants. So, in both situations, mobility can be a way to escape controls imposed by states through a formal structure of certainty (Fernandez 2020).

Although states seek to control the distribution of societal hope through regulations and by communicating potential risks, they can only do so in a partial way. In a context where informal institutions have a much stronger influence on people's everyday lives, they are likely to overrule the distributional forces of distant formal institutions. Even if the state sets out the contours of what people can hope for, societal hope embedded in informal institutions is often recognised by migrants as more relevant, due to the proximity of those institutions. Thus, at the micro level in rural Ethiopia, young women's labour migration to the Middle East is in the process of generating a redistribution of societal hope in the form of changing gender relations within families.

Conclusion

This chapter set out to explore how different conceptions of the uncertainty–mobility nexus intersect in the formal politics of migration management, and how this results in contestations of the power of states and in sentiments of hope, anticipation, precarity and disappointment that are fundamental in contemporary mobilities.

Especially in formal policy debates, the production and outcomes of uncertainty are often conceived in a narrow spatial sense, focusing on either the place of origin or the place of residence. Within this focus, migrants are presented as social actors, whose life-worlds are circumscribed by the risky conditions of where they are. The state, in turn, is capable of regulating living conditions and mobilities, or at least is able to make life uncertain for those who are not seen as legitimate.

If we extend the analytical scope across multiple spaces and include a focus on informal institutions it becomes clear that migrants and their families construct uncertainty and risk very differently. From this perspective, the potentiality of mobility outweighs the inherent uncertainty, and migrants seek to mitigate risks and uncertainties through social networks, as well as through faith, courage and patience.

As the chapter has shown, migratory projects are highly gendered and the risks and uncertainties that young men and women encounter are different. At the intersection of formal and informal distributors of societal hope, the availability of legal mobilities into domestic work in the Middle East for young women, for example, situates them in a context with little societal hope due to the Kafala system. However, a focus on informal institutions reveals that these mobilities are in the process of expanding societal hope for women in the community of origin by gradually changing gender relations within families towards greater equality.

In conclusion, therefore, a politics of uncertainty needs to grapple with the complexity of the intertwining factors that fuel hope and that make potentialities sufficiently imaginable for migrants and their families to contend with uncertainties.

Notes

1 The roundtable discussion was chaired by the author and involved Sébastien Bachelet from Manchester University, Bina Fernandez from Melbourne University, Hans Peter Hahn from Frankfurt University and Nauja Kleist from the Danish Institute of International Studies.

2 Massive attacks consist of several hundred young men 'attacking' the six-metre high border fences in the depth of the night, using makeshift ladders to get across. Their sheer numbers sufficiently diffuse the efforts of the Moroccan and Spanish border guards to let a small proportion of the migrants, usually in the region of 40–60 persons, proceed to the safety of the reception centre, where registration decreases the risk of informal expulsion to Morocco.

References

Adepoju, A. (2005) 'Migration in West Africa', Geneva: Global Commission on International Migration, www.GCIM.org

Aguillon, M.-D. (2018) 'Encouraging "Returns", Obstructing Departures and Constructing Causal Links. The New Creed of Euro-African Migration Management', Brighton: Migrating out of Poverty Research Programme Consortium

Awedoba, A.K. and Hahn, H.P. (2014) 'Wealth, Consumption and Migration in a West African Society. New Lifestyles and New Social Obligations among the Kasena, Northern Ghana', *Anthropos* 109.1: 45–56

Bachelet, S. (2016) 'Irregular Sub-Saharan Migrants in Morocco: Illegality, Immobility, Uncertainty and "Adventure" in Rabat', PhD thesis, The University of Edinburgh

Bloch, E. (1972) *The Principle of Hope*, vol. 3, Cambridge MA: MIT Press

Bredeloup, S. (2014) *Migrations d'Aventures. Terrain Africains*, Paris: Comité des travaux historiques et scientifiques (THS) | Géographie

—— (2012) 'Sahara Transit: Times, Spaces, People', *Population, Space and Place* 18.4: 457–467

Bredeloup, S. and Zongo, M. (2005) 'Quand les Frères Burkinabè de la Petite Jamahiriyya s'arrêtent à Tripoli', *Autrepart* 36: 123–147

Cooper, E. and Pratten, D. (2015) 'Ethnographies of Uncertainty in Africa: An Introduction', in E. Cooper and D. Pratten (eds) *Ethnographies of Uncertainty in Africa*, Basingstoke and New York: Palgrave Macmillan: 1–16

Darkwah, A.K., Thorsen, D., Boateng, D.A. and Teye, J.K. (2019) 'Good for Parents but Bad for Wives: Migration as a Contested Model of Success in Contemporary Ghana', Brighton: Migrating out of Poverty Research Programme Consortium

Fassin, D. (2011) 'Policing Borders, Producing Boundaries: The Governmentality of Immigration in Dark Times', *Annual Review of Anthropology* 40: 213–226

Fernandez, B. (2020) *Ethiopian Migrant Domestic Workers: Migrant Agency and Social Change*, Cham: Palgrave MacMillan

Glick Schiller, N. and Salazar, N.B. (2013) 'Regimes of Mobility Across the Globe', *Journal of Ethnic and Migration Studies* 39.2: 183–200

Hage, G. (2003) *Against Paranoid Nationalism. Searching for Hope in a Shrinking Society*, Annandale and London: Pluto Press and Merlin Press

Hage, G. and Papadopoulos, D. (2004) 'Ghassan Hage in Conversation with Dimitris Papadopoulos: Migration, Hope and the Making of Subjectivity in Transnational Capitalism', *International Journal for Critical Psychology* 12: 95–117

Inda, J.X. (2011) 'Borderzones of Enforcement: Criminalization, Workplace Raids, and Migrant Counterconducts', in V. Squire (ed) *The Contested Politics of Mobility. Borderzones and Irregularity*, Advances in International Relations and Global Politics, London and New York: Routledge: 74–90

Kleist, N. (2017), 'Disrupted Migration Projects: the Moral Economy of Involuntary Return to Ghana from Libya', *Africa* 87.2, 322–342

—— (2016) 'Introduction: Studying Hope and Uncertainty in African Migration', in N. Kleist and D. Thorsen (eds) *Hope and Uncertainty in Contemporary African Migration*, Routledge Studies in Anthropology, London and New York: Routledge

Kleist, N. and Thorsen, D. (eds) (2016) *Hope and Uncertainty in Contemporary African Migration*, Routledge Studies in Anthropology, London and New York: Routledge

Landau, L.B. and Freemantle, I. (2010) 'Tactical Cosmopolitanism and Idioms of Belonging: Insertion and Self-exclusion in Johannesburg', *Journal of Ethnic and Migration Studies* 36.3: 375–390

Mar, P. (2005), 'Unsettling Potentialities: Topographies of Hope in Transnational Migration', *Journal of Intercultural Studies* 26.4: 361–378

Mazzella, S. and Perrin, D. (2019) 'Introduction', in S. Mazzella and D. Perrin (eds) *Frontières, Sociétés et Droit en Mouvement. Dynamiques et Politiques Migratoires de l'Europe au Sahel*, Bruxelles: Bruylant

Squire, V. (ed) (2011) *The Contested Politics of Mobility. Borderzones and Irregularity*, Advances in International Relations and Global Politics, London and New York: Routledge

Thorsen, D. (2017) 'Is Europe Really the Dream? Contingent Paths among sub-Saharan Migrants in Morocco', *Africa* 87.2: 343–361

Thorsen, D., Desta, M.K. and Bogale, A.A. (forthcoming) 'Gender Norms in Ethiopia in Migration and Remittance Decision-making', Brighton: Migrating out of Poverty Research Programme Consortium

Tine, B. and Thorsen, D. (2019) 'Faith and Mystical Preparations to Kindle Success in Migration', Migrating out of Poverty Research Programme Consortium, www.sussex. ac.uk/global/intranet/migratingoutofpoverty/videos/Vidéo3_GG_Senegal_Final.mp4 (note, some internet browsers may play audio only)

Whitehouse, B. (2009) 'Discrimination, Despoliation and Irreconcilable Difference: Host-Immigrant Tensions in Brazzaville, Congo', *Africa Spectrum* 44.1: 39–59

11

DISPUTING SECURITY AND RISK

The convoluted politics of uncertainty

Helena Farrand Carrapico, Narzanin Massoumi,
William McGowan and Gabe Mythen

Introduction

Uncertainty has become a prevalent, but arguably oblique, signifier in recent years, with economic crisis, climate emergency and the threat of terrorism contributing to a tangible − yet simultaneously free-floating − sense of incertitude. To speak in the abstract about 'uncertainty' in such politically charged times is thus problematic. In this chapter, we argue for a grounded, context-specific account of uncertainty, drawing on vignettes that enable us to think practically about the nature of uncertainty and to explore the ways in which incertitude connects to other political, cultural and economic processes and forces. We will grapple with the impacts of discourses of uncertainty in three areas: cyber security, counter-terrorism and coping mechanisms in the aftermath of structural violence. It is our intention not only to engage with, but moreover to problematise, dominant understandings of 'risk' and 'security' in each of these domains. Elucidating salient problems and issues, our intention is to be forthright in challenging settled assumptions around the nature of uncertainty, and also its pervasiveness. Counselling against conceptual overreach, we contend that the explanatory power of more traditional sociological frames of analysis − such as power, ideology and social control − should not be marginalised by the omnipresence of debates about uncertainty.

In order to tease out the political dimensions of uncertainty, as they intersect with issues of risk and security, we turn first to the case of cyber security, with a specific emphasis on the implications of the UK's exit from the European Union for the regulation of future UK−EU security relations. From here, we explore further the mobilisation of uncertainty as a lever for politics and policy, focusing on the deleterious effects of pre-emptive anti-terrorism and counter-radicalisation measures in the UK. Finally, we reflect on survivors' accounts of managing uncertainty in the aftermath of surviving structural violence.

In order to organise our discussion we direct attention to two key themes that cut across and cement together research undertaken by the chapter contributors in these three areas. These relate, in turn, to governance, power and accountability, and the ideological mobilisation of uncertainty. In prioritising these themes we highlight some of the ways in which states engage with situations of 'not-knowing' and illuminate the ways in which political elites are able to harness the politics of uncertainty not only as a mode of governance, but also as a means of bolstering social control. These topics constitute central problems for modern nation states, with efforts to counter them commanding a sizeable amount of political energy, large tranches of public expenditure and considerable material resources for the police, criminal justice system and intelligence services. The UK government's National Risk Register – which assesses large-scale threats – considers the threat of cyber and terrorist attacks as 'high', both in terms of likelihood of occurrence and severity of impact. In relation to cyber security, the frequency and the scale of attacks continues to proliferate. Given enhanced connectivity between digital systems, there is a clear possibility of attacks of greater magnitude, with public and private sector organisations considered to be 'at risk' (see National Risk Register of Civil Emergencies 2017: 63). There is, of course, discernible overlap between cyber security and national security – especially given instances of attacks designed to destabilise military and intelligence – with both organised groups and lone individuals who are committed to violence seeking to launch cyber-attacks that destabilise state security and disrupt processes of capital accumulation. Further, widespread concerns have been expressed in political discourse and policy about the emergence of new types of terrorist violence:

> Many of those networks and individuals who are judged to pose a terrorist threat share an ambition to cause large numbers of casualties without warning. Some have aspirations to use non-conventional weapons such as chemical, biological, radiological and nuclear substances. Others aspire to attack our national infrastructure using both traditional methods and more novel methods such as electronic attack (National Risk Register of Civil Emergencies 2017: 26).

Given pronounced institutional anxieties, it is unsurprising that the current UK threat level for international terrorism – set by the Joint Terrorism Analysis Centre – is classified as 'substantial', meaning that an attack is 'highly likely'. While framing matters of security in this way may incline us to an understanding of risk and uncertainty that is slanted towards institutional regulation determined by expert systems, such a proclivity may encourage a somewhat partial view. The state has a formal duty to protect citizens from harm through implementing protective policies and practices, but risk and uncertainty are also lived and experienced by individuals in the course of everyday life. As we shall argue, risks and uncertainties are not naturally occurring, flat and horizontal phenomena; rather, they emerge in specific locales under particular political, economic and cultural conditions (McGowan 2018). This is significant, as it infers that uncertainties are both produced by and affect different people to different degrees and in different ways. As Ian Scoones (2019: 4) reasons, extant forms of stratification – such as gender, class, ethnicity and age – are salient factors in understanding the uneven impacts of uncertainty.

Governing cyber security: competing narratives

The first section of the chapter, led by Helena Farrand Carrapico, explores the governance of Brexit uncertainty in the context of cyber security policy. Cyber security is considered to be an intensely uncertain field, with ever-increasing levels of attacks on information systems and their users being reported (EC 2018). Not only is cyber insecurity understood as affecting the daily running of societal infrastructures and citizens' lives, it is also construed as having the potential to undermine fundamental rights, democracy and the rule of law: 'malicious cyber activities not only threaten our economies and the drive to the Digital Single Market, but also the very functioning of our democracies, our freedoms and our values' (EC 2017: 2). Nowadays, 'cyber security is about defending our way of life' (UK National Cyber Security Centre 2019: 1). This potential for harm has been framed as an existential form of uncertainty that is often associated with societal dependence on fast-evolving technology, mass production of personal digital data, anonymity of attackers and a lack of technical knowledge and resilience among the public. It is also portrayed as a pervasive type of uncertainty, with cyber-attacks presented as affecting all levels of society, from large companies to state infrastructure and the general public (EC and HREU 2013).

Given the discursive context, it is easy to understand why the current threat level has been flagged as a major concern at international, European and national levels (UK National Cyber Security Centre 2019), and also why cyber security has, in recent years, jumped to the forefront of many political and business agendas (Carrapico and Barrinha 2017). It is equally unsurprising that EU citizens' perceptions of cyber security and their attitudes towards internet security have changed considerably, with a recent poll indicating that 79 per cent of those surveyed believed that the risk of becoming a victim of cyber-crime is increasing (EC 2019). The framing of cyber security as a deeply uncertain field has enabled a wide range of actors, including both state and private actors, to propose and apply a range of policies directed towards addressing cyberspace-calculated risks. This process has been particularly evident within the EU, with uncertainty being used as one of the key justifications for the introduction and development of a joint macro-level cyber security policy and strategy (EC and HREU 2013). Given the borderless nature of cyber-attacks, closer cooperation between EU member states has been presented as the logical answer to the uncertainties of cyberspace.

The governance of Brexit, following the 2016 EU membership referendum, has introduced new forms of complexity in an already uncertain field, with business and practitioner concerns being vocally articulated (Harcup 2019). The main difference between 'new' forms of uncertainty and cyber security emanates from the idea that Brexit constitutes a step into the complete unknown. Whereas cyber security is often couched in terms of risks, which are considered to be calculable and insurable, the Brexit process brings considerable uncertainty to the sector. The rupture in the relationship between the EU and the UK triggered by Brexit means that the full consequences of the process on both the sector and the wider economy are unpredictable and largely unknown (see Anan 2019). The lack of historical, political and legal reference points reinforces uncertainties and serves to render the task of imagining post-Brexit futures necessarily speculative.

In practice, the governance of Brexit has resulted, above all, in a crisis of knowledge, which in turn has led to a crisis in decision-making. More specifically, incertitude in this case has both political and operational dimensions. Operationally, Brexit is likely to disrupt seriously, if not to interrupt entirely, the flow of cyber security-related information regularly exchanged by national authorities responsible for countering online threats (Stevens and O'Brien 2019). Regarding the explicitly political dimensions, Brexit has the potential to damage the UK's reputation as a key policy entrepreneur in cyber security. As an EU outlier post-Brexit, the UK is likely to have limited or no access to EU institutions and agencies. In addition, even if the UK is able to secure a degree of access, it will not be allowed to take part in decision-making, including involvement in voting processes. Clearly, Brexit has the potential to reduce the levels of trust that the UK–EU relationship has previously benefited from and which has enabled strategic and operational cooperation to flow in the field of cyber security (Carrapico *et al.* 2019).

The practitioner-led narratives on uncertainty recounted above have, however, not circulated without contest or challenge. As part of the UK government's process of negotiating an exit from the EU, considerable political efforts have been put into creating a counter-narrative that emphasises that the UK and the EU will continue to exchange cyber security-related intelligence and that the UK will still be able to shape EU standards and incident responses, as other formal and informal channels can be used to cooperate in cyber security beyond the EU, including the Five Eyes framework and NATO: 'pretty much everything we do now to help European partners, and what you do to help us, on cyber security can, should, and I am confident, will, continue beyond Brexit' (Martin, cited in Ashford 2019). Whatever the upshot of Brexit in the domain of cyber security, such narratives and counternarratives demonstrate competing ways in which uncertainty is not only understood but, moreover, is being ideationally massaged to suit particular political and economic ends. The fact that this is a nascent – but increasingly vital – policy field allows us to observe some of the ways in which discourses of certainty and uncertainty are created and disseminated. In addition, a critical analysis of the cyber risks triggered by Brexit enables us to envision how these discourses are co-produced and mutually responsive, as each jostles to become the dominant and commonly accepted security narrative.

Counter-terrorism: the strategic exploitation of uncertainties

In this section, Narzanin Massoumi discusses the strategic exploitation of uncertainties through the UK government's counter-radicalisation strategy, Prevent, focusing primarily on the relationship between government and two sets of non-governmental actors that played a significant role in delivering and developing anti-terrorism initiatives. The first set of actors are state-supported civil society organisations that rely on government support through funding, institutional access and other resources. In the first iteration of Prevent, such organisations were overtly linked to the government and included agencies like the Quilliam Foundation (now Quilliam). Following a shift in strategy from 2011 onwards, the government adopted a set of discreet relations with a new set of state-supported organisations in order to compensate for previous failures in gaining legitimacy. The second key group of actors are neo-conservative think tanks – such as the Henry Jackson Society – which have successfully lobbied for changes in government policy in this area. As we shall see, these non-governmental organisations have played a significant role in supporting and enacting Prevent. The publicly autonomous nature of these organisations means that they are not subjected to official forms of scrutiny, raising to the fore issues of power and accountability.

The Prevent strategy was devised in 2003 under the presiding Labour government, but was formally launched in 2007 following the '7/7' London bombings. The strategy is underpinned by the presumption that the roots of politically and religiously motivated violence lie in the propagation of 'extremist' ideas – in other words, that a continuum operates that stretches from initial adoption of radical ideas through to committing acts of terrorism. Prevent is based on pre-emptive principles and serves as a 'pre-crime' measure, designed to promote early intervention to avert later occurrence of harm. While the Prevent strategy seeks to model future threats by identifying indicators of vulnerability to extremist ideology and 'drivers' of violent behaviour, its design, implementation and impacts have been widely criticised since its inception (Mythen *et al.* 2017; Kundnani 2009; 2015; Dodd 2009). In the first iteration of the Prevent strategy, the stated objective was to 'work with Muslim communities to isolate, prevent and defeat violent extremism' (DCLG 2007). As a result, there was a concerted drive to fund Muslim civil society organisations – via the Department for Communities and Local Government – that would work directly on tackling 'violent extremism'. This saw the largest ever injection of funding into Muslim civil society in the UK, with £60 million being directed to 'third sector' agencies to counter extremism (O'Toole *et al.* 2013). At the same time, Prevent funding was controversially allocated to local authorities on the basis of the proportion of Muslims living in the locale (Mythen *et al.* 2017; Kundnani 2009). While 'capacity building' initiatives were focused on empowering Muslim minority communities, the government's drive to recruit partners to assist in the counter-terrorism agenda proved difficult. The Prevent programme faced widespread criticism from human rights groups, academics and activists for being selective in its engagement with Muslim groups and excluding those critical of UK foreign policy or domestic counter-terrorism measures. The strategy was also criticised for its heavy policing of civil society organisations and its surveillant ambitions in gathering data for intelligence purposes (Kundnani 2015; Dodd 2009).

Following a review conducted by the then independent reviewer of terrorism legislation, David Anderson QC, the Conservative/Liberal Democrat coalition government issued a second iteration of Prevent in 2011 (HM Government 2011). The revised strategy included significant modifications. First, following lobbying by neo-conservative groups, there was a move from exclusively tackling 'violent extremism' to also combating 'non-violent extremism'. Second, the revised strategy purported to address a wider variety of forms of extremism, including that emanating from the far right; although, as we shall see, the policy has always disproportionately targeted 'Islamist extremism'. Third, overall responsibility for Prevent was centralised in the Home Office, with community cohesion activities remaining with the Department for Communities and Local Government. Fourth, and not expressed in the formal strategy, a shift towards working covertly with Muslim civil society groups occurred. Following the failure of government counter-radicalisation measures to gain legitimacy among Muslim civil society, in 2012 the UK government adopted a policy of covertly funding Muslim civil society organisations that would politically align with state priorities as the statement below by the former British prime minister, Theresa May, shows:

> Often it is more effective to be working through groups that are recognized as having a voice … rather than it being seen to be government trying to give a message. Indeed, it's always better to be using those people to whom people look naturally to hear the message, rather than simply doing it as RICU itself (Intelligence and Security Committee 2012).

The Research Information and Communications Unit, based in the Home Office and referred to by Theresa May above, led these covert elements of Prevent, employing the services of a public relations company called Breakthrough Media to create social media campaigns in order to promote pro-government messaging (Massoumi and Miller 2019; Massoumi *et al.* 2019). RICU covertly supported, via Breakthrough Media, campaigns purporting to emanate from grassroots Muslim civil society groups challenging 'extremism' in local communities. One such campaign was fronted by Families Against Stress and Terror, which describes itself as an independent organisation that offers 'support to vulnerable families and individuals'. Yet, in a leaked internal Office for Security and Counter-Terrorism document marked 'not for public disclosure', FAST's 'Families matter' campaign is described as a 'RICU product' that has been 'led and developed' by FAST but 'supported by … PR and online activity' (Miller and Massoumi 2016). FAST is but one of many ostensibly grassroots organisations that play a role in counter-radicalisation initiatives, and that have been afforded discreet Home Office support (Hooper 2017; Cobain *et al.* 2016). The covert nature of these initiatives creates uncertainty throughout Muslim civil society, as people are unaware which initiatives are linked to government and which are not.

In 2015, the Prevent programme was placed on a statutory footing, following the Counter-Terrorism and Security Act 2015. This required public institutions to pay 'due regard' to 'prevent people being drawn into terrorism'. Although Prevent in the public sector is supposed to be guided by the Prevent Duty Guidance (HM Government 2015a), in practice there exists uncertainty about if, how and when to implement it. This trajectory of the Prevent programme has been heavily influenced by neo-conservative think tanks with strongly defined neo-conservative viewpoints on issues such as religion, immigration, integration and terrorism. In Britain, neo-conservative organisations such as the Henry Jackson Society and Policy Exchange routinely lobby government and promote authoritarian, exclusionist polices. Such think tanks have published a series of reports purporting to show 'evidence' of extremism among British Muslims – calling on government to sever links with particular individuals and groups and urging intensified surveillance of Muslims. In addition to being morally dubious and socially retrogressive, the evidence presented for such calls is highly questionable. To give but one example, a report by the Policy Exchange was withdrawn by the think tank after the BBC established that receipts claiming to establish that 'extremist' literature was being sold in British Mosques had been forged (see Mills *et al.* 2011). There are numerous instances in which the 'research' of right-wing think-thanks alleging extremist activities by British Muslims has been challenged for being either inaccurate or highly exaggerated. The specific examples that have come to light signal broader concerns about the integrity of their research practices (Miller *et al.* 2017). Mediating and endorsing Islamophobic discourses in the public sphere and attempting to influence security policy are, lamentably, embedded activities for many neo-conservative think tanks. For example, the Centre for Social Cohesion – later incorporated into the Henry Jackson Society – and Policy Exchange were at the forefront of pushing for the revision of the Prevent strategy to include 'non-violent' extremism. Following these mobilisation efforts, the Prevent policy was expanded to include 'non-violent extremism', with the Centre for Social Cohesion being cited no fewer than six times, indicating its role in influencing the formation of the policy. More recently, it was uncovered that the Home Office Extremism Analysis Unit – the body created to monitor extremism following the introduction of the Prevent Duty Guidance (2015) – was receiving data directly from the Henry Jackson Society in its efforts to identify extremists (*Butt v Secretary of State for Home Department* 2017). This demonstrates the extent to which non-accountable neo-conservative agencies have not only influenced the direction of the Prevent policy but also tangibly shaped its practical implementation. The range of oblique activities and practices undertaken by non-governmental actors acting outwith democratic protocols and procedures generates palpable concerns with regards to responsibility, scrutiny and accountability. The predominant focus of ideational activities in the public sphere for right-wing think tanks has been oriented towards expanding the nebulous concept of extremism and indexing it to Islam and Muslims. Such disingenuous activities have fuelled Islamophobic discourses and acted as a lever to lobby government to move 'security' policy in increasingly authoritarian directions. At the same time, Muslim public figures and legitimate civil society organisations have been targeted by deliberate smears, further restricting and discouraging Muslim political participation in public life. This, coupled with the official counter-terrorism apparatus – an already powerful and largely unaccountable set of institutions – targeting individuals considered as extremists and those apparently radicalised has had serious repercussions. Concepts such as extremism and radicalisation are imprecisely defined in official discourse, generating widespread uncertainty at the level of identification and intervention. The flexible fashion in which these concepts are operationalised in the state bureaucracy, together with the routine practices of the police and other public servants, means that many thousands of people in the UK are now regarded as legitimate targets for suspicion, surveillance and intelligence-gathering. To this end, there is already a wide and deep body of evidence indicating that UK counter-terrorism policy has disproportionately affected and discriminated against Muslims (Qurashi 2018; Massoumi *et al.* 2017; Kundnani 2015). Nested within Prevent – and designed to combat radicalisation – 'Channel' serves as but one example of this. Channel is the UK government's pre-criminal 'diversionary' programme, which 'provide[s] support for people vulnerable to being drawn into any form of terrorism' (HM Government 2015b). Figures released under the Freedom of Information Act – and now routinely published by the Home Office – show that there has been a sharp increase in Channel referrals since the introduction of the Counter-Terrorism and Security Act and the Prevent Duty Guidance in 2015. Between July 2015 and June 2016 there were 4,611 referrals – a 75 per cent increase on the previous year. Notably, of these cases some 2,311 were children under the age of 18 (including 352 under nine years old) (Massoumi *et al.* 2017: 11). Subsequently, the figures have continued at a similar rate, meaning that on average 12 people a day are being referred to the programme. While the revised Prevent strategy purports to deal with all forms of terrorism, the large majority of referrals to Channel relate to suspicions of Islamist extremism: 65 per cent in 2015/16 and 61 per cent in 2016/17. Alarmingly, from 2014 to 2016, young Muslims were 44 times more likely to be referred to the Channel programme than individuals of other religions (Blakeley *et al.* 2019). Although there was an increase in referrals and Channel support decisions for right-wing extremism in 2017/18 (Islamist extremism referrals reported at 50 per cent, compared to 32 per cent for right-wing extremism, with Channel supporting 45 per cent of decisions for Islamist extremism and 44 per cent for right-wing extremism), the Prevent programme still disproportionately targets Muslims. Yet, despite apparent rising awareness of the threat presented by individuals and groups motivated by racism and Islamophobia, none of the RICU covert activity described above was directed towards the problem of right-wing extremism. Moreover, groups racialised as White are not universally implicated in right-wing extremism, in the way that Muslim groups have had their cultural beliefs and practices spuriously used as potential indicators for extremism or radicalisation. As empirical studies have illustrated, the implementation of undemocratic counter-terrorism measures has created widespread anxiety and uncertainty for young British Muslims, who have been subjected to disproportionate forms of policing, harassment and surveillance (Khan and Mythen

2018; Qurashi 2018; Kundnani 2009; Mythen *et al.* 2009). Examples of how this has transpired in practice are abundant. Section 44 of the Terrorism Act 2000 enabled the police to stop and search any person or vehicle without any requirement for 'reasonable suspicion'. Asians and Blacks were disproportionately targeted compared with Whites, with Asians being over six times more likely to be stopped and searched, and Black people on average almost eight times more likely (Massoumi *et al.* 2017: 8). In January 2010, Section 44 was declared unlawful by the European Court of Human Rights, in the case of *Gillan and Quinton v UK*. The court noted in its judgement that 'none of the many thousands of searches has ever resulted in conviction of a terrorism offence' (*Gillan and Quinton v UK*, 2010: para. 148). Further, Schedule 7 of the Terrorism Act 2000 sanctions draconian powers which apply to port and airport border controls allowing the detainment of individuals for up to nine hours to conduct searches of their person, allowing belongings to be seized for up to seven days. Those detained under Schedule 7 have fewer legal rights than criminal suspects: they are not entitled to a publicly-funded lawyer, are obliged to answer questions and, if detained at a police station, to provide biometric data, including fingerprints and DNA – all without a requirement of 'reasonable suspicion' (Massoumi *et al.* 2017: 9). While the religion of those detained under Schedule 7 is not recorded in official statistics, publicly available figures on the ethnicity of those examined or detained indicate that individuals of Pakistani ethnicity are over 150 times more likely to be detained under Schedule 7 than White British citizens (Massoumi *et al.* 2017: 10). As flagged earlier, forms of state control and para-statal involvement in ideational projects of regulation and division underscore the ways in which uncertainty connects to issues of governance and accountability, and also index to the operation of power and the enactment of political priorities.

All of this suggests that, when we think about concrete examples where uncertainty seems rife, it is worth asking whether the issues in front of us can be viewed through a different lens and/or interpreted in a different way. Uncertainty is often associated with unknowns and futurity, but this often obscures tangible and observable phenomena. For example, how might our understanding of a given situation change if we were not to use the optic of uncertainty and risk, but instead to use that of harm and injustice? As the long-standing discrimination faced by British Muslims in the UK illustrates, history, dominant ideologies and institutionalised prejudice matter. To this end, it is vital to stress that, while the state may formally aver that it is the guardian of 'public' security, in practice the role of state intelligence and surveillance agencies in producing insecurity for certain individuals and groups is evident.

Survivors of structural violence: emotion, trust and the politics of accountability

Historical and temporal factors are also present when thinking about the consequences of political and religiously motivated violence, as Will McGowan shows in this final part of the chapter. His research focuses on the different treatment – both legal and cultural – received by those living in the aftermath of such violence. In this regard, the shooting of innocent protestors by the British Army in 1972 in Ireland on 'Bloody Sunday' and the coordinated bombing of London's transport system in the 2005 '7/7' attacks offer contrasting points of reference. In making sense of these various pasts in the present, the two respective 'survivor groups' have had both to negotiate and traverse life since these tragic events, but in quite different ways. While the 7/7 attacks were subject to close scrutiny by the state – including profiling of the perpetrators, transparent and widely publicised inquests and post-event analysis for the emergency and security services – the survivors of Bloody Sunday have spent more than four decades seeking justice through successive inquiries. Indeed, it was not until 2010 that an official apology was received from the British prime minister and, more recently, a case for prosecution belatedly brought against one of the British soldiers involved in the incident. The information made available to the public following 7/7 provided at least a satisfactory 'completeness' of knowledge about how their loved ones were killed and the contextual factors surrounding the event. No such completeness was available to Bloody Sunday survivors. Within the Catholic community of Derry, it was not uncertainty that beset efforts to expose the abuses and persecution they faced, or to establish what took place at that Civil Rights march. Instead, their ability to make public those harms and to ensure an accurate and just recording of them has meant that survivors and campaigners have had perpetually to look back on events retrospectively, with little chance of 'moving on' with life as before.

Locating uncertainty within these two examples becomes very much a 'tale of two tragedies': with one in which knowledge enables at least the potential for prospective and future recovery, and the other in which the cultural and legal precedent of remembering history displaces any such hopes for transcending its impacts within living memory. Contemporary political conditions have also intermingled with these survivors' sense of collective identity and ontological security differentially, with uncertainty, fears and hypothetical resolutions relating to Brexit and the Irish border looming ever larger. The relationship between politics, emotion, (non)knowledge and power in such landmark cases is thus contingent upon the state's arbitration of them. Hannah Arendt's (1958: 237) oft-cited analysis of political promises usefully illuminates this relationship further:

> The remedy for unpredictability, for the chaotic uncertainty of the future, is contained in the faculty to make and keep promises … binding oneself through promises, serves to set up in the ocean of uncertainty, which the future is by definition, islands of security without which not even continuity, let alone durability of any kind, would be possible in the relationships between men [*sic*].

In the immediate aftermath of catastrophe or injustice, such events again raise pressing questions about accountability and democracy, partly because of the relationship Arendt highlights between those in positions of power and the *demos* to whom they make promises. When these promises are broken – as they are with alarming frequency – trust is not only eroded: it is difficult to win back. However, looking beyond specific actions and reactions concerning individuals, Arendt's analysis of uncertainty merits closer attention in relation to the relationship between governance, emotion and trust. Unlike Arendt's remedy for unpredictability, which provides islands of security, today's political landscape presents us with insecurity as an unceasing and inevitable feature of social, economic and political life. Catastrophe, vulnerability and surprise perpetually await us and must be embraced; preparation to deal with the jolts and shocks generated by twenty-first century turbo-capitalism must be prioritised, and represent something of an emotional retraining exercise. As Mark Neocleous (2012: 188) posits, the nature of today's security politics might be epitomised in the maxim: 'don't be scared, be prepared'. The *actual* emotions engendered under such political conditions – the preponderance of which are likely to be negative ones, such as fear and anger – may encourage an inward-turning and acquiescent citizenry. Whether or not this is the case, they provide no basis for long-term stability, or happiness.

Four concluding provocations

In drawing the chapter to a close, it has been our intention to deploy concrete examples of the ways in which problems of uncertainty have an impact upon 'security' in its many guises, from policy and practice to the ontological and emotional. Having discussed several problematiques that arise when we seek to engage in debates about uncertainty in the context of security, we wish to end by offering up four caveats that serve as simultaneous provocations. First, it is our contention that, rather than analysing uncertainty as a purely abstract concept, we need to situate it in specific contexts of knowledge and grounded cultural milieu. The dangers of presentism – through which histories of uncertainty might become masked – are obvious in this regard. Second, having identified a set of specific practices to focus on, it is important to remain alert to the different characteristics of uncertainty, and to speak consistently about particular strands across a chosen set of observations. Third, as we have demonstrated, it is important to be aware of – and alert to – the pursuit of narrow, sectoral interests that may lurk beneath the veil that uncertainty enables. Fourth, and relatedly, we would counsel against 'uncertainty imperialism', whereby the term becomes used as a catch-all *lingua franca* that is devoid of specificity. Mirroring academic overuse of 'risk' as an heuristic device, if we are loose in bandying about the discourse of 'uncertainty' there is a palpable danger of catachresis. While theoretically exploring the constitution of uncertainty adds to the corpus of academic knowledge, as we have intimated, overstretching its explanatory potential may serve to shroud rather than elucidate more pressing and critical analyses of power relations, inequalities and injustices.

References

Anan, M. (2019) *Cost of No Deal Revisited. UK in a Changing Europe*, https://ukandeu.ac.uk/wp-content/uploads/2018/09/Cost-of-No-Deal-Revisted.pdf (15 September 2019)

Arendt, H. (1958) *The Human Condition*, Chicago: University of Chicago Press

Ashford, W. (2019) 'UK Committed to Working with EU Cyber Security Partners', *ComputerWeekly.com*, 21 February 2019, www.computerweekly.com/news/252458102/UK-committed-to-working-with-EU-cyber-security-partners (accessed 13 September 2019)

Blakeley, R., Hayes, B., Kapoor, N., Kundnani, A., Massoumi, N., Miller, D., Mills, T., Sian, K. and Tufail, W. (2019) *Leaving the War on Terror*, London: Transnational Institute

Butt v Secretary of State for the Home Department [2017] EWHC 1930 (Admin)

Carrapico, H. and Barrinha, A. (2017) 'The EU as a Coherent (Cyber)Security Actor?', *Journal of Common Market Studies* 55.6: 1254–1272

Carrapico, H., Niehuss, A. and Berthelemy, C. (2019) *Brexit and Internal Security – Political and Legal Concerns in the context of the Future UK-EU Relationship*, Basingstoke: Palgrave

Cobain, I., Ross, A., Evans, R. and Mahmood, M. (2016) 'Inside Ricu, the Shadowy Propaganda Unit Inspired by the Cold War', *The Guardian*, 2 May 2016, www.theguardian.com/politics/2016/may/02/inside-ricu-the-shadowy-propaganda-unit-inspired-by-the-cold-war (accessed 23 October 2019)

DCLG (2007) *Preventing Violent Extremism: Winning Hearts and Minds*, London: HMSO

Dodd, V. (2009) 'Government Anti-terrorism Strategy "Spies on Innocent"', *The Guardian*, 16 October 2009, www.theguardian.com/uk/2009/oct/16/anti-terrorism-strategy-spies-innocents (accessed 12 February 2020)

European Commission (2019) *Europeans' Attitudes Towards Internet Security*, Special Eurobarometer 480DG for Migration and Home Affairs and DG for Communication, March edition, Brussels

—— (2018) Speech by Vice-President Ansip at the Cyber Security Conference in Vienna, 3 December. Vienna, https://ec.europa.eu/commission/commissioners/2014–2019/ansip/announcements/speech-vice-president-ansip-cyber-security-conference-vienna_en (accessed 10 September 2019)

—— (2017) Joint Communication to the European Parliament and the Council: Resilience, Deterrence and Defence: building strong cybersecurity for the EU, JOIN(2017)450 final, Brussels (13 September 2017). https://ec.europa.eu/transparency/regdoc/rep/10101/2017/EN/JOIN-2017-450-F1-EN-MAIN-PART-1.PDF (accessed 10 September 2019)

European Commission and HREU (2013) *Joint Communication to the European Parliament, The Council, The European Economic and Social Committee and the Committee of the Regions: Cybersecurity Strategy of the European Union: An Open, Safe and Secure Cyberspace*, JOIN(2013)1 final

Gillan and Quinton v UK (2010) European Court of Human Rights Transcript, 12 January

Harcup, A. (2019) 'Brexit Uncertainty and Resulting Cybersecurity Concerns', *SC Media*, July 2019, www.scmagazineuk.com/brexit-uncertainty-resulting-cybersecurity-concerns/article/1588883 (accessed 16 September 2019)

HM Government (2015a) *Revised Prevent Duty Guidance: For England and Wales*, London: The Stationary Office Limited, https://assets.publishing.service.gov.uk/government/uploads/system/uploads/attachment_data/file/445977/3799_Revised_Prevent_Duty_Guidance__England_Wales_V2-Interactive.pdf (accessed 23 October 2019)

—— (2015b) *Channel Duty Guidance*, London: The Stationary Office Limited, www.gov.uk/government/publications/channel-guidance (accessed 17 August 2018)

—— (2011) *Prevent Strategy*, London: The Stationary Office Limited, www.gov.uk/government/publications/prevent-strategy-2011 (accessed 2 May 2018)

Hooper, S. (2017) 'Google-Hosted Muslim Leaders Summit Linked to Home Office Prevent Unit', *Middle East Eye*, 11 January 2017, www.middleeasteye.net/news/google-hosted-muslim-leaders-summit-linked-home-office-prevent-unit (accessed 23 October 2019)

Intelligence and Security Committee (2012) *Annual Report 2011–2012*, https://assets.publishing.service.gov.uk/government/uploads/system/uploads/attachment_data/file/211559/ISC-2011–12.pdf (accessed 27 September 2019)

Khan, F. and Mythen, G. (2018) 'Micro Level Management of Islamophobia', in I. Awan and I. Zempi (eds) *The Routledge International Handbook of Islamophobia*, London: Routledge

Kundnani, A. (2015) *A Decade Lost: Rethinking Radicalisation and Extremism*, London: Claystone

—— (2009) *Spooked! How Not to Prevent Violent Extremism*, London: Institute of Race Relations

Massoumi, N. and Miller, D. (2019) *Counter Terrorism and Muslim Civil Society*, London: Spinwatch

Massoumi N., Mills T. and Miller, D. (2019) 'Secrecy, Coercion and Deception in Research on "Terrorism" and "Extremism"', *Contemporary Social Science*, DOI: 10.1080/21582041.2019.1616107

Massoumi, N., Mills, T. and Miller, D. (2017) *What is Islamophobia? Racism, Social Movements and the State*, London: Pluto Press

McGowan, W. (2018) 'The Perils of "Uncertainty" for Fear of Crime Research in the 21st Century', in M. Lee and G. Mythen (eds) *The International Handbook on Fear of Crime*, London: Routledge

Miller, D. and Massoumi, N. (2016) *Briefing on the Home Office, RICU and Muslim Civil Society Groups*. Submission to the Home Affairs Select Committee Countering Extremism Inquiry, CEX0062, 10 June

Miller, D., Massoumi, N. and Mills, T. (2017) 'The Challenge of Islamophobia', in M. Wakefield (ed) *Why We Need A New Foreign Policy: A Stop the War Coalition Briefing*, London: Stop the War Coalition

Mills, T., Griffin, T. and Miller, D. (2011) *The Cold War on British Muslims: An Examination of Policy Exchange and the Centre for Social Cohesion*, Glasgow: Public Interest Investigations

Mythen, G., Walklate, S. and Khan, F. (2009) '"I'm a Muslim, but I'm not a Terrorist": Risk, Victimization and the Negotiation of Risky Identities', *British Journal of Criminology* 49.6: 736–754

Mythen, G., Walklate, S. and Peatfield, E.J. (2017). 'Assembling and Deconstructing Radicalisation in PREVENT: A Critique of the Logic of Drivers', *Critical Social Policy* 37.2: 180–201

National Risk Register of Civil Emergencies (2017) London: Cabinet Office

Neocleous, M. (2012) '"Don't Be Scared, Be Prepared": Trauma-Anxiety-Resilience', *Alternatives: Global, Local, Political* 37.3: 188–198

O'Toole, T., DeHanas, D.N., Modood, T., Meer, N. and Jones, S. (2013) *Taking Part: Muslim Participation in Contemporary Governance*, Bristol: University of Bristol

Qurashi, F. (2018) 'The Prevent Strategy and the UK "War on Terror": Embedding Infrastructures of Surveillance in Muslim Communities', *Palgrave Communications* 4.17: 1–13

Scoones, I. (2019) *What is Uncertainty and Why Does it Matter?*, STEPS Working Paper 105, Sussex: STEPS Centre

Stevens, T. and O'Brien, K. (2019) 'Brexit and Cyber Security', *RUSI Journal* 164.3: 22–33

UK National Cyber Security Centre (2019) 'Ciaran Martin's Speech at the Billington Cyber Security Summit', 6 September, Washington DC, www.ncsc.gov.uk/speech/ciaran-martins-speech-at-billington-cyber-security-summit-2019 (accessed 14 September 2019)

12

UNSETTLING THE APOCALYPSE

Uncertainty in spirituality and religion

Nathan Oxley

Introduction: the end

A wave of apocalyptic language has emerged around a heightened sense of crisis in climate change and biodiversity loss, and the inadequacy of effective responses to it. Among the participants in recent Extinction Rebellion protests are Christians, Muslims, Buddhists and others who overtly link their activism to religious and spiritual convictions. In May 2019 a UK shadow cabinet minister warned of impacts of 'biblical proportions: droughts, pestilence, famine, floods, wildfires, mass migration, political instability, war and terrorism' (Hansard 2019). It seems that earthly language alone is not sufficient to capture the immensity of the problems that the world faces.

The search for religious ways to express fears of catastrophe is not a new phenomenon, even in modern times. In response to the threat of nuclear weapons, Sallie McFague (1987) proposed a change in theological language away from patriarchy and monarchy towards more caring, ecologically sensitive, nurturing 'models' of God. Stefan Skrimshire wrote a decade ago about a flurry of apocalyptic rhetoric on the climate at the time, as the latest punctuation point in a long story in which apocalyptic thought had been 'stitched' into foundational ideas about history, progress and science (Skrimshire 2010). In the same volume, Mike Hulme cited 'presaging apocalypse' as one of four ways that problems around climate change were being framed: as a 'call to action', but not one that left much room for discussion about what that action should be (Hulme 2010: 43–46).

Today, there are at least four related things going on in the current outpouring of religious terms in response to environmental problems. First, religious stories about the 'end of days' are a useful shorthand to dramatise and simplify the powerful, disruptive or destructive forces being felt in many parts of the world. Second, the rhetoric points to the proper meaning of 'apocalypse' as a revelation or uncovering – with a call to action that emphasises 'listening' or 'paying attention' to experts, or to the experiences of vulnerable people. Third, the overt religiosity of recent climate protests, combining and appropriating various traditions and rituals, suggests that people are searching for emotional and spiritual responses to feelings of crisis, attempting to create spaces for consolation or reflection. Fourth, putting environmental problems in religious terms brings their moral and cultural dimensions to the surface – dimensions that are often neglected by dominant approaches based on technical or market-based 'solutions'.

Climate change is not the only challenge facing the world, and apocalyptic stories are not the only way that religious language can help to explore the emotional and moral dimensions of uncertainty. In a wide variety of contexts – from migration to science and technology, disaster response, disease emergence, care of nature and the valuation of resources – uncertainties are more than just risks to be calculated and overcome. Fears and hopes are not just global: they can be local, very specific – personal even. Religious language and practices have long been a resource for capitalising on these emotions or helping people deal with them, by connecting local, personal struggles to wider institutions, bigger stories and deeper histories. Apocalyptic visions may stir strong feelings, but they lead too easily to despair, and it is hard to connect them to the myriad everyday struggles that people face and the many possible ways things can turn out. Happily, as discussed below, other visions and other stories are available.

Asking what makes people uncertain across so many areas of life raises some big questions. How do we know what is real and true? How do people deal with disagreement and different points of view regarding facts or values? How do people interpret why things happen and work out how to respond to them? How do people reflect, console, shelter or care for people when the unexpected happens? How do people create flexible, resilient structures and practices in the face of unpredictable events? In a world that is often marked by injustice and destruction, how can one hope to imagine that things could be different in the future?

Looking at religious answers to these questions shows a rich variety of responses – often shaped by experiences and wider culture. These responses challenge the modern pressure to conform to a single ideal or optimal way of dealing with uncertainty, ambiguity and ignorance, either by managing them as risk or sweeping them under the carpet. They show possibilities for responding to uncertainty with humility about what can be known, and creating flexible spaces or practices to prepare for when things go wrong. They can also show the dangers of rigid, doctrinaire approaches to problems that demand flexibility and humility in the face of the unknown or unexpected.

Amid pressures to accept dominant narratives about capitalism, single-track solutions, global crisis, progress and development, understanding religion may prove to be a vital tool, among others, for breaking fixed and predictable visions apart, and showing plural ways of seeing and alternative ways of valuing the world and each other. This chapter focuses on how religious thought (in particular, drawing from my own partial knowledge of Christian traditions, with some tentative comparisons with other faiths) can help to foster these qualities of humility, care and sanctuary, and considers their practical implications. The central idea is that religious thought-worlds can *unsettle* the assumptions that are built into dominant modes of progress and development, to reveal and highlight new possibilities for thought and action.

Certainty and uncertainty

It is a stereotype that religions offer certainty to their adherents. Like many stereotypes, this is partly based on truth. Religious beliefs and structures can offer a kind of security to believers facing uncertain futures or deep questions about the nature of consciousness, the origins of the universe or how to know the difference between right and wrong. A part of spiritual and mystical experience across traditions is a feeling of certainty that can be emotionally overwhelming, even if it only lasts a moment. To some, the sense of belonging to a community also offers a sense of protection against the unknown.

Religious convictions can also provide a space for reaction and entrenchment. Fundamentalism is not just a fervent belief in God(s) or doctrines, it aids decision-making: non-believers are considered as either satanic enemies or targets for conversion; questioning believers are seen as betrayers of the faith and abetters of impurity, not just incorrect but evil. In response to these perceived dangers, believers are urged to return to sacred texts, authority figures or individual prayer to determine the clear path to be taken, often in terms of opposing, dominating, expelling or conquering malevolent forces.

Authoritarian politics has made good use of these qualities, from Bolivia to the United States (Berlet and Sunshine 2019) and India (Vanaik 2018), and in other examples elsewhere and throughout history (for example in the important role of theology in justifying Apartheid in South Africa). In these settings, religious assertions of certainty are inextricably bound up in party, racial, class and gender politics, foreign policy, history, borders, security and cultures around food, drink, sexuality, dress and other forms of consumption. Rather than provoking a challenge to power or the liberation of the spirit, authoritarian politics uses religious institutions and ideas as vehicles for judgement and domination in its demands for conformity of behaviour, othering of outgroups and uniformity of thought.

But this is not the whole story. Religions also point deliberately towards the unknown and unknowable. John Gray (2007: 207) says that rather than aiming for consensus and comprehensive knowledge of the world, 'Religions are not claims to knowledge but ways of living with what cannot be known'. Fundamentalism acknowledges this lack of control by denying it. In other, perhaps more subtle, ways religious thought can serve to unsettle fundamental assumptions that are built into logics of risk management, humanitarian efforts, migration policy, technology and conservation, alongside other domains of life. These assumptions may themselves originate in a moral world that is shaped by religious thought, but in the many settings where plural cultures and worldviews are present it is worth examining how religious ideas can also expose uncertainties and alternative ways of seeing.

What is unsettled by the religious and spiritual imagination are not just ideas about moral choices or values in any simple sense. Religious thinking upsets conventional modern notions of how history and time behave: the logical relationships between cause and effect; what is considered to be natural, alive or conscious; where truth comes from; how to respond to danger and the threat of death; what freedom or emancipation means; the relationships between humans and animals, plants and land; and who deserves our attention or care. These are themes that might point the way beyond the certain doom implied by apocalyptic visions, on the one hand, and controlled – purportedly neutral and unbiased – technical approaches to reducing risk and managing security, on the other.

For example, what does it mean to see animals, plants, celestial bodies and the weather not as resources or threats, but as fellow worshippers of God, as in the Benedicite?[1] What does it mean to see the material world as an illusion, or as a good creation, or alternatively as evil or corrupted? What does it mean to perceive that souls can migrate from humans to animals, and back again; or that there is a sacred quality in all living things, or in particular ones? What does it mean to imagine that a rock or an artefact is endowed with a spirit or consciousness? What does it mean to say that all people are brothers and sisters, or that animals and humans are siblings? How do myths about dangerous parts of nature – large animals, storms, fire and so on – help people to deal with fears about them and engender respect for them?

All of these questions affect how people see the building blocks of life, how things are perceived to work, how they should work, what connects them and how they are able to change. If not simply dismissed as illogical or archaic, these questions can shed light on the things that different people prioritise as important, and what motivates the decisions they make. In some cases, as in indigenous worldviews that are often marginalised in policy, religious stories and concepts are repositories of sophisticated knowledge about the natural world – to take one example, the rich descriptions of nature–human relations in Māori cosmology (Harmsworth and Awatere 2013: 274–286). Religious myths are often full of descriptions of nature, but in contrast to scientific texts, they tend to assign value to it and underline how humans are supposed to exist in relation to other parts of nature.

The point here is not to aim for a consensus on any of these stories and concepts, or treat them as equivalent to each other. Indeed, many people in modern societies are exposed (to some extent) to plural accounts. Even within religions themselves, accepted truths are maintained and reinforced through storytelling, creeds, educational institutions and so on; but many religions also have a history of challenge, debate and dissension that is visible in texts and doctrines. Looking at the unsettling aspects and contradictory claims of religion is a step towards a pluralistic approach to uncertainty that recognises the value of different perspectives, not as a way of integrating them or adding them to an ever-growing set of data, but in the desire to '[hold] different ways of knowing as equal' and value the 'discontinuities and contradictions' that arise (Nightingale *et al.* 2019: 3).

'Neither light nor darkness, but both together'

Religions do not just provide a way of living with uncertainties about what is out there in the world, but, internally, religions can also unsettle themselves. Deeply embedded in many religious traditions is a darkness: the idea that the truth itself is never fully knowable, that God or gods are hidden or mysterious, or that truth is best expressed in terms of paradoxes or contradictions. This idea is present at the heart of many religions and spiritual traditions, downplayed in some (for example in some evangelical traditions in Christianity) and emphasised in others (for example in contemplative and mystical traditions in many faiths[2]).

The assertive claims to 'truth' that are sometimes made, and the colonising and dominating violence committed in the name of religion, may mask or repress this central insight. But an important set of ideas embedded in religious traditions maintains that the most significant truths are beyond human comprehension, pointed to by revelation. Canonical texts are full of mysteries, myths, poetry and parables; images or statues of God are prohibited in some traditions; Zen *kōans,* riddles or puzzles used in certain meditation practices, offer a path to wisdom via apparent paradoxes, puns and allusions, not by straightforward assertions. In John Henry Newman's words, applied to Christian notions of truth:

> The religious truth is neither light nor darkness, but both together: it is like the dim view of a country seen in the twilight. Revelation, in this way of seeing it, is not a revealed system, but consists of a number of detached and incomplete truths belonging to a vast system unrevealed (Oakley 2012: vi).

In this view, there may be an objective reality, but it lies outside our comprehension. Darkness, blinding lights, oceans, clouds, mirrors, nothingness are the operative metaphors.

This notion of incomprehensible truth is in tension with the constant repeated impulse to *experience* the divine. The words 'For now we see only a reflection as in a mirror; then we shall see face to face. Now I know in part; then I shall know fully, even as I am fully known' (1 Corinthians 13:12, NIV) imply that it is an inescapable part of the human condition to have only a partial, clouded understanding of the divine: and yet this is accompanied by the hope of a more intimate and perfect knowledge through grace. But this is not as much of a contradiction as it seems. The point is that one can experience something without fully comprehending it. This is more than an intellectual process. The unsettling experience of *awe* or the *sublime* may be approached through meditation and fasting, through art or immersion in nature; religious traditions provide a framework through which to connect these experiences to people's understanding of the nature of spirit, gods or God. Liturgies and rituals depend on bodily and sensual experiences (or the deliberate absence of them, as in intentional periods of silence) as part of the process of listening or knowing. The 'knowing' of Corinthians is not about understanding a collection of facts.

Knowledge becomes less about adding information, and more about a process of deepening relationships – including between humans, and sometimes in relation to other creatures, living and non-living.

Shaping responses

What does this mean for a politics of uncertainty? If the very core and ground of truth is accepted to be mysterious, then assertive statements about what is natural or self-evident may be open to challenge. It may also encourage some scepticism about claims to power on the part of authorities. It may allow some humility about the idea of being able to fully understand or predict mechanisms in the natural world and human society. If the deepest kind of knowledge is achieved through a relational process, this may serve to highlight the importance of *encounters* in producing and deepening knowledge.

These ideas are by no means dominant everywhere in religious contexts, but highlighting them can spark an important conversation about how people arrive at knowledge and truths. Opening these ideas up could enable religious people to take part in a deeper conversation with others about uncertainty in the material and social world.

Why does this matter? For a politics of uncertainty, it is important not just to understand what people do, or even just why they do it, or even just what is involved in the process of deciding to do it, but also what it means to them to act (or not). If we describe uncertainty as being produced 'under a particular view', rather than as a 'condition out there in the world' (Stirling 2019), this means examining what shapes that view, and what therefore shapes the ongoing response to a perceived uncertainty.

For example, religious narratives about the dangers of technology may be 'implicit' and at cross-purposes with other ways of thinking about risk, so 'proponents of technology attempting progress at a level of simple risk analysis will simply be talking past any voices propelled by … deeply swimming stories of warning' (McLeish 2015: 193). In responses to migration too there is no unified religious response. Concepts that emphasise the brotherhood/sisterhood of all people, the diaspora of believers (in Islam and Judaism, among others), long traditions of asylum (Rowlands 2015) and scriptural stories about the experience of exile can be brought to bear in fostering more caring approaches.

For example, a church in The Hague held a service continuously for 96 days to shelter a family of asylum seekers. Religious establishments, even temporary ones like that in the 'Jungle' camp in Calais in 2015, have been important gathering points for people on the move. Examples of sanctuary and refuge are a counterpoint to more exclusionary politics, some of which also invoke religion defensively against perceived threats. The idea of providing sanctuary, shelter and support also applies to disasters such as floods; here, religious institutions are often well-placed to provide practical space for people to gather, as well as pastoral support or the mobilisation of funds.

These responses may be motivated (at least in part) by religious convictions, but the relationship between doctrines and action is complicated. Religious and spiritual views are in dialogue with a wider set of identities, politics and worldviews that inform a person or group. A 'perspective' or 'worldview' is rarely a simple thing.

Within religions themselves, there are tensions and disagreements about how to respond to sources of uncertainty. This plurality means that it is risky to make assumptions about how someone will behave just based on a religious (self-)identity. It also means that inclusive, flexible approaches to uncertainty need to be reinforced and debated within religious communities themselves. An example is the Pope's Lampedusa sermon and Laudato Si' (see Rowlands 2015), which emphasise the importance of care for migrants and the challenge of ecological integrity: these have not met with universal approval even from Catholics. In these circumstances, advocates of care and solidarity within religious communities need to reach for traditions and stories that support their cause.

Hope

In the Christian tradition, as in others, these kinds of practical responses and expressions of mutual aid are seen as being part of a bigger story. Efforts to challenge power or to care for vulnerable people are acts of hopeful prefiguration. The animating vision, that of the Kingdom of Heaven, is not merely a utopian vision of the future. The community is meant to see itself as part of the action of making it present here and now, even though in sometimes small, imperfect ways.

One of the most powerful expressions of this kind of hope is the meaning given to the *Magnificat* ('He hath put down the mighty from their seat / And hath exalted the humble and meek') – abundance, mercy or justice, an end to conflict and the fading away of earthly riches. Many early Christians expected this to be quite imminent, and hope is always somehow looking towards the final end; although it is important to note that some traditions within Christianity largely ignore or attempt to neutralise the radical potential of these ideas, while others value them as an urgent call to participate in revolutionary justice, linked to specific political struggles (Cardenal 2008).

Hope is one of the three things that 'remain' or 'abide' in earthly experience in 1 Corinthians 13 (with faith and love), in expectation of fulfilment at the end. Rather than an abstract wish for things to be better ('I hope that the world will not end tomorrow'),[3] or necessarily pinned to a particular programme of action, hope is found *in* God, rather than in human power or authority, and is therefore by nature unpredictable and ungovernable. This means that when Christians talk about hope they are probably not talking about a vague wish or assurance that somebody else will make everything alright, as hope is inseparable from *faith* and *love*.

In other words, hope is in a threefold relation with what might be termed 'trust within a collective search towards God' (faith), and 'the active giving of oneself in a relation of interdependence' (love). The obvious danger is that hope on its own becomes merely individualised, or a fantasy of justice in the afterlife, permitting great injustices to be tolerated; but linking hope to faith and love may help to bring it down from the clouds, for nobody can tolerate for very long the suffering of someone they love.

This kind of hope does not deny the reality of present suffering or the possibility that things will continue to be hard long into the future. It is a hope that emerges through accompaniment of those who need it. It rests on the hard truth that the future is genuinely not fully known, that there are cracks in the confident stories we tell each other about the future, through which alternatives might emerge and flourish, if they are nurtured.

Giving shape to hope: stories and histories

> *Sometimes the most direct way to tell the truth is to tell a totally implausible story, like a myth* (Interview with Ursula Le Guin, in Freeman (2008)).

Expressions of hope in Christianity, as in other religions, look backwards as well as forwards (note the past tense of the *Magnificat*). This may seem strange – how do you hope for something that has already happened? But stories give shape to hope: they provide patterns and continuities that are always being reinterpreted and retold in response to new events.

Stories are central to how knowledge is embedded in religions, perhaps even more than rituals or institutional structures; indeed, rituals are often a way of dramatising or remembering the shape and meaning of a story. Stories come before doctrine. Stories may permit uncertainty, confusion, debate and multiple perspectives in a way that doctrines cannot easily achieve. Tom McLeish (2015: 193) describes the book of Job in the Hebrew Bible as a text that uses the device of legal debate to create 'an area in which different accounts can emerge … six differentiated views of human response to the natural world'. The four Christian Gospels have resisted efforts to combine them into a single narrative. Ancient stories have been reinterpreted and retold by newer religions. And a key part of the colonising influence of religion has been to try to erase old stories and impose new ones. Stories can imprison as well as liberate.

Stories also encode knowledge in ways that allow it to be passed on through generations. In the Sundarbans, the delta region across the India/Bangladesh border, stories about Bonbibi (the 'lady of the forest') shape the way people treat the perils of the forest and the aggressive tigers who live there (Jalais 2010). These stories also unite communities, across religious boundaries, in traditions and rituals that reinforce the identity of islanders, in the face of encroachments from conservation NGOs and civil authorities. The story of Bonbibi, in bringing together Islamic and Hindu elements, reflects the history of migration into the region and the way that cultural conflicts were dealt with in the process (Ghosh *et al.* 2018: 10). But, as wider economies and environments change rapidly, patterns of worship are changing too. Prawn seed collectors are increasingly drawn to venerate the goddess Kali, a figure associated with more violent and risky behaviours (Jalais 2010: 119–120).

Here, stories and worship practices are bound up with perceptions about class and livelihoods.

The challenge for cultures in which religion is a shaping force – which applies in many parts of the world – is how these stories and myths might survive the accelerating change brought on by new technologies, changes in societies and the large-scale destruction of places and habitats. More than just surviving, how might religious stories and cultures respond to, challenge or shed new light on these processes of change?

A broader politics of uncertainty needs to be critically aware of the stories – whether spiritual in origin or not – that shape people's imaginative worlds and the practices or structures that enable action or connection. Stories need to be recognised for their value without being fossilised. Some lost or forgotten stories with emancipatory power might be rediscovered. Some will be rejected or altered beyond recognition. Through dialogue with other traditions or encounters with new sources of uncertainty, stories can retain their power to move and inspire action. Through exchanging stories and noting their differences, people can identify what makes their own stories more distinctive. In reckoning with the multiple perspectives and ways of interpreting the world that exist, rediscovering different stories and myths can reveal the values and limitations of these perspectives. Together, they can help to navigate through a life that remains full of uncertainty and rich with the promise of other possible worlds.

Acknowledgements

I offer my particular thanks to Rose Cairns, for discussions that shaped this chapter; to Chris and Paula Oxley, Ian Christie, Upasona Ghosh and Becky Ayre, for motivation, discussion and reading suggestions; and to Ian Scoones and Andy Stirling, for thought-provoking and helpful editorial comments and suggestions.

Notes

1 www.churchofengland.org/prayer-and-worship/worship-texts-and-resources/common-worship/common-material/canticles/benedicite-song-creation.
2 e.g. 'O thou who art hidden in that which is hidden, thou art more than all. All see themselves in thee and they see thee in everything. Since thy dwelling is surrounded by guards and sentinels how can we come near to thy presence?' (Attar 1971: 4); 'He moves, and he moves not. He is far, and he is near. He is within all, and he is outside all … The face of truth remains hidden behind a circle of gold' (Mascaro 2005: 4)); 'The godliest knowledge of God is that which is known through ignorance' (Spearing 2001: 96).
3 See also Romans 8:24 (RSV): 'Now hope that is seen is not hope'.

References

Attar, F.U.-D. (1971) *The Conference of the Birds*, C.S. Nott (trans.), Berkeley, CA: Shambala
Berlet, C. and Sunshine, S. (2019) 'Rural Rage: The Roots of Right-Wing Populism in the United States', *Journal of Peasant Studies* 46.3: 480–513

Cardenal, E. (2008) 'The Gospel in Solentiname', in I. Marquez *Contemporary Latin American Social and Political Thought*, Lanham, MD: Rowman & Littlefield

Freeman, C.H. (2008) *Conversations with Ursula K. Le Guin,* Jackson, MS: University Press of Mississippi

Ghosh, U., Bose, S. and Bramhachari, R. (2018) *Living on the Edge: Climate Change and Uncertainty in the Indian Sundarbans*, STEPS Working Paper 101, Brighton: STEPS Centre

Gray, J. (2007) *Black Mass: Apocalyptic Religion and the Death of Utopia*, London: Allen Lane

Hansard (2019) Hansard HC Deb. vol. 659 col. 285, 1 May 2019, https://hansard.parliament.uk/commons/2019-05-01/debates/3C133E25-D670-4F2B-B245-33968D0228D2/EnvironmentAndClimateChange (4 December 2019)

Harmsworth G. and Awatere S. (2013) 'Indigenous Māori Knowledge and Perspectives of Ecosystems', in J.R. Dymond (ed) *Ecosystem Services in New Zealand – Conditions and Trends*, Lincoln, New Zealand: Manaaki Whenua Press

Hulme, M. (2010) 'Four Meanings of Climate Change', in S. Skrimshire (ed) *Future Ethics: Climate Change and Apocalyptic Imagination*, London: Continuum

Jalais, A. (2010) *Forest of Tigers: People, Politics and Environment in the Sundarbans*, Abingdon: Routledge

Mascaro, J. (trans.) (2005) *The Upanishads*, London: Penguin

McFague, S. (1987) *Models of God*: *Theology for an Ecological, Nuclear Age*, Minneapolis, MN: Fortress Press

McLeish, T. (2015) 'The Search for Affirming Narratives for the Future Governance of Technology: Reflections From a Science-Theology Perspective on GMFuturos', in P. Macnaghten and S. Carro-Ripalda (eds) *Governing Agricultural Sustainability: Global Lessons from GM Crops*, Abingdon: Routledge

Nightingale, A.J., Eriksen, S., Taylor, M., Forsyth, T., Pelling, M., Newsham, A., Boyd, E., Brown, K., Harvey, B., Jones, L., Kerr, R.B., Mehta, L., Naess, L.O., Ockwell, D., Scoones, I., Tanner, T. and Whitfield, S. (2019) 'Beyond Technical Fixes: Climate Solutions and the Great Derangement', *Climate and Development*, DOI: 10.1080/17565529.2019.1624495

Oakley, M. (2012) *The Collage of God*, Norwich: Canterbury Press

Rowlands, A. (2015) 'Forgetting the Good: Moral Contradictions in the Response to Mass Migration', *ABC Religion & Ethics,* 10 November 2015 www.abc.net.au/religion/forgetting-the-good-moral-contradictions-in-the-response-to-mass/10097648

Skrimshire, S. (2010) 'Eternal Return of Apocalypse', in S. Skrimshire (ed) *Future Ethics: Climate Change and Apocalyptic Imagination*, London: Continuum

Spearing, A.C. (trans.) (2001) *The Cloud of Unknowing,* London: Penguin

Stirling, A.C. (2019) 'Politics in the Language of Uncertainty', *STEPS Centre blog*, 11 February 2019 https://steps-centre.org/blog/politics-in-the-language-of-uncertainty/

Vanaik, A. (2018) 'Hindu Authoritarianism and Agrarian Distress', *OpenDemocracy* www.opendemocracy.net/en/openindia/hindu-authoritarianism-and-agrarian-distress/

INDEX

Printed in the United States
By Bookmasters